Happy 86th Lunch.

1-15-14

Much Love,

Pam

*Down the Wild Cape Fear*

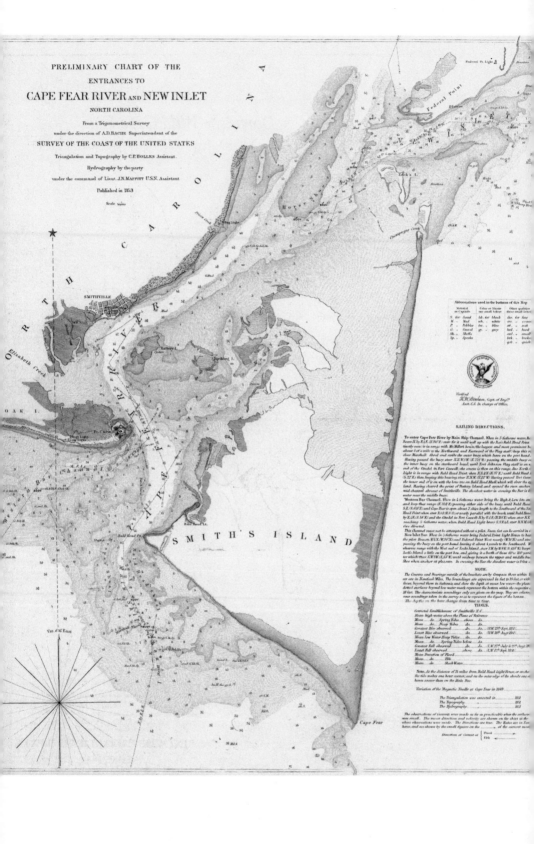

# PRELIMINARY CHART OF THE
## ENTRANCES TO
# CAPE FEAR RIVER AND NEW INLET
### NORTH CAROLINA

From a Trigonometrical Survey

under the direction of A.D.BACHE Superintendent of the

### SURVEY OF THE COAST OF THE UNITED STATES

Triangulation and Topography by C.P.BOLLES Assistant.

Hydrography by the party

under the command of Lieut. J.N.MAFFITT U.S.N. Assistant.

Published in 1853

Scale

# Down
# the Wild
# Cape Fear

*A River Journey through the Heart of North Carolina*

# Philip Gerard

THE UNIVERSITY OF NORTH CAROLINA PRESS   CHAPEL HILL

Designed by Kimberly Bryant and set in Merlo and Aller types
by Tseng Information Systems, Inc.
Manufactured in the United States of America

The paper in this book meets the guidelines for permanence and durability
of the Committee on Production Guidelines for Book Longevity of the
Council on Library Resources. The University of North Carolina Press has
been a member of the Green Press Initiative since 2003.

Library of Congress Cataloging-in-Publication Data
Gerard, Philip.
Down the wild Cape Fear : a river journey through the heart of North Caro-
lina / by Philip Gerard. — First edition.
pages cm
Includes bibliographical references and index.
ISBN 978-1-4696-0207-3 (cloth : alkaline paper) 1. Cape Fear River (N.C.) —
Description and travel. 2. Gerard, Philip—Travel—North Carolina—
Cape Fear River. 3. Boats and boating—North Carolina—Cape Fear River.
4. Natural history—North Carolina—Cape Fear River. 5. Human ecology—
North Carolina—Cape Fear River. 6. Cape Fear River Valley (N.C.)—
History. 7. Cape Fear River Valley (N.C.)—Politics and government. 8. Cape
Fear River Valley (N.C.)—Social conditions. 9. Cape Fear River Valley
(N.C.)—Environmental conditions. I. Title.
F262.C2G37 2013
975.6'2—dc23
2012032751

Brief passages of this work appeared in different form in "Cape Fear: Historic Gateway to the Atlantic," *Wildlife in North Carolina*, November 1999,
and "Sailors on Horseback: The Mounties of Bald Head Island," *Haven* 3,
no. 1 (2006).

Frontispiece: "Preliminary Chart of the Entrances to Cape Fear River and
New Inlet" made by the Survey of the Coast of the United States, by the
party under the command of Lieutenant John Newland Maffitt, U.S.N., 1853
(courtesy of NOAA)

Chapter opening art (silhouette): ©iStockphoto.com/Jonathan Haste

17 16 15 14 13  5 4 3 2 1

*for Jill,*
*with love & gratitude*

# Contents

**Illustrations**

**Maps**

*Down the Wild Cape Fear*

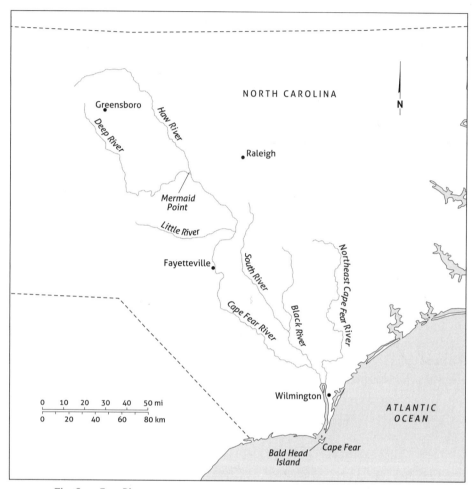

The Cape Fear River

I have lived beside the Cape Fear River for more than twenty years. I have run its length, 200-odd miles of foaming rapids, placid eddies, tannin-dark water hiding snakes and snapping turtles, in canoe, kayak, sailboat, runabout, fishing boat, and ship—and I've run parts if it many times.

On a soft autumn evening, with the clear October light casting the Wilmington waterfront in a luminous clarity, I've cruised aboard the *Henrietta III*, a replica of an old-time steamboat, the breeze riffling the North Carolina state flag at the jackstaff. The occasion was a cocktail reception and a concert by The Schoolboys, a rock cover band of fellow professors. But the river scrolling past the windows was the main event. On another evening, a dinner "blues cruise" was abruptly terminated when a sudden squall swept across the deck and literally blew the tables over and knocked the band off the bandstand.

I have kayaked through the Holly Shelter preserve on a lovely tributary creek and drifted in a johnboat on the Black River just upriver from the confluence where it joins the Cape Fear, the two rivers separated by a line as hard as a seam of rock, the water on one side tea-colored, on the other black as Guinness stout. Upriver on the Black, my paddling companions and I have floated among giant cypress trees that were already a thousand years old when Columbus sailed accidentally to the New World.

I have shadowed a biologist up Town Creek, a lower tributary, and counted five alligators forted in their muddy wallows just a long handshake from our johnboat. Down at the mouth of the river, I have ridden the ferry from Southport to Federal Point on idle Sundays when I didn't have to, just to be out on the estuary and watch the brown pelicans make their insane vertical dives, slapping into the drink like stones and emerging with wriggling fish in their gullets, and to feel the live salt breeze across the deck and the restless current under the keel.

I've made the crossing to Bald Head Island at the mouth of the river by ferry, sailboat, and fast powerboat and wrestled a reef into a racing sailboat in the roadstead just beyond during a forty-knot blow that raised the river-sea into black-gray humps that broke over the deck with drenching power and scattered the regatta.

I have shouldered my own sailboat *Suspense* upriver against the ebbing tide to find a "hurricane hole."

In the fairway at the mouth of the river, I've climbed up a Jacob's ladder from the heaving deck of a moving tugboat to board a container ship and marked its progress upriver from a bridge deck so high above the main deck we rode an elevator up to it.

On my way out to sea on various sailboats, I've watched ospreys and yellow-crowned night herons patrol the skies and followed the bow-riding dolphins out the fairway past Bald Head Island to the sea buoy. Once, crossing the Cape Fear bar inbound at dawn, my crew and I harnessed ourselves in for a wild ride, surfing down twelve-foot seas on an incoming tide with a thirty-knot wind sweeping downriver against us, piling up the water in long heaving mounds, and when we were finally safe in the quieter waters of the estuary, I enjoyed the best cup of coffee of my life.

I have helped raise the mains'l on *Pride of Baltimore II* as we crewed the 1812-era topsail schooner under the Cape Fear Memorial Bridge, past the blue and orange gantry cranes of the port, and through the fairway out to sea.

The Cape Fear River is many rivers with many seasons. In the course of more than four centuries, it has been called the Sapona, Rio Jordan, the Charles, the Clarendon, the Thoroughfare, and the Cape Fair. It begins just above Buckhorn Dam, an obsolete hydroelectric project at the edge of the Piedmont, and rushes through white-water rock gardens to Raven Rock, now a state park built on high bluffs overlooking the river. The river widens past Lillington and courses in a meandering current down to Fayetteville, formerly Cross Creek and Campbellton, settled by Scots.

Then it passes through three massive sets of locks and dams on to Tarheel, Elizabethtown, Navassa, and Wilmington, where it is joined by the Northeast Cape Fear, and continues down the ship channel to the estuary at Southport, sweeping in a graceful S-turn past Oak Island and Smith's Island, now called Bald Head Island, and Fort Fisher, through an estuary that stretches thirty-five miles to the sea.

The Cape Fear River drains one of seventeen river basins in North Carolina. It's one of only four rivers contained entirely within the borders of the state, and the only one of the seventeen that empties directly into the ocean. It spreads out over 9,322 square miles, cutting right through the heart of the state, containing in its drainage basin 116 towns and cities in 26 of North Carolina's 100 counties, covering 15 percent of the state and containing fully one-fifth of its people—nearly 2 million souls.

It runs inland like the main artery of history from the sea to the mountains. On its banks, the early rivalry between England and Spain was played out with swords and cannon. Pirates anchored in the lee of Bald Head Island to prey on the treasure ships of the Spanish Main.

Along the lower reaches, white European settlers wiped out or drove away a thriving, diverse population of Native Americans, hunted certain wild species to extinction, and repeatedly tried—and mainly failed—to tame the river.

And the river was a political lifeline as well. The first organized resistance to the Stamp Act in the nation was plotted not in Boston or Philadelphia but by Patriots along the lower Cape Fear.

Upriver at Fayetteville, other Patriots signed the Liberty Point Resolves, an early declaration of independence, more than a year before the Continental Congress in Philadelphia got around to it. After being driven out of Boston in 1776, the British reinvaded America through New York and North Carolina, establishing a fort on Bald Head. In New York, they were victorious. But in a pivotal battle along a little tributary of the Cape Fear called Widow Moore's Creek, the Scots Tories were driven off, and the British invasion fleet weighed anchor and left the Cape Fear.

When it came time to adopt the United States Constitution, the North Carolina convention met in a Cape Fear River town, Fayetteville, to ratify it.

Likewise, during the Civil War, four crucial battles took place along the river, which was the last international supply line to Robert E. Lee's Army of Northern Virginia. The Confederates' final battle—to stop General William Tecumseh Sherman from joining up with General Ulysses S. Grant and ending the war—was staged along the river in a series of running fights from Fayetteville across the river to Averasboro, ending in a full-scale Confederate disaster at Bentonville. Not long after that battle, at the Bennett place on the Hillsborough Road, above present-day Jordan Lake in the headwaters of the Cape Fear, more Confederate troops surrendered to Sherman than had been surrendered by General Robert E. Lee at Appomattox Court House seventeen days earlier. And so the last state to secede became the stage for the war's final act.

During the two world wars, the lower river turned into a shipbuilding powerhouse, and during later wars—Vietnam, the Gulf War, the campaigns in Iraq and Afghanistan—the Sunny Point Military Ocean Terminal supplied, and still supplies, allied armies across Europe and Asia.

On the river, too, was chartered the University of North Carolina, the oldest public university in the nation.

Nearly every crucial political or environmental issue has been played out—or is being played out—on the river, from Indian removal and racial strife to water and air pollution, from global warming to industrial development, from the conservation of species to the preservation of cultural heritage.

In the poet Walt Whitman's words, the river contains multitudes.

Though it begins as a fast-rushing stream, for the last miles, the Cape Fear is a coastal river, meandering in lazy loops, tea-colored from the cypress tannin that leaches into it from the adjacent swamps. On the river the scenery is wild and green, a lush tangle that caches a remarkable variety of birds, along with deer, otters, beavers, foxes, mink, and even black bears. From the air, the lower river is a surprisingly lovely maze of recursive loops, a work of art on an amazing scale, broadening into an estuary that never fails to astonish with its diversity of birds and sheer panoramic beauty.

I've long wanted to write about this river to which I've felt such a visceral connection, and the best way to do that was to go back on it again, starting where the river is born and riding it to the sea.

No book can contain the whole river or tell all its stories. The best I can do is follow the current and pay attention to where it carries me, to squint through the lens of 400 years of history and catch a glimpse of the many rivers it has been, to reclaim a few of the people and events that have left their marks upon it, and to attempt to discover and reveal something of its nature. To explore some of the shady tributaries of history and nature and recover something of their contribution to the lore of the river.

I do this not for the paddlers or fishermen or sailors who already are intimate with the river. Rather, for most of the rest of us 2 million people who live within its basin and have seen it only from a bridge or muddy bank as a slice of brown rushing stream pushing relentlessly to the sea.

The Cape Fear River is more than just a certain volume of water coursing along a muddy track, more even than a sum of acreage drained by its tributaries.

It's a living system, a wild and delightful thing. A breathless story.

# PART 1 The Upper Reaches

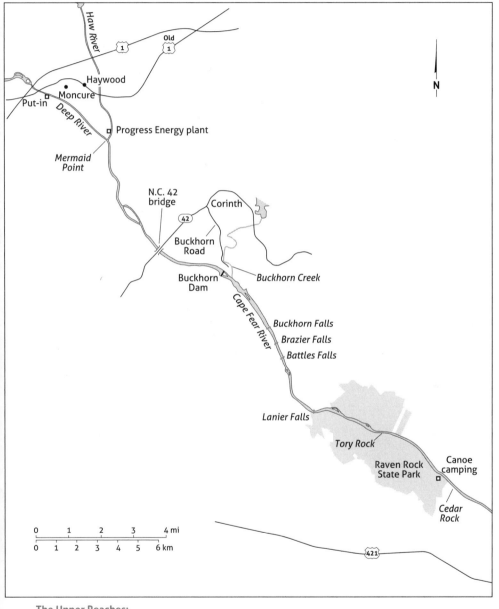

**The Upper Reaches:**
**Old Route 1 to Raven Rock State Park**

Nearly 200 miles inland from the Atlantic Ocean, at the confluence where the Deep and Haw Rivers come together in the North Carolina Piedmont—literally, the foot of the mountains—lies a small wedge of beach called Mermaid Point. For more than a hundred years now it's been submerged by a hydroelectric dam just downstream, but the sandy bottom is still there.

In the 1700s, when only a handful of white settlers made their home in the vast Cape Fear basin, travelers reported hearing beautiful, ghostly singing emanating from this beach. A legend grew up that this was the place where mermaids would gather under a full moon. They had swum up the river till it was cleansed of salt and clarified of the tea-stain of tannin leaching from the cypress swamps in the lower river, to this beach where the mountain-cold water ran purified by fifty miles of fall and drip and seep through a watershed spider-webbing out north, east, and west. Here they would lounge, washing and combing one another's long hair, all the while keening their siren song in a lovely, mesmerizing language no human ear could comprehend.

I like to imagine them there, creatures of the sea, far up the long reach of the Cape Fear. The mermaids carry the legacy of the first European explorers who paddled their way up from the low coast to this hilly, wild green country more than three centuries ago in search of their fortunes. It was those settlers, after all, who first heard the beguiling song and created a fanciful legend to explain its mystery. Unlike so much country lore—cautionary tales intended to scare listeners into staying close to their campfires—this tale of sweet-singing mermaids carries an invitation to venture out and look, to discover the enchanting truth at the core of the mystery.

And the mermaids carry, too, the future of the river, the promise of the millions of gallons of water per day that flow past the Point and downriver, drained from more than 6,000 miles of tributaries above their submerged beach, with names like Persimmon Creek, Rocky River, Stinking Creek, Alamance Creek, and Nursery Branch. The waters roll from Mermaid Point over the fall line to refresh the estuary far downriver.

The legend doesn't say how the mermaids got back down to the sea, any more than it describes their initial journey up that long, stubborn current. But I imagine them slipping into the cold water like river otters, gliding supplely among the foaming rapids of the upper reaches, stretching out now in the deeper water, tails working with a steady rhythm, riding the current past the bluffs at Raven Rock, sliding through the sluices and chutes of the rock gardens and little falls above Fayetteville, coasting around the long bends of the middle river, then swimming again down the slow, loopy meanders of the lower reaches, the river at last opening like a story into the broad estuary.

In my imagination, I see them porpoising past the long S-turn at Southport, where the channel narrows against the bulkheads of the town front and the pilot boats are tied up at the wharf under the steel lookout tower. I watch them head out to sea past Battery Island on the left and the slim upright cylinder of the Oak Island Light on the right, with the misty silhouette of Bald Head Island in the offing, Old Baldy light glinting from the squat white tower, as they dive into deep water again—clean, invigorated, now singing a different song, equally enchanting, far out to sea.

That's the journey we're going to take, from the confluence to the sea, finishing at the Cape of Fear that lends its name to the river. But this journey, like these pages, will not be a fast, straight, rushing line from here to a distant objective. A river basin is an organism. The tributaries threading through the landscape are capillaries to the main artery that is the river. The wetlands and swamps spreading out around the live water are the lungs, full of vegetation through which the land breathes. To really know the river, to understand its essential nature and place in our lives, we need to know these.

So we will venture off the mainstem from time to time, exploring literal backwaters of geography and the more figurative ones of history, but always coming back to the main channel.

It's the journey we're after, not merely the destination.

The four of us arrive at Buckhorn Dam just before 10:30 A.M. on a gorgeous May morning: David Webster, a wildlife biologist and my colleague at the university; Ethan Williamson, an experienced white-water river guide who is also head of Friends School of Wilmington; his wife, Amy, our expedition photographer and birder; and me, a silver-haired writer with two strong paddling arms, one good knee, and a yen for adventure. We have help from Kyle Mustain and Will Flowers, students in the MFA in Creative Writing program at the University of North Carolina Wilmington, who will ferry our vehicles home and return a few days from now to fetch us at the take-out below Fayetteville, some sixty-five miles downriver.

The air is cool but fast warming, the sky clear of any threat of storm.

The drive up from Wilmington took about three hours. We had planned to put in on Old Route 1 on the Deep River and paddle six and a half miles or so down to the dam, thereby passing Mermaid Point, but we were running a bit late and didn't want the first day's paddle to be an ordeal driven by a clock. That would defeat the whole purpose of the trip, to find the rhythm of the river. We are in no particular hurry, don't want to be forced to hurry. We're drawn not by the lore of legend but by the lure of the river itself, a yearning to push out into its current and, quite literally, get carried away.

Anyway, I don't really mind. In fact, part of me is glad.

Now I know I'll have to come back and paddle that stretch alone, and having it all to myself will be like having a wonderful unread book on the bookshelf waiting for the right moment, one last adventure before the finish. When you embark on a journey, you have to trust yourself to it, relinquish a little control, and I'm trusting that the journey will complete itself in its own time, in its own way.

We're splashing the boats just below the confluence of the Deep and Haw Rivers, just downstream of Mermaid Point. The Deep River falls from 800 feet to 160 feet above sea level, and seventeen dams regulate its flow: an average of 936 million gallons of water per day into the Cape Fear—a hell of a lot of water.

The Haw River, including part of the upper Cape Fear, was once known as the Saxapahaw, after the namesake Indian tribe that lived on its banks. Today the Haw River channel is backed up for five miles above the 1,330-foot-long B. Everett Jordan Dam, built at the mouth of the New Hope River as a flood control project in the 1970s. It regulates the Haw River's flow into the Cape Fear.

It's already plain that the Cape Fear has felt the heavy touch of the human hand before it even gets started. Almost from the moment of its discovery, humans have tried to change the river, to reengineer it to their purposes. One of the things I hope to discover is just how that has worked out—for us and for the river.

At Mermaid Point, the two rivers, the Deep and the Haw, join their flows, mingling into a sluggish backwater called Buckhorn Lake, formed by the dam of the same name.

The road we followed for most of our way to the headwaters is U.S. Route

421, a fast, asphalt road overlaid on one of the oldest Indian trails in the eastern part of the state. It follows the eastern bank of the river for a little ways out of Wilmington, through the industrial corridor on the west bank, then veers farther east toward the Black River before looping back to cross the Cape Fear at Lillington on its way to Sanford and beyond.

We're accustomed to highway maps that break up the state into regions defined by mainly north-south roads, such as the swath of coast east of the I-95 corridor. Interstate 85 is an interior version of I-95, angling northeast. The I-77 corridor is a straight north-south shot. The exception is I-40, a north-arcing east-west corridor that crosses the others and is hung with a populous chain of cities: Raleigh, Durham, Chapel Hill, Greensboro, Winston-Salem, and finally, Asheville.

But the river basins provide a different template, organizing the land into watersheds, each like a single body served by a coherent circulatory system. The Cape Fear basin, like most of the other basins in the state, angles north and west, 200 miles long and 50 to 60 miles wide, more or less. The map created by the basins shows up as a series of wide corridors reaching inland from the sea—not running northeast or due west.

The basins collectively resemble the splayed swollen fingers of several giant hands gripping the state from the sea to the mountains.

Early commerce used the rivers, and the corridors of trade followed the river basins. So it makes sense that ancient inland corridors such as Route 421 and Route 87 should follow the river. Later, in the 1800s, many of the railroads were laid down according to the same template, angling inland along the river valleys, following the level paths of least resistance, rather than straight north and south—a major drawback when the time came to supply the Confederate army during the Civil War.

So all during our drive, we've never been very far from the river. We reach Buckhorn Dam down Buckhorn Road, which runs paved for about a mile and then gradually deteriorates into a gravel lane. Along the way we encounter a somewhat daunting sign:

NOTICE TO ALL
IN THE EVENT OF AN IDENTIFIED EMERGENCY
REQUIRING EVACUATION OF THE RIVER AREA,
YOU WILL BE NOTIFIED BY SIRENS,
RED SMOKE OR ORANGE FLARES.
IF THESE SIGNALS ARE OBSERVED, PLEASE:
1. LEAVE THE RIVER AREA IMMEDIATELY.

## 2. TURN ON RADIO OR TELEVISION FOR INFORMATION AND INSTRUCTIONS.

We stop the car, listening for a moment out the open window. No sirens. Nothing but a soft breeze and some distant motor noises. The sky is blue with a few puffy clouds, but no sign of red smoke or the contrail of an orange flare. Apparently we are not in an "identified emergency"—presumably a flash flood, or perhaps an accident at the Shearon Harris nuclear power plant, invisible but nearby. We continue, and the road finally peters out in a pitted dirt road that dead-ends in a muddy Jeep-track at the water's edge.

Off to the right looms the dam, anchored by a kind of square concrete tower on the near bank, stretching across the river in a hard straight line, the water rushing over it in a beautiful glimmering falls that seems almost frozen, it is so uniform.

Buckhorn Dam presents a somewhat dangerous optical illusion: It appears rather diminutive with a short fall beyond it. In fact, it stands 14 feet high from the original riverbed, 1,200 hundred linear feet of concrete founded solidly on a base that is 12 feet wide. It crosses the current just a little ways below the site of a much older dam built more than a century ago by the defunct Cape Fear and Deep River Navigation Company. Because we see it at relatively low water, it looks tame, but time and again it has proved to be a killer.

"Four men were drowned, on last Tuesday, at the Buckhorne dam in the Cape Fear river," reported the *Chatham County Record* on April 25, 1907. "They were Capt. Thorson, the foreman of the works at Buckhorne, Mr. Emory A. Brady and two colored men, one named George Champion and the other Henry Lashley."

The story goes on: "They and a colored man, named Joe Andrews, were in a gasolene boat that was in the river above the dam, carrying some lumber across the river, when the machinery got out of fix, or for some cause the boat got beyond control and began drifting with the strong current towards the dam. All efforts to stop the boat were in vain, and with accelerated motion it swept to the dam and plunged over, dashing the five men into the seething waters below."

It's an old story to any boater. The engine dies, the current sweeps you away, and things get dangerous in a hurry. For these men, it was a disastrous day: "Only one of them, Joe Andrews, escaped a watery grave. He was able to swim ashore, but the other four were drowned, and their bodies were swept down the river and may not be found for many days, if ever."

But it turned out that before long all four bodies were recovered and buried by their loved ones, and locals maintained a healthy respect for the power of the falls. They understood that the river was a force of nature, and "gasolene" engine or not, it could take you where it wanted to go. All that's required for disaster is for something to get "out of fix."

And drowning wasn't the only danger posed by the hydroelectric dam or the river. In September 1907, a hellacious lightning storm dropped more than two inches of rain in a few hours. Lightning arced from a poplar tree into the powerhouse near the dam and killed seven men instantly. Another twenty-five workers were stunned by the strike, seven of them seriously injured. A horse was said to be uninjured but "frantic" and had to be brought under control. The accidental death toll at Buckhorn by now was reckoned at twenty men, including the four washed over the dam, not to mention all those injured or burned by lightning.

The *Record* tallies the grim toll and adds a snarky postscript: "About fifty feet of the dam was washed away next day after the men were killed by lightning, which will delay for some time longer the completion of this important (and we may add unlucky) enterprise."

The dam was built by the Cape Fear Power Company in 1905 and 1906 at a cost of half a million dollars ($1.85 million in today's dollars) to provide power to cotton mills in Fayetteville, though it took a couple more years to get the power-generating equipment installed and fully operational. But almost from the start, the company and its dam ran into trouble. Because the dam backed up water in the farmland above it, farmers whose lands were flooded out launched numerous lawsuits. Not only that, but the dam was blamed for a local epidemic.

As the *Record* reported on September 6, 1906, in an article titled "Dam a Nuisance," "There is said to be an epidemic of chills and fever in Cape Fear township among the people residing on and near the Cape Fear river, between Lockville and the Buckhorne dam. This sickness is said to be caused by the backwater from the new dam of the Cape Fear Power Company, which has overflowed many thousand acres along the riverbanks. Such sickness was predicted and feared by the people of that section when the dam was being constructed, and their fears are now being realized."

The claim, fanciful on its face, may have had some validity: Still water breeds mosquitoes, the vectors of malaria and encephalitis.

The company went into receivership, and the dam was sold for half its value. The reorganized Cape Fear Electric Power Company managed to operate the dam as a paying proposition into the 1950s, when it became obsolete as a hydroelectric power generator. A contractor named Ebasco demolished the main power plant, finishing the job on January 1, 1963—fifty-five years to the day from the commissioning of the turbine.

But the dam, rebuilt in 1960, remains important to Progress Energy, which owns the site. The backed-up water provides cooling for its coal-fired power plant upstream on the Haw, and when that plant goes off-line in a few years, the water will become even more crucial as a cooling reservoir for the Shearon Harris nuclear power plant, located at the head of Buckhorn Creek, which joins the Cape Fear River just below Buckhorn Dam. It's all a little confusing. To confound matters even further, there used to be a second Buckhorn Dam on Buckhorn Creek, but it was dismantled a couple years ago.

In any event, we have arrived at Buckhorn Dam to launch our adventure.

We wrestle the two canoes off the roofs of the vehicles, carry them to the flat beach downstream of the dam, and load them. We take our time stowing the gear, tying all the bags and sealed buckets to the thwarts in the event of capsize. David, my colleague at the university and now paddling partner, has assured me more than once, "I've never capsized a canoe in my life." And he's paddled on rivers and lakes on several continents in every weather and season.

To save strain on our backs, we strap onto the built-in canoe seats a second set of folding nylon seats with backrests.

At last, David and I are ready to shove off in his old aluminum Grumman canoe—moss green, built like a dreadnought. I'll be the bowman and he, with his considerably greater experience, will steer from the stern. Our canoe is heavily laden, but it's big enough to still ride well.

One of the joys of mounting an expedition is the weeks of anticipation and planning, the patient preparation that always takes longer than the trip itself, buying or gathering up gear, shopping for provisions, crafting a stowage plan. Our stowage plan was devised by Ethan and Amy, who have used it on countless trips. Basically, food is sorted into logical combinations, usually by meal, and double-bagged in sturdy, contractor-grade trash bags, the opening twisted tight and tied in a big knot. Then each bag is stuffed into a five-gallon plastic paint bucket sealed with a snap-on lid. The sealed buckets are secured in the boats by a rope run through their wire bales and tied off on the thwarts.

Every other item—including and especially sleeping bags—is double-bagged as well.

On the river, I know I'll be getting wet often (more often if we capsize), so quick-drying clothing is essential. We need camping gear, cameras and notebooks to record the trip, and the ability to keep it all dry. And most of all we must include reliable safety gear: life vests, first-aid kit, throw-rope. There's no handy Coast Guard station on the river, and however pleasant and pic-

Intrepid explorers: David Webster and the author prepare to launch the
Green Monster just below Buckhorn Dam (Amy Williamson photo)

turesque the river seems, we can never let ourselves forget that it is a force of
nature—quite literally—and is utterly indifferent to our fate.

A canoe right-side-up is a comfortable and safe conveyance. Upside-down
it is just one more chunk of flotsam careening down the river. And the difference between the two can be a few distracted seconds.

A gallon of freshwater weighs about eight pounds. Getting slapped in the
face by, say, five gallons would be like being slugged by a forty-pound weight,
enough to knock you out of the boat and worse.

Ethan has already related to us all how, on a recent trip on another river, he
hauled a drowning kayaker ashore and revived him with CPR before the man
was airlifted out to a hospital. It was a close call, and it could easily have gone
the other way.

Under my seat I have stowed a sleeping bag and a two-man nylon tent.
Clipped with carabiners to a rope running from bow to thwart are my red
drinking bottle; my first-aid kit in a dry bag; a small dry bag containing personal items such as a cell phone in its own watertight case (which will prove
largely useless on the river, since cell signals will be few and far between); and
a large, clear, dry bag containing a wallet and extra paddling clothes—T-shirt
and khaki trunks.

The long, olive-drab paddling pants I'm wearing have zip-off legs. I'm also wearing a blue, long-sleeved, quick-dry shirt with many pockets and new Keen river shoes, which have sturdy rubber bumpers protecting the toes. The long pants and long-sleeved shirt are meant to ward off sunburn. Snug on my head is a North Face olive-drab boonie hat with mesh vents and a floppy brim. The hat is essential in the strong sun that will bear down on us for many hours each day. Buttoned in my shirt pocket is a pair of aviator sunglasses that will help dampen the glare off the river in the afternoons.

In the pocket of my life vest (worn at all times under way), encased in two ziplock bags are one of several moleskin notebooks and a pen.

I have to admit that I love all the gear, love having a good reason to buy it and trick myself out like a genuine explorer, Teddy Roosevelt maybe, headed into the dark heart of the River of Doubt. We're off on an adventure not nearly so fraught with danger and misery. Still, it feels thrilling.

Behind my seat are stowed ten gallons of water—a box of eight one-gallon jugs and one two-gallon jug—more than we'll need, probably, but better to err on the side of plenty. Water is the heaviest item we carry, and the most crucial. It is a supreme irony that we will be riding this river for days, swimming in it, and bailing it out of our boats; but we dare not drink it, not unfiltered. There's just too much questionable stuff that has already been dumped in it upstream: fertilizer runoff, oil and gas from roadways, drainage from hog farms and chicken houses, outflows from storm drains.

Also amidships are stowed three five-gallon plastic buckets packed with food, their bales roped in across the thwarts. David's clothes are double-bagged inside contractor bags as well just ahead of him in the stern.

On the drive up in David's Jeep, he made a running joke of logging each crossing of the Cape Fear River. At the Memorial Bridge in Wilmington, he said, "Crossing the river at 6:42 A.M." Then, heading up Route 421 on Eagles Island: "Crossing the river at 6:45 A.M." Later at Lillington, same deal. A total of thirteen highway bridges span the Cape Fear, from Wilmington up to the Deep, and today we have crossed four of them.

David is a man of medium build with dark hair, about my own age, which is to say mid-fifties, sunburned and a little weathered from years in the field. He settles comfortably into the stern under a broad-brimmed straw hat. He is a man of extraordinary resourcefulness and patience, a problem solver with a congenial manner and a quick sense of humor, all of which make him invaluable as an associate dean at our university in charge of infrastructure that supports research, a broad portfolio that includes everything from computers and grants to office space.

He has been doing biology for thirty-odd years. On the university website

David Webster,
a biologist who
likes to trek
into wild places
(author photo)

you will find his declared area of research: "My research primarily involves the evolution, systematics, and ecology of New World mammals, especially rats, bats, and shrews. I encourage my students to use a combination of molecular, chromosomal, morphological, and ecological analyses to examine the phylogenetic relationships among closely related taxa."

But he doesn't talk that way in real life, especially not on the river. One of his special talents is explaining complicated scientific processes in a manner that even I—who never quite sorted out the difference between *mitosis* and *meiosis* in high school biology class—can comprehend. There's not an ounce of pretension in him. He loves the wild outdoors, is nuts about the critters he studies, and knows more about the natural world than any five other people I could name. That's one of the benefits of working at a university: You get to hang out with smart people, and if you pay any attention at all, on a trip like this, you can't help but learn something.

David's research has taken him into nearly every watershed in the coastal South on every kind of boat, from the Great Dismal Swamp, the Croatan National Forest, and the Alligator River in North Carolina to Congaree National Park in South Carolina; to rivers in coastal Georgia, Alabama, and North Florida; and down into Mexico and Central America. Among his more local research projects, he studied turtles on the Cape Fear and Northeast Cape Fear Rivers and determined that the turtles in the Northeast Cape Fear carry fewer parasites than their cousins on the main stem, since the greater acidity of the water limits the intermediate hosts necessary to breed them.

He's a scientist, used to patient observation and drawing conclusions only from reliable data. He deals with the world not just through the Big Picture but also through a level of meticulously gathered detail.

David now actively participates in monitoring sea turtle nests on Figure Eight and Masonboro Islands, the latter a stretch of barrier sandbar that has been turned into a natural preserve, accessible only by boat from the mainland. He routinely patrols the beach before sunrise on a four-wheeler ferried across on a johnboat with a special platform built onto the bow. Then he showers, puts on a coat and tie, and drives to campus to wrangle us professors. He is the guy you always want to look up and see standing in your office doorway, because he almost always has a solution for you, something to help you do your job better.

He's also an avid birder and a wildlife biologist who specializes in endangered species. He mainly studies small mammals, especially bats, shrews, and rodents. "I get most of my research information from small mammals because they're more poorly known," he explains. "White-tailed deer are everywhere, so I'm not learning anything from white-tailed deer." He tramps or paddles way off the beaten track into heavy interior thickets too dense for bear and deer—truly undisturbed, unbroken habitat.

"We would cut trails up in the Alligator River," he remembers, "and in the days when we were cutting vegetation we would come out and not be covered by ticks at all. And go back a week later to check our traps and be covered by ticks and we would be chasing bears out of there! It was unbelievable that we were providing *them* with trails, when you think typically they provide *you* with trails."

Off campus, David is widely sought after as a consultant. Other scientists collaborate with him, and commercial outfits hire him to inventory bird and animal species on land they own. Golf courses bring him in to help them figure out what to do with the beavers that are damming up the canals leading to ponds, or how to discourage the foxes that are denning in the bunkers. Utility companies retain him to help in their permitting process with regulatory agencies. He is no ivory tower academic; he spends a great deal of time in the field, tramping along remote trails and slogging through swamps, doing his best to protect critters from unnatural enemies like us and to preserve habitat.

He is a force for good, a diligent watchdog on the Coastal Resources Commission and the board of the North Carolina Coastal Land Trust, which has negotiated conservation easements along a wide swath of the lower Cape Fear, including thousands of acres of plantation land on the west bank.

In collaboration with two colleagues, he literally wrote the book on the critters we're likely to encounter along the river: *Mammals of the Carolinas, Virginia, and Maryland.* So while he is at home in the laboratory, his real love is the outdoors, and he's the perfect companion to help me find and identify wildlife along the river.

This begins with *seeing* the animals and birds, which are not always obvious. Mostly what you see of a turtle is a head the size of a wine cork barely breaking the surface, then disappearing in a small roil of bubbles. A water snake may be just a slight ripple moving across the current. An alligator gar will rise abruptly, showing a bony jaw that doesn't much resemble a fish's. A deer might show just a flash of white tail as it vanishes into the foliage after coming down to drink. Otters may be invisible altogether, but their telltale slides scar the cutbanks.

Other animals onshore will stay out of sight; all you know of them is the rustling sound made by their quick retreat through the brush. You judge their size by how much noise they make, then narrow down the list of suspects: squirrel, fox, deer. Mink abound in the riverside thickets, but you'll rarely see them. A mink is a member of the weasel family that weighs just one to three pounds, and its narrow, tubular body can disappear quickly into the smallest opening. All it leaves behind are distinctive, sharp, five-toed tracks, each barely an inch across.

"Mink are much more secretive, they're more solitary," David tells me. "They don't occur in family units the way otters do. They're smaller, head and body twelve to fourteen inches long and then a four-inch tail. I've only seen a handful of mink in the wild in my life." They may be furtive, but they're also fierce hunters: "They feed primarily on muskrats and other small mammals and birds, frogs, snakes, toads. They're very predacious."

Coyotes, too, are ubiquitous in the Cape Fear basin, which is not surprising, since coyotes have been observed in all 100 counties in the state. The adults are long and rangy, weighing up to forty-five pounds, and move furtively through virtually any habitat. They are a replacement species that fills a niche vacated by the red wolf, the native canid that was hunted to extinction in eastern North Carolina more than a century ago.

Also out in the thickets along the river lurk bobcat and black bears — lots of them.

Likewise, in the air, the soaring shadow of wings is either a turkey vulture, if it has a red head and the trailing edge of the wing flashes silvery white, or an osprey, if it is dark. Hard to tell an osprey from a juvenile bald eagle from afar, or against the glare of the full sun, so you follow it with field glasses until it reveals itself.

And of course in the river itself plenty of species will be swimming, slithering, floating, or just sitting on the bottom—like the oval-shaped, notched, rainbow mussel (*Villosa constricta*), an inch and a half or so long, first identified in 1838. It favors a sandy bottom and can be found in many of the upland streams draining into the Cape Fear. It can also be found in the muddy river bottom.

So the river we will be riding is full of life—underwater, in the air, and secreted in the shoreline thicket.

Now ready to enter the wild at Buckhorn Dam, we carefully board our canoes and push off into the mild current below the dam. The water is low, just a foot and a half or so deep. I'm a little nervous, not having been in a canoe on a river with real current for a few years. The last time I put in at Buckhorn, doing a television documentary more than fifteen years ago, my paddling partner and I dumped the canoe at the first sluice only a few hundred yards downriver.

Just below the dam we encounter a wide boulder field—Brazier Falls—tricky in low water, what are called Class I rapids, the mildest kind, easily navigated by an alert beginner. In really high water it would be challenging indeed, a real trap. We follow Amy and Ethan, who has been running rapids since he was a kid. Amy is also an expert paddler with many miles of wild rivers on her résumé.

Ethan is tall and broad, easygoing, deceptively strong and agile. He has that knack for making physically difficult things look easy that is the hallmark of a real pro. He's a born teacher with a gift for explaining how complex things work, which makes him an ideal mentor on the river. He's also a font of practical wisdom. He knows how to handle a boat and how to read a river.

For running rapids, Ethan's modus operandi is to stand up in the back of his canoe about a hundred yards upstream of any "horizon line" that indicates fast water ahead. When you're on the river, the water always appears to be above and in front of you, so when it ends in a flat horizon, that's an indication that beyond that horizon the river falls.

And the crucial question is always how much, how fast? Is it a gentle fall through an easily threaded rock garden, a dramatic drop requiring focus and skill, or a true falls to be avoided altogether?

Ethan studies the river downstream, looking for surface ripples or humps indicating submerged rocks, circular eddies that are the telltales of back-flowing currents, foaming shallows over a sandbar, and so on. He picks out a route, and then David and I do our best to follow him. We do not stand up in our canoe. We are not morons. We understand that what seems easy when Ethan does it is in fact a minor feat of acrobatic balance. And were we to try it, a great way to transform ourselves in an instant from paddlers to swimmers.

David and I soon learn that we are in a "sticky" boat, a canoe that grips a rock face with great friction and doesn't let go easily. By contrast, Ethan and Amy's canoe, an old green Mohawk with duct-tape seats (the original fabric wore out ages ago), is plastic and slides off a rock. It's also far more flexible, so it has some bend and bounce to spring it off rocks, and it doesn't lie so deep in the water—what mariners call "draft." They skim over many rocks that grab us hard and won't let go.

The upside is that the Grumman, which David calls the "Green Monster," is tough and pretty stable, so that whenever we do have to get out of it, getting back in is a matter of flopping aboard and grabbing on. It's not tippy or tender, and there's no danger that the rocks can do anything more than scrape off some paint or add a ding to the battered hull. It's at least half a century old, a true classic.

Below the dam, we veer off from the rock garden, following Ethan into a side channel that turns out to be a very fast, very long canal or millrace, a vestige of the days when settlers attempted to navigate the upper river in flatboats. It's like the log-flume ride at Great Adventure: a fast run with the current tugging us along. We dodge rocks, slide around a long left-hand bend, and I get my first dousing of the trip, a slap in the face with cold water.

Great stuff.

It's a sporty ride through the second rapids at Battles Falls, and at one point we actually do a three-sixty (our first but far from our last of the trip). We drop to the bottom of the race and, just yards from the still waters of the bottom eddy, stick hard on an underwater rock. For the first of many times, we hop out of the canoe, shove it forward into deeper water, then slip back in. We become very adept at this, so that in time whenever we stick hard on a rock, we don't even have to speak; we just free the boat and continue on our way.

The rapids have gone from Class I to Class II. Ethan explains later that anytime you get doused with a wave of water while going through a white-water passage, that counts as Class II. So I've been baptized with cold Class II water.

We're cruising right along, finding our rhythm, fully entering the environment of the river both physically and psychologically. For the first time in all

Running the first chute below Buckhorn Dam (Amy Williamson photo)

the weeks of preparation, I find myself completely absorbed in the moment, free from anxiety and distraction, completely *present*. There's just too much to claim my attention on the river for my mind to wander anywhere else.

Not far below the dam, we pass a lone black fisherman in a small johnboat setting out lines. He throws us a friendly wave, but he's intent on casting his line. He's fishing in the St. Jude Children's Hospital Tournament—all for a good cause and the chance to win a few thousand bucks. We wish him luck and proceed downriver, which we will now have to ourselves for miles.

After two hours of good paddling, we stop for lunch on a grassy shaded bench pocked with fresh deer tracks.

Amy has been adventuring outdoors with Ethan long enough that for most routine activities, such as paddling the river, they hardly have to talk at all. She is fit and relaxed, thoughtful and watchful, and speaks quietly. Her dark hair is short-cropped, and she is self-possessed, curious, and alert.

She has a great eye for spotting birds in any layer of the canopy, and her ear is just as remarkable. Amy is a birder by avocation, self-taught, particularly good at hearing and recognizing signature songs and calls. She's keeping a list for the trip, and it's already filling up: prothonotary warblers (little yellow things), waterthrushes (in mating pairs all down the river), spotted sandpipers, Carolina wrens, red-eyed vireos, the ever-present soaring ospreys, yellow-billed cuckoos, northern flickers, red-bellied woodpeckers, and great blue herons. I have always associated herons with the seashore, but they are equally at home on rivers, lakes, and ponds.

Onshore we have already seen evidence of northern raccoons, bullfrogs, and the ubiquitous yellow-bellied sliders, flat-shelled turtles that crawl up onto logs and then plink themselves into the water just before you get close. They often line up comically by size—largest, then medium, then smallest, and sometimes the really tiny turtles will actually climb onto the larger turtles' backs. So our paddle is punctuated all day by the soft plash of multiple turtles, some as small as a biscuit, some as large as a dinner plate, plopping into the brown water.

Turtles are good. They indicate clean water. When the turtles disappear, watch out.

In the water itself we see carp rising, along with catfish and long-nosed gar, which make quite a ruckus when they rise. The gar is a primitive-looking fish with a bony head that protrudes like an armored ram from its face, if a fish can be said to have a face. It would look right at home among dinosaurs, and in fact its relatives were around during the Cretaceous period of the Mesozoic era, well established by the time the dinosaurs died out. The gar grows to be about a yard long, and its only enemy on the river—besides human fishermen—is *Alligator mississippiensis*—the American alligator, which is lurking many miles downriver.

David reaches down into the shallow, clear water and pulls up river mussels. There are two varieties: the native species, *elliptio*, which used to cover the Cape Fear River so extensively it was said to be able to filter the entire volume of the river every mile, and *corbicula*, the Asian clam, what is kindly called an "introduced" species, less kindly an "invasive" species. Either way, it has just about taken over the river from poor little *elliptio*. *Corbicula*, like the zebra mussel that infested the Great Lakes when it was discharged from the bilge water of oceangoing ships, can clog intake valves and choke water pipes.

On the upper reaches of the Cape Fear, the river is serene—eddies and a slow current regularly quickened by rapids, the banks covered in thick foliage, deciduous trees draped with lush vines. We are only a couple dozen miles from the busiest metropolitan area in the state, yet we are in a wild place, a place with hardly any access by road. This will be true most of the way down the river, and it's the best protection the river has.

The pace of a drifting canoe affords time to look, really look. The banks are greening up with spring, deep shadowy bowers limned by the bright greens of willows and hanging clouds of poison ivy.

The banks here are cut but not high, and the river carries a heavy silt load. As a rule of thumb, mountain rivers carry heavier sediment particles—gravel, coarse sand, grit—because they can. They move fast. As the river slows downstream and gravity lets up a bit, the heaver bits of sediment drop to the bottom and only the lighter stuff—dirt, clay—remains roiling in the slow current. This is how the river builds up bottomland in its delta, the topsoil carried in the quick current sinking in the slow, lazy meanders as the grade flattens and the river approaches the sea.

We paddle with the current, coasting fast through rapids and gliding along at a more leisurely pace in the long stretches in between, the riverbank wild on either side. We settle into our task paddling the Green Monster, listening to the birds, the soft splash of our paddle blades, the music of the water gliding along the sleek drum that is our hull.

For miles, we have the river all to ourselves.

Our adventure is under way.

We let the current take us.

This becomes a theme of the trip.

John Steinbeck, who roamed America in a camper truck called *Rocinante* searching for the soul of his own troubled nation to write *Travels with Charley*, put it nicely: "We find after years of struggle that we do not take a trip; a trip takes us."

So it is with our little expedition. Even when we pick a course through the white water, invariably the current does something unexpected, slews us around, grabs our bow, and sucks us toward a rock or, if we're lucky, a sluice. If the former, we bump around it or push off it, snake our way back toward the main current. If the latter, we feel that little thrill in the stomach as we drop fast and rocket forward in a chirpy spray of cold water.

Sometimes the current stalls us in an eddy, and all our paddling gets us nowhere until we cooperate with what the river is trying to do; just dip a blade like a rudder into the current to steer us along. Sometimes the river takes us down a chute backward and we simply ride along, hunkered forward, paddles shipped across the gunwales, until the river spits us out downstream, pointing again in the right direction.

Some of this is our inexperience. But really a lot of it is simply the river being what it is: an elemental force propelled by gravity, a tremendous mass that moves downhill inexorably, pushing past rocks, carving out the far bank of a bend because a physical law dictates that the water on the outside has to go a longer distance than that on the inside, and so must move faster to keep up with the river. And sometimes the river narrows and the water speeds up again because, as described by the Continuity Equation, if you decrease the radius of the conduit, the fluid moving through it must speed up according to a predictable formula.

Running a river is a great lesson in fluid dynamics without any numbers or arcane symbols. You're right there inside the equation, feeling it whirl and dip you. There's nothing abstract about it: The water is moving in complex ways, and with power.

For example, at the foot of Buckhorn Dam the water flow over the dam produces what paddlers call a recirculating current, or "hydraulic." Ethan explains all this to me in an ongoing series of lessons, sometimes drifting along beside us, other times as we rest on the bank. The water pours over the dam and into the pool at the foot of the dam with such force that it actually hits the bottom and curls back toward the dam in a permanent wave. Thus, you can position your boat at the foot of the dam, facing upstream, and remain stationary almost indefinitely with only a minor stroke or two, surfing the current, for the downstream lip of the wave has caught your bow and is pulling it upstream, though not hard enough to actually move the boat—just enough to a achieve equilibrium.

But if you get caught inside the "boil-line" of the hydraulic, you will just be tumbled over and over, unable to break free of the powerful cycle. This can be true in the water at the foot of any sluice or ledge, but it's actually most dangerous at the foot of a long, even dam (like Buckhorn), because the only way to break the cycle is to move parallel to the ledge or dam until you move out of the pull of the hydraulic—much like swimming parallel to shore to break free of a rip current in the ocean. But if the dam is unbroken across the whole river, there's no way to break free of the hydraulic.

In that case the journey really does take you—and may not give you back.

Another ever-present danger on the Cape Fear is foot entrapment—which is just what it sounds like: Your foot gets snagged between underwater rocks, the current rushes you downstream, head underwater, and you drown because, with the tremendous force of the water tugging you tighter into their grip, you cannot break free of the rocks.

The worst danger of all, perhaps, is getting caught in what paddlers call a "strainer"—usually a tree that has fallen across the current. And on the Cape Fear, with all the hurricanes that have barreled upstream in the past fifteen years, there are plenty of those. Water can pass through the tangle of submerged branches, but they will trap a swimmer. And a paddler approaching a strainer will inevitably become a swimmer as, bow stalled against the obstacle, the canoe or kayak broaches broadside and the current tips out the paddler. The only recourse, explains Paul Ferguson in his river-running bible, *Paddling Eastern North Carolina* (which is safely encased in my dry bag), is to either make it to the bank or else launch yourself onto the downed tree, clambering to safety above the deadly roil of the strainer.

Ethan reinforces this wisdom on the river. He has guided many trips for kids' adventure camps, and every so often a boat has come to grief against a downed tree and paddlers have managed to self-rescue, scrambling aboard the branches, while he and others retrieved their boats downstream.

So we are alert to fallen trees, especially those that are partially submerged,

Ethan Williamson, river guide (Amy Williamson photo)

and we spot plenty of them. Luckily we manage to avoid the many strainers we pass by diligent scouting of the water ahead with binoculars.

There's not much human activity visible on the banks. From time to time we see a primitive fish camp, usually a small cabin with some kind of dock attached, a barbecue, and some outdoor chairs. Some folks have ingeniously engineered solutions to the problem of getting down to the water from a high bank. (What an old native North Carolina friend of mine calls "redneck engineering," and it seems to work.)

For instance, one house features a dock/deck that protrudes over the water beside the house, its cantilevered surface supported by two cables strapped to big trees on the bank and slanting down to the ends of the deck. Others have homemade ladders, boatlifts, even elevators. None looks very sturdy, but on the other hand, all look as if they've been there a good long while, judging by the rust and rot. On one stretch, the docks are all metal, welded rusty contraptions, one with an elevator that looks frozen with rust, a relic from another age. Some are creepy and appear abandoned, like the wrecks of old ship's boilers in the Wilmington harbor on Eagles Island.

One flies a sun-faded, tattered Confederate flag, which is either defiant and proud, blatantly racist, an emblem of defeat, a gesture of nostalgia, or maybe some combination of all four. Or maybe it's just an expression of clannish pride, the way a bunch of boys will plant a flag over their tree fort.

THE UPPER REACHES

The shoreline reels by like a movie without voices. The trip takes you. The current, the river, takes you. The rocks snag you. Your companions take you.

The old Grumman is half a century old and hard-edged proof. We snag every rock in the river, seemingly, and shine them up. On our way downriver, we also spy on the bottom both a frying pan and a baking pan, unmistakable artifacts of someone else's spill, reminding us we're far from the first to paddle down this river. We slip by them too fast to recover them in the deep, clear water.

~~~~~~~~~~

Humans have been navigating the Cape Fear River for a very long time, probably centuries before it was called the Cape Fear. The old Indian trails that are now paved over as U.S. Route 421 and N.C. 87 bracket the Cape Fear River east and west. They suggest that traffic with the interior was going on for hundreds of years at least before Europeans arrived. Logic suggests that the river would have been a natural highway returning to the coast. We know that the various Indian tribes made dugout canoes by burning hollows in logs.

James Sprunt, who probably researched the history of the region more thoroughly than anyone before or since, reports that the Indians called the Cape Fear River "Sapona." The Spaniards called it the Rio Jordan. Early English settlers called it, interchangeably, the Charles or the Clarendon. Sometimes Clarendon referred to what we now call the Brunswick River, a short detour off the Cape Fear's main channel at Wilmington that rejoins the river farther down.

Remember, this was back during an age when maps were very provisional, based on a mixture of hearsay, wishful thinking, commercial promotion to prospective settlers and underwriters, outright fabrication, whimsy, and even, on occasion, actual exploration of the region in question. Names were coined to flatter kings and underwriters; then along came other explorers with different agendas, as well as new kings and underwriters, and the old names were scratched out and the new ones penned in.

So, for a long period, various mapmakers called Cape Fear "Cape Fair," perhaps to reinforce the glowing descriptions of the lower river brought back to England by Captain James Hilton after his expedition from Barbados of 1663. He called the point on Bald Head Island (then called Smith's—everything on the river has a lineage of names) "Cape Fair." Hilton's crew was greeted by Indians who provided fresh fish—shad and mullet—and the expedition took on an Indian guide for its exploration of the main branch and assorted tributaries, making it halfway to the current site of Fayetteville before retiring back to the coast.

Hilton dealt with an Indian chief he called Wat Coosa and, to his mind at least, purchased the river and surrounding lands. Wat Coosa is the only Cape Fear Indian whose name has been recorded. His village was called Necoes. Probably the Cape Fear Indians were Siouxan, related to more northerly tribes by language. But not much is known about them. Indeed, the name itself was conferred upon them; we don't know by what name they called themselves. And the term "Cape Fear Indians" may refer to several groups scattered along the lower river and adjacent coast. It might even include a conglomeration of other tribes all the way up the river, all lumped together by European settlers not interested in making fine distinctions.

Hilton's party looked for cattle that had been left behind by an earlier expedition from New England, which had come up the river with the intention of colonizing it. What Hilton's band found instead was writing on a post, "the contents whereof tended not only to the disparagement of the land about the said river, but also to the great discouragement of all as should hereafter come into these parts to settle." Hilton was outraged by the "scandalous" writing left behind by this splinter group of pilgrims, and thus it was probably intentional that he called the place not *Fear*, but *Fair*. In this way he became the region's first civic booster.

Sprunt—of whom much more later—opens his *Chronicles of the Cape Fear River, 1660-1916* with the very question of the name: "Is it Cape Fair? Or Cape Fear? Adjective or Noun?" And he proceeds with a lawyerly treatise on the merits of each claim, complete with citations from all the prominent cartographers of the Age of Exploration.

Of the cape that lends its name to the river, he at last concludes, with a magisterial flourish, "It is the playground of billows and tempests, the kingdom of silence and awe, disturbed by no sound save the sea gull's shriek and the breakers' roar. Its whole aspect is suggestive, not of repose and beauty, but of desolation and terror. Imagination can not adorn it. Romance can not hallow it. Local pride can not soften it. There it stands today, bleak, and threatening, and pitiless, as it stood three hundred years ago. . . . And, as its nature, so its name, is now, always has been, and always will be, the Cape of Fear."

His point is well taken, and with a flourish.

Every account of early exploration of the river mouth seems to open with a comment about just how treacherous the passage through the shoals proved to be—every account, that is, except the very first.

The first European to visit the area was Giovanni da Verrazano in 1524 aboard *La Dauphine*, sailing in the service of King Francis I of France. He reports in a letter to the king, "The sea is calm, not boisterous, and its waves are gentle. Although the whole coast is low and without harbours, it is not dangerous for navigation, being free from rocks and bold." Of course, Verrazano had just sailed through "as violent a hurricane as any ship ever weathered" on his way to the Carolina coast, so he was likely seeing the flat aftermath of a storm, the quiet high that settles in behind a big low as it sucks the weather up the coast with it.

And Verrazano did not make his report in English; the translation comes courtesy of "Joseph B. Cogswell, Esq., of the N.Y. Historical Society &c." in 1841. The original letter does not survive, just two Italian copies of it, the first published in 1556. So plenty of historians have stepped forward over the years to claim it was a forgery, that Verrazano never made any such voyage, that the whole document was contrived to give France claims in the New World. Some even assert that there were not one but two distinct Verrazanos: one a reputable narrator, the other a corsair executed for piracy in 1527 for looting Cortez's treasure ships on the Spanish Main.

But the letter rings true and carries the spirit of the Age of Discovery.

Like most maritime explorers of his era, Verrazano was seeking a passage to Asia to exploit the riches to be found there, including and especially spices. Instead he found the Cape Fear River, anchored at its mouth for a time, and had some contact with the local Indians. At first he observed fires burning at intervals all along the shoreline, indicating a fairly large local population. He drew close enough inshore to be able to see them gesticulating, then he apparently entered the river and got some further encouragement to anchor. He and some of this crew went ashore, where they discovered a crowd of inhabitants eager to share provisions and satisfy their curiosity about these odd-looking strangers who had come in off the sea.

The encounter was apparently pleasant enough for all concerned. Verrazano found the inhabitants charming and good-looking and in his letter describes them in considerable detail: "They go entirely naked, except that about their loins they wear skins of small animals like martens fastened by a girdle of plaited grass, to which they tie, all round the body, the tails of other animals hanging down to the knees."

In addition, he notes, with the alertness of an anthropologist, "Some wear garlands similar to birds' feathers."

He records that they were dark-skinned as Ethiopians and wore their thick black hair comparatively short, "worn tied in the back of the head in the form of a little tail."

He goes on, "In person they are of good proportions, of middle stature, a little above our own, broad across the breast, strong in the arms, and well formed in legs and other parts of the body." Their faces, however, he decides are mostly too broad to satisfy a European standard of beauty. "They are not very strong in body but acute in mind, active and swift of foot, as far as we could judge by observation."

His letter to a faraway king feels like old hat to us, the stuff of seventh-grade history books. But actually it's a remarkable encounter—compared to the ones had by the likes of Columbus, Pizzaro, Cortez, and a horde of other more rapacious explorers. Remember, practically the first thing Columbus did on discovering the New World was to preside over the rape of a native Taino girl, a practice that became a favorite method of rewarding subordinates, and just about the second thing he did was to enslave the inhabitants of every island where he landed.

Verrazano, by contrast, is enamored of the local inhabitants and writes about them with respect and an eye for noticing rather than judging (okay, he finds their broad faces rather unattractive, but he's also quick to point out that some of the Indians have more angular faces with piercing black eyes, and those *do* appeal to his aesthetic sense). He is grateful for their largesse and treats with them as equals—indeed, he acts like a guest, not a conqueror. And he leaves them as well off as he found them, which can't be said for very many of his peers in the explorers game.

Verrazano sailed south as far as Charleston, then coasted north to the Hudson before returning to France.

A subsequent voyage a few years later landed him in the Lesser Antilles, and there his diplomatic skills apparently broke down. He went ashore at Guadeloupe Island and was promptly captured and eaten by cannibals.

Two years after Verrazano cruised on to New York, Captain Francisco Gordillo, sailing under the sponsorship of Lucas Vázquez de Ayllón, entered the "Rio Jordan" and explored it as far up as Town Creek, halfway to present-day Wilmington. Vázquez de Ayllón attempted to colonize South Carolina, and he even brought African slaves to help in carving out a colony near the mouth of the Pee Dee River at Winyah Bay; but his efforts produced the typical saga of violent bloodshed, oppression of the native peoples, a slave revolt, and finally failure, fever, and death.

Later explorers uniformly treat the Cape Fear approaches with trepidation.

In June 1585, on his first expedition to the region, Sir Richard Grenville writes, "The 23rd we were in great danger of a wreck on a breach called the Cape of Fear." Note (as Sprunt does) that he calls it a "breach," as in, a passage through the shoals, not a "beach."

Likewise, two years later, in July 1587, on another voyage of exploration sponsored by Sir Walter Raleigh, John White, the expedition artist, reports that "had not Captain Stafford been more careful in looking out than our Simon Fernando, we had been all cast away on a breach called the Cape of Fear."

Simon Fernando was a recalcitrant pilot and something of a troublemaker. He balked at taking White's party to the Chesapeake Bay, the original destination, stranding them instead on Roanoke Island—where an earlier colony had already failed. White went on to become governor of the colony on Roanoke Island. His daughter, Eleanor, married Ananias Dare and bore the first child born to English parents in the New World, named Virginia. White returned to England later that year to arrange for more provisions to be shipped to the faltering colony, but his return was delayed for three years. When he did at last make it back in 1590, all the inhabitants, including his daughter and granddaughter, had vanished without a trace, the only clue the enigmatic word CROATOAN carved on a tree.

Thus was born the legend of the Lost Colony of Roanoke Island, recounted each year in the outdoor drama of the same name by playwright Paul Green.

In the same year as White's voyage to Roanoke, 1787, the cape appears on a map identified only as *promontorium tremendum*—"terrible" or "awe-inspiring cape."

I'll take either. From the shore, it's awe-inspiring. From the deck of a sailing ship at sea, it's terrifying. But the passage through the shoals to the river was the beginning of European travel on the Cape Fear.

~~~~~~~

Many miles and days upriver from the Cape of Fear, our little party of canoeists has settled into a routine of paddling and watching, feeling the water under us carry our boats along with an easy motion, as the scenery onshore reels by and the turtles go splish-splash.

We keep moving at a steady pace, but we don't spend the whole time paddling.

Though we are proceeding according to the necessary fiction that we have all the time in the world, we do in fact have something of a schedule to keep—we are four busy people who all have responsibilities off the river, and as much as we have tried to carve a leisurely hole in our collective schedules, we can't avoid the clock entirely. But by lopping off the first stage above Buckhorn Dam, we've built in some play time the first day, to get used to the river and enjoy the fast water on the upper reaches. We stop for lunch at a little island made by fallen trees and eat sweet homemade bread baked by my wife, Jill, in imitation of the loaves my mother used to bake for me in coffee cans when I was a wild, roving, backpacking college kid—full of fruit and nuts—along with delectable cold bruscetta, boxes of fruit juice, and other snacky goodies.

We hang out for an hour or so in the shade. I stretch my surprisingly stiff legs. I blew out my right knee many years ago chasing down a fly ball in left field, and several surgeries later it tends to lock up on me if I sit too long. I rub circulation back into it. Then it's time to get under way again, leaving us plenty of time to dawdle downstream on our way to Raven Rock before dark.

We drift for a time, and Amy, feeling the heat of the sun-drenched day, slips out of their canoe into the water for a swim. Then, a few minutes later, she adroitly flips herself back into the canoe without so much as a wobble, as Ethan steers, oblivious, completely relaxed, in the stern. This is over-your-head deep water, and I find this remarkable—that a grown woman can exit and reboard a canoe in motion without upsetting it. But they've been adventuring companions for years, run many a river together, and hiked and camped and sailed and come to rely on each other. Each can anticipate what the other will do and react without words. A shift of weight in the canoe, a paddlestroke to change direction.

Slipping overboard and flipping back in.

All the while we're hearing birds, watching birds. The river teems with birds, swooping, soaring, circling, perching, scurrying over rocks and sandbars. Red-headed turkey vultures spiral overhead—I always confuse them with hawks, but for a trained eye, the trailing silvery white edge of the underside of the wing is unmistakable—while Canada geese and mallards and wood ducks with tufted crowns skid onto the shimmering surface of the river and then float there in small rafts. The ducks are always paired with mates, so they raft in even numbers. There are lots of juveniles, small and skittish. The mallards are easily distinguished by sex: striking green-blue-headed males and speckled brown females. They seem to dote on their mates, swimming close together, sitting side by side on the bank.

It's tempting to overlay human qualities on the ducks: tenderness, fidelity, even love. But we can't know what goes on in the minds of birds. All we know is what we can see: close companionship that will outlast the season. But their presence endows the river with a sense of ordinary beauty, of a kind of natural business-as-usual that is both routine and wonderful.

In our daily lives away from the river, all too often we go through whole days without any routine beauty, growing accustomed by degrees to coarseness, to the bland ugliness of highways lined with concrete strip malls, to dirty pavement, to being trapped inside walls with no view of the world out-

doors. It helps to be outside, carried along by a current that would be coursing toward the sea with or without us aboard, kept company by squadrons of oblivious loyal ducks.

Between Buckhorn Dam and the take-out at Fayetteville, with David vigorously helping her spot, Amy will log sixty-three species of birds, not including several others that we only hear but never see. Amy has a spectacular ear for birdcalls, a kind of perfect pitch when it comes to recognizing the signature songs of a given species: the harsh rattle of the belted kingfisher, perched invisibly on a branch overhanging the current, or the *churr-churr-yarrow-yarrow-yarrow* of the red-headed woodpecker off in the treeline, followed by the staccato tapping of its beak into pine bark.

Early spring is the ideal time to find nesting songbirds and migrating species of all kinds. The most spectacular ones that we spot are bald eagles (six), ospreys (six), great blue herons (five), and the much smaller green herons (two). Migrating geese and ducks are ubiquitous, as are glossy black cormorants, diving for fish and disappearing for long moments underwater, only to emerge like periscopes a dozen yards from where they submerged.

We also spot a red-tailed hawk, a smaller Cooper's hawk, and six red-shouldered hawks, all hunting the riverbanks. There are tanagers, orioles, buntings, flycatchers, cuckoos, doves, kingfishers, phoebes, sandpipers, crows, vireos, blue jays, chickadees, titmouses, starlings, thrashers, cardinals, grosbeaks, grackles, Carolina wrens, purple martins, flickers, and four varieties of woodpecker. Even their names make a kind of music, as Amy and David pronounce each sighting.

Cliff swallows nest under the concrete abutments of bridges, and barn swallows and chimney swifts erupt in small squadrons from the steel bridges and bluffs. The forested banks are haunted by both the eastern screech owl and its much larger cousin, the great horned owl, which has a wingspan of more than four and a half feet and preys on any creature up to the size of a large rabbit. The screech owl emits an eerie cry, and the great horned owl calls the signature *Who-who?*

Amy's notes record just how plentiful some species are: "In particular, we saw an astonishing number of Louisiana Waterthrushes and Prothonotary Warblers, no doubt because we were cruising right through their prime habitat during the height of breeding season, when they had staked out territory and were singing and visibly patrolling. These birds occupied every bit of territory along the way. I mean this literally—there were NO areas along the river where there were not territorial Louisiana Waterthrushes and Prothonotaries."

The mating pairs claim territories 100 to 150 yards apart all along the upper river. Different mating pairs claim the opposite banks. And each species patrols a certain level of the territories. The prothonotaries sweep back and forth from the low to mid-level branches, their golden orange heads and breasts bright accents among the deeper greens and browns of the spring thicket. The Louisiana waterthrushes, olive-brown on top and white and streaked below, are visible on the banks and twisted tree roots and among the low branches of the canopy. They are twitchy birds, easy to spot because of their frequently bobbing tails. Spotted sandpipers hop along the sandbars, cobble bars, and rocks at water's edge and in midstream.

So who cares about bird-watching? What does it matter that sixty-three species of birds have accompanied us so far downriver?

Think of it this way: The birds add a third dimension. The river is not just long and broad; it also has *height*. There are layers to the canopy of foliage and trees lining the river, covering the wetlands of its floodplain. There are lenses in the air column above the river. The birds emphasize this added dimension, swooping and soaring and circling, or just flitting by. There is a grid of airspace above us, invisible three-dimensional boxes of "aer-ritory," glide-slopes and cruising lanes, a whole intricate aerobatic display carried on by thousands of birds, many flashing bright and startling in the sun, others bursting like dull gunshots from the foliage, almost too fast to see.

And their constant song—twitters, screeches, chirps, squawks, abrupt chattering outbursts, and long melodic trills—creates a constant soundtrack for the river, against the rhythm of rushing water and soughing breeze, the punctuation of splashing turtles and jumping fish, and the soft percussion of regular paddle strokes. Their combined song fills that third dimension.

In fact, the third dimension of the river rises higher than we might suppose.

The river creates its own weather, in the sense that the temperature of the surface of its waters varies a lot from the temperature of the adjacent land. At this time of year, the river is much cooler, and this has a fairly dramatic effect on wind and air temperature over the water. The riverbanks heat faster than the river water, and hot air rises, just as cool air sinks. We experience this as a fairly significant breeze that follows the contours of the river. That is, the air on the bank may seem still as stone, but in midstream, at the same moment, we may be paddling against a stiff breeze rushing toward the heated interior.

Hawks, turkey vultures, eagles, and other raptors take advantage of the updrafts of warmer air—thermals—to gyre and soar with minimal effort as they hunt for fish and small prey far below. And sometimes, to be honest, they look as if they are doing it just for the pure enjoyment of it, airborne for long intervals, just being high in space, lofted along by winds they can feel but not see.

And why not? Why deny animals the thrill of exhilaration?

The one species of bird we do not spot is the Carolina parakeet, a green bird with a bright yellow head and orange cheeks—the only native American parakeet. It was hunted to extinction by the early settlers of the Cape Fear River because it fed on cornfields and apple orchards. Commercial hunters also killed it for its colorful feathers, used in making ladies' hats. By the Civil War it was just a ghost in North Carolina, though it survived in Florida until 1904. The last known specimen died in the Cincinnati Zoo in 1918—in the same aviary that had once housed Martha, the last of the passenger pigeons.

Ultimately we pull up onto a rocky spur and park the boats and all swim for awhile, lolling in the cool brown river in a two-knot current. We tell jokes and banter about the three local boys we met on the river a little ways upstream, tooling along in a Johnboat. They cut their motor when they spotted us, drifted over, and wished us a good day.

"Pretty day to be on the river," Ethan said.

"Pretty river," one of them said. We talked about nothing for a minute or two. We told them we were headed all the way downriver. They were just out fishing and for a lark.

"Good luck," they said, then revved up their motor and went on their way.

In some sense, such people are more genuine environmentalists than a lot of the rest of us. They recognize the allure of the wild space of the river, get out onto it. Like the commercial fishermen on the coast, they're the first to know when a species of fish goes missing, when the water is fouled by an overspill of hog waste upstream or oiled and roiled by torrential rain washing down bare, unbuffered banks.

Nowadays, very few people ply this stretch of the river out of necessity. Roads are faster than river travel. The great flatboats and lumber rafts of by-gone days are no longer. Many miles downstream lies the broad working river, full of tugboats and container ships and commercial trawlers and Coast Guard cutters. For those men and women, the river is a jobsite. But with few exceptions, whoever goes onto the river up here does so by choice: to fish or explore or just find refuge from the clatter and din of contemporary life. Just to mess around in a small boat, out of cell phone range.

We're apt to be an agreeable lot, as long as we're on the river.

We also stop for a long time—an hour and a half perhaps—to play at Lanier Falls, just above Raven Rock. We pull in above the falls and run the chute over and over and surf the hydraulic in Ethan's unloaded canoe. Lanier is formed by a ledge that crosses the whole channel, with white-water chutes on either side. Ethan is an expert, and I run the left-hand chute with him, then body-surf it with only the life vest on, feet up to avoid getting them trapped in underwater crevices between or under rocks.

Then I spend a good long time relaxing in the cold whirlpool bath formed in the eddy of the chute against the downstream rocks. The sensation is refreshing and quite wonderful, the cool water boiling around me, leaving me semi-weightless, nudged into the slick curve of rock at my back, my ears full of the music of fast-running water.

There's another party of canoes and kayaks on the far side of the falls. One guy in particular is a real expert, shooting the sluice over and over again, surfing the recirculating current at the bottom. All at once David recognizes him as a former student from twenty-odd years ago. They enjoy a little reunion there at the falls, catching up on two decades' worth of family and jobs.

David and I unload the Green Monster and slip it down the chute perfectly, only to come to grief on an underwater rock at the bottom. We strike the rock hard and head-on and get caught the way a canoe will. It broaches sideways against the rock, and then the full force of the current pushes directly at the gunwale of the canoe and upends it. We bang hard and dump the canoe. The key thing is not to get pinned between the heavy canoe and the rock, and this we easily manage to do. Once we're out of the canoe, standing waist-deep in the rushing water, it isn't hard to tow it out of the boisterous current, bail it, and then haul it to the downstream eddy behind the same flat rock onto which we unloaded our gear, so we can reload and push off in milder waters.

No harm, no foul. We unpacked the canoe deliberately before daring the chute, so if we did indeed capsize we wouldn't get any gear wet, and now this looks like a genius move.

We were all already wet, delightfully so in the heat, so it

Surfing the hydraulic at Lanier Falls (Amy Williamson photo)

doesn't matter that we took another swim. My one worry is that my new hat has been swept away, and I fear that a few days on the river without a good hat will fry my brain. But as we're towing the canoe toward the eddy, David alertly fishes it out of the current and I slap it back on my head, cool and dripping.

I had a feeling we would capsize at some point on the river, because all day, from the moment we got into the car, David kept saying stuff like, "I've never dumped a canoe in my life." He meant it to be reassuring, since I was not very experienced—or at least, most of my experience came a long time ago—and he has been on many rivers, many lakes, in many weathers. But, as I explained to him, he never had me for his bowman.

So it had to happen. You just can't tempt fate like that. Oh, the hubris.

But the chute at Lanier is a heavy Class II, and after we recover our canoe and finish bailing the river out of it, David declares manfully, "If I had to dump a canoe today, I don't mind saying that I did it here."

I originally planned to run the upper reaches in my kayak, in which I have paddled a number of the lower tributaries. It is fast, light, and sleek and has a sturdy backrest; but when a fifth member of the expedition had a conflict and could not make the trip, I moved from solitary paddler in a sleek kayak to bowman in an aluminum canoe, and when all is said and done, it has made the trip both more exciting and more memorable—not to say more satisfying

THE UPPER REACHES

Ethan runs the chute at Lanier falls, his canoe fully loaded (Amy Williamson photo)

on account of David's good companionship and the lessons he and Ethan have imparted to me about canoe handling. And canoe bailing.

One more set of rapids awaits us between Lanier Falls and our stopping point at Raven Rock. It's called Fishtraps, the rocky bones of an old lock and dam dating from the era of the Cape Fear Navigation Company, before it finally yielded to the river in 1834 and confined itself to the channel below Fayetteville, the natural head of navigation of the Cape Fear. We run Fishtraps cleanly, pass Tory Rock, and fetch up near the entrance to the canoe camps, shadowed by the high bluffs that block the sinking sun. We recognize the take-out by the cockeyed white buoy anchored just a few yards off the bank against a fallen tree that juts into the river. It's low water, and the buoy is stranded on mud.

We have arrived at Raven Rock State Park.

It's well after six in the evening when we tie off our canoes at the foot of steep stairs that lead up twenty feet or so above the water. To get to the canoe campsites at Raven Rock State Park, reserved in advance, we have to haul our boats out of the river a couple of feet onto the muddy bench that forms the

The stairs leading to the Raven Rock Park canoe camp (author photo)

bank. In higher water, the bench would be a beach, and we could simply slide the bow home and step out. Our choice is either to tie off our canoe to one of the trees, to make sure it doesn't float away in the night if the water rises, or to haul it up that first series of stairs made of landscaping timbers etched into the bank. These take you to another landing large enough for perhaps two boats. A second set of steep stairs brings you to a meadow with an outdoor privy and trails branching off to the various secluded campsites.

David and I leave the heavy Grumman down by the water, securely tied to a tree, then make several trips to hump up food, tent, and bedding to our site, canoe camp #4.

Ethan single-handedly carries his plastic Mohawk up both sets of stairs and finds a niche for it beside the trail leading to our campsite. It's an old habit of his, keeping his gear close. Manhandling the boat is a matter of strength and balance, but he doesn't seem to give it much thought, just lifts it over his head and clambers up the timber steps and lays it down in the grass gently.

Setting up camp takes only about twenty minutes. My tent is brand-new, two interlocking poles through sleeves, gray and red nylon with mesh windows and a rain fly, and it goes up in a matter of minutes. Ethan cooks up a pot of pasta, and we use the sturdy plastic buckets as seating. The mosquitoes start at dusk but are bad only for a little while, and we enjoy a small campfire in the fire ring. We're surrounded by fallen trees, including a few massive ones—pines and some beech or sycamore, judging by their gray, scaly bark—

that came down recently in storms. Our campsite, so thickly forested now, was once a meadow, and it has returned to forest in a natural cycle of succession that takes about a generation: First bushes and thickets rise up, then saplings, and finally a young canopied forest.

A group of young kayakers has set up camp in site #2, just fifty yards or so from us. We can't see them through the trees and thick brush, but we can sure hear them. They commence to chopping energetically with a hatchet, and we joke that they must be building a cabin, they are hacking so much. Soon they have a smoky fire, which we can smell more than see, and we hear them talking for awhile and then go quiet.

So we chow down on three-cheese tortellini and bruschetta, black olive sauce and parmesan. (We open a good pinot and an even better Malbec, which we sip discreetly, since no alcohol is allowed in state parks and we don't want to get thrown out. Where would we go?) It's good company after a day on the river.

Ethan takes a stroll in the gathering darkness down the trail to the boats. When he returns, I ask him if he wants a flashlight. Ferguson's paddling guide warned against snakes at the landing for Raven Rock. In addition to copperheads, the park is a haven for the nonvenomous northern water snake, the rat snake, and the hog-nosed snake, which mimics a rattler when cornered, first rising from its coil and hissing while faking a pretty convincing rattle.

"No," he says. "There's nothing out here at this time of day."

David smiles and says, "Actually, this is the time of day you're most likely to see a copperhead."

"Well, in that case . . ." From then on, we all carry lights.

David goes off to visit with his former student, who is camped nearby, and returns in the gathering darkness.

We hear the sudden bloodcurdling screech of an owl, and Amy tries in vain to get it to call again—I'm not making this up—by playing a recorded owl screech app on her phone. She plays it several times and we listen hard in the darkness, but whatever bird was out there a couple of minutes ago isn't talking back to us now.

~~~~~~~~~~~~

Raven Rock lies along the fall zone of the river, that in-between space where the Piedmont, the last geologic folds of hard-rock mountain, forged in a cauldron of unimaginable heat and pressure some 400 million years ago, gives way to the softer alluvial coastal plain. In fact, since Buckhorn Dam, the river has dropped almost forty-five vertical feet—more than two and a half feet per mile—hence the rushing momentum of gravity on the river.

So in fifteen miles or so we have done the equivalent of falling off a four-story building.

The evidence of this drop looms high over our heads. The actual rocky bluff named Raven Rock is unusual along the river, towering 150 feet above the water for more than a mile on the western bank, the signature geology of a park that now spreads out across almost 5,000 acres threaded by ten trails for hikers and horses, including the Northington Ferry Trail. This trail leads to the spot where, in bygone days, the Raleigh to Fayetteville Road used to intersect the river just below Lanier Falls. Like everything else along the river, this place used to be called something else—Patterson's Rock—until in 1854 it was renamed for the ravens that roosted by the hundreds in the crags of the bluffs.

The park is a riot of wildflowers.

The description on its website seems at first blush a little too enthusiastic, even gushy: "Look over patches of Dutchman's breeches, bloodroot, saxifrage and trailing arbutus. Gaze down paths lined with Solomon's seal, bellwort and spring beauty, or let your eyes wander through a haze of greens and yellows as leaves break their winter dormancy and begin to color the forest." But then you see the park, and it's all true. You rehearse those glorious names as you walk its paths, even say them out loud, and you can practically taste the names as they roll off your tongue. The place is gorgeously wild and overgrown, every turn in the trail opening upon a new discovery.

As I hiked along Little Creek trail during an earlier trip to scout the campsite, the air was still and dappled with shadow, the stream alive with minnows and frogs and salamanders, the trees thick with warblers. More than twenty species of warblers are known to inhabit the park in spring. Other denizens include muskrats, weasels, raccoons, white-tailed deer, cottontails, shrews, and bats, as well as fence lizards, skinks, and Carolina anoles.

We toyed with the idea of running down to Raven Rock mostly unloaded, then meeting friends at dusk to carry down our tents and sleeping bags and load us up with provisions for supper and the rest of the trip, but in the end we abandoned that plan. Little Creek Loop Trail, leading from the picnic area parking lot to the canoe camp, is only a mile and a half long, give or take; but it drops steeply toward the river, and it would prove a long haul for multiple trips carrying cartons of full water jugs and five-gallon tubs of food. And the return trips would be all uphill—half an hour of steep climbing to blow your wind and rubber your legs.

Little Creek, running beside the steep trail like a watery shadow, sometimes hidden by overhanging boughs, is a beautiful rill winding along the trail, sparkling with miniature falls and dropping here and there into pools shaded by river birch, red maple, beech, elm, sycamore, and mountain laurel blooming in white and pink clusters.

Thousands of these rills feed into the Cape Fear, and when it rains in the Piedmont, the volume of water that suddenly cascades into the river is momentous. Even in these dry months, the flow of Little Creek is easily several dozen gallons a minute. Multiply that by thousands, then add a hammering downpour. And imagine the muscle of the river growing exponentially.

Time and again since European settlers began keeping records, the river has turned into a raging torrent, sweeping away all before it. Even on this trip, we have seen giant trees cracked and pulled out of the banks, monstrous deadfalls hung up high in the branches of other trees, where they were lifted by Hurricane Fran in 1996. That storm banged hard into the coast near Wilmington and then shot straight up the Cape Fear, wreaking havoc all the way to Raleigh and beyond. Residents of the coast who had evacuated to the "safety" of Raleigh found themselves square in the middle of a raging Category 2 hurricane with sustained winds of more than 100 knots. It dumped ten inches of rain along the whole middle watershed, cracked trees onto powerlines, washed away millions of dollars in property, and killed twenty people.

And it turned the Cape Fear into a debris-choked swollen torrent.

In 1846, 1901, 1908, and again in 1945, the Cape Fear swelled into floods and inundated entire towns along the river.

But this spring has been a dry season mostly. Unless we get a heavy rain upstream, the water level will stay moderately low. Of course, we won't know if it's raining upstream—or more importantly, if the engineers who run the B. Everett Jordan Lake Dam will need to release water to lower the lake to a safe level.

Our camp at Raven Rock is quiet, once the woodchoppers next door have turned in. We can't hear the river, though it runs briskly just a hundred yards or so through the trees. David's wallet got soaked at some point during our run, so once the tent is erected, he carefully extracts all his credit cards and money from the wallet. He peels the soggy bills apart and one by one lays out each credit card, ID, and bill on the roof of our tent to dry.

By and by I fall asleep in my tent, which I'm sharing with David. I sleep fitfully, not out of anxiety or because I'm not dog-tired from more than eight hours on the river, but because I'm not used to sleeping on the ground, and I neglected to bring my foam sleeping pad.

I haven't slept in a tent in years, and I forgot the wonderful feeling of cocoonlike enclosure, the odd fiction that somehow you are safe and protected. In fact, all that stands between you and the raw force of nature is a thin sheet of nylon, still now that the breeze has died.

But tonight it will do nicely.

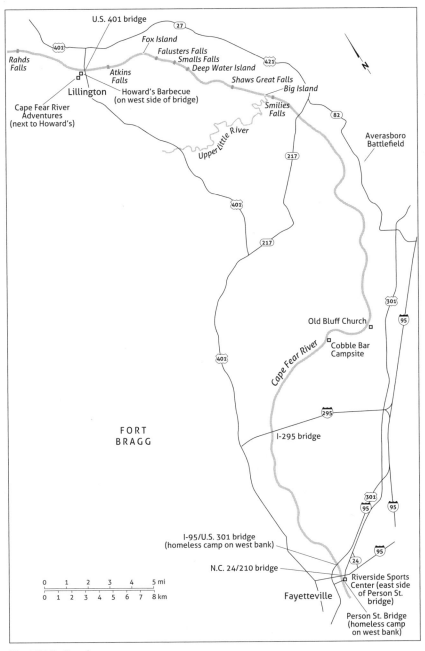

**The Middle Reaches:**
**Raven Rock State Park to Fayetteville**

We get a later-than-planned start from Raven Rock—8:40 or so. We're slugabeds. The kayak campers are just getting roused out of their tents when we shove off from the muddy bank into a lovely morning. Proceeding downriver, we tend to stay in the shade of the trees on the east bank in the morning and then, after lunch, shift to the shade of the west bank, unless we're in fast water and need to thread the rocks. We're careful not to run too close under overhanging branches, for fear of snakes dropping out of the trees into our boats.

Amy lolls out of the canoe, feet propped on the gunwales, taking photos. Ethan hardly has to paddle—he keeps the paddle almost always on the right side and, with a repertoire of deft strokes, can steer it in one direction or another. They glide along, and we let them go ahead and wait while we catch up. Nobody is talking much yet, just listening to the river wake up around us. The country remains wild, and it takes us a few minutes to paddle beyond the boundaries of the park.

Today is a "push" day—we have a lot of miles to cover if we're going to be within striking distance of Fayetteville tomorrow. The plan is to go through Fayetteville and about six miles farther south to a Wildlife ramp on Old Route 87, variously called Wilmington Highway and Elizabethtown Road, named for two of the destinations it will take you to.

If we are running too late—Ethan has a Friends School board meeting at 6:00 P.M. in Wilmington and will need about two hours to get there—we will take out at the Riverside Sports Center on Person Street upstream, where there is a ramp. Our Plan B is an uncomfortable reminder of just how hard it is to break free of the surface tension of contemporary life, in which all of our schedules seem ridiculously crowded and it's hard to map out a blank space of time even for a few days. The river gives us the best excuse to shoehorn some free outdoor time into our indoor calendars.

But push day or not, we find ourselves stopping in midstream just a little ways below Raven Rock, somewhere near Cedar Rock, spectators to a remarkable aerial drama. We paddle in place and stare upward. An osprey has appeared, a brown gliding shape, flashing white on its undersides, circling, lower and lower, then climbing. Even high overhead, its wingspan looks enormous—probably five feet. All at once, it dives on the river ahead and comes up with a fat silver fish in its talons. Its great wings grab air and lift the fish-carrying bird off the river and high over our heads, almost in slow motion.

Suddenly, a bald eagle appears out of nowhere, larger and faster, and blind-sides the osprey with a body check. The osprey loses its hold on the fish, which falls wriggling from its talons. The osprey tumbles, wings flapping wildly, then recovers. The fish free-falls earthward. The eagle is swift: It swoops down and grabs the fish, then rockets off to its nest high in a tree. The osprey follows, circles the nest, feints and dives repeatedly, trying to lure the eagle out of the nest. But the eagle stays put, posturing, wings enfolded across the nest and the fish.

The osprey dives, swoops, circles, dives again, at last gives up and flies away.

It's the most exciting thing I've ever seen in nature, thrilling, delightful, utterly mesmerizing. Nobody says anything for a long minute, then somebody says, "You could spend your whole life on the river and never see that again."

Osprey, fish, eagle. That's why we came.

～～～～～

We have one more set of mild rapids to negotiate, Rahds Falls, on a straight run into Lillington.

By 11:30 A.M. we spot the high bridge going into Lillington, full of the racket of fast cars on the highway that carries U.S. 421, U.S. 401, N.C. 210, and N.C. 21. The bridge is named for Highway Patrol Trooper Harry T. Long, a twenty-two-year-old rookie who was killed by a hit-and-run-driver in 1959 while making a routine traffic stop. I suppose a bridge is an apt memorial—so many are: a literal metaphor of connection to the "other side."

We pull up the canoes on the ramp upstream, which serves Cape Fear River Adventures, an outfitter of canoe and kayak trips. On the grassy bluff over-looking the river stands Howard's Barbecue, a local institution that has been going strong for twenty-four years at this location. It's closed today, Sunday, so I can't treat the team to the barbecue sandwiches I promised them. But I'll be back to spend some time onshore.

～～～～～

So in the dead of winter, I find Howard's Barbecue full of locals: a district attorney from the county courthouse and a couple of lawyers, a sher-iff's deputy, contractors on lunch break. It's a perfect day for a hot barbecued chicken sandwich chased down by homemade banana pudding.

David Avrette, the owner, slides into the booth across from me. He's a hardy, thickset man with a neat, graying goatee, a ruddy complexion, and steady, humorous eyes. He holds out his hand, and his handshake is strong. As we talk, he tends to look me directly in the eye, an effect of concentration heightened by the curved brim of the slate ballcap that frames his face. He looks like he'd be right at home in the outdoors—which is where he most loves to be.

His voice is soft, flavored with the local idiom. He says, "I grew up on this river. When I was nine years old, I was down here squirrel hunting on the banks. We'd get out of church and we'd go catch salamanders in the creek and come down here and get a stick, make a bobber off of it, and hang it in a tree and catch a catfish and then race it back home. I've been doing it all my life. I love the river, and I always have."

Through the long bay of windows, we can see the terrace and swingset in the play area, the wood-decked stage on the riverbank where not long ago a troupe of actors performed the bluegrass gospel musical *Smoke on the Mountain*, and beyond that, the river running brown and gelid on this frigid January day—not at all like the silky May warmth we enjoyed on our paddle. Outside, the air temperature is 35 degrees, and the surface of the river seems to be running in slow motion, patches of frozen slush rafting along its current.

Every time I look at the river, I see a different river. It changes by season, and it changes simply by turning a bend.

"Each section has its own personality really," is how Avrette puts it. "You've got this section that's flat and not navigable, then you've got other areas with eighteen to twenty rock ledges in about five miles—makes good rapids. Below that you've got high banks, deep water, and you can go all the way to the coast. We'll be in Wilmington if we just stay on it." He reflects for a moment, smiling with his whole face. "You get the imagination, just like Tom Sawyer had, you know?"

Here at Lillington, the river looks deep and free of rapids, but that's an illusion, as Avrette reminds me: "It's a hard rock bottom. It looks like a very deep river, but the average depth is probably two and a half to three feet. You can walk all the way across and not get your cigarettes wet."

Crews are working big cranes at either end of the bridge, setting concrete forms for a parallel span. Already five double-pillared concrete piers have been sunk into the riverbed to hold the deck, but the bridge won't open for traffic for at least another year.

The bridge carries motorists between Raleigh and Fayetteville, from the I-95 corridor to Sanford and other cities. It's one of the few crossings on this stretch of the river and can back up for miles at rush hour if there's an accident. But there's an odd north-south divide among the locals, a holdover from the old days when northside communities like Buie's Creek were self-contained and separate enclaves with their own schools and social circles. Avrette tells me, "There's people that never cross this bridge. They live in Buie's Creek, they go to the grocery store over there, they eat over there, they never cross this bridge unless they need to use the post office. And people on this side of the river that never go over there unless they have to get to the courthouse, the tax office, to the department of motor vehicles. They just don't go there. It's not in their circle."

That's changing slowly. He himself lives in Buie's Creek and crosses the bridge every day. Still, Lillington is one of those river towns, like Elizabethtown and Tar Heel and even Moncure on the Deep—that seem oblivious to the fact that they are even on the river.

Avrette explains why: "The reason for that back then, before they built the Jordan Lake Dam, was that we had floods. I remember hunting back here with my dad and finding parts of a liquor still up in a tree, finding all kinds of stuff, because you'd get a big fresh and it would pick it all up, and then the water would leave and it would be stuck in the trees."

And it makes sense. Intellectually I've known all along the river that, however wild it seems, the entire mainstem has been altered irrevocably—and invisibly—by engineering, the flow regulated far upstream of its own beginnings at Mermaid Point by a gargantuan dam holding back 14,000 acres of deep water. But it has been easy to forget, to just pay attention to the boisterous current, the lush foliage, the birds and turtles.

David Avrette explains just how wild and unpredictable the river could be in those days: "The river used to come up fourteen foot, fifteen foot." He points upstream. "Back in '45, it went all the way up to the top of the railroad bridge. There was car up there and goats, and the river was running by on both sides."

So that was the prevailing wisdom in those days: If you got too close to the river, it might take you.

"People are afraid of it. And there's people who have lived here all their lives and never been this close to the river till they came in here to eat. I mean, it wasn't tamed, it wasn't navigable, it was just something to be scared of and worry about, not something to enjoy. Things changed a lot when they put that dam in."

With a friend, Avrette started the canoe rental business that is now Cape Fear River Adventures. He was just out of college. They had a handful of boats and worked off the end of the service road under the bridge. He smiles ruefully and shakes his head. "We worked ourselves to death, really, for nothing, other than to get people going out on the river."

But though he sold off the canoe business, he still sees the economic future of the Lillington area tied with the fortunes of the river. "As people get less and less scared of this river, they'll get pulled to it more and more," he says. "I've already seen it pick up in recreational paddling. In this economy, people can't afford to go deep sea fishing or drive all the way to the beach." But they can hoist a small boat onto the roof rack and drive an hour or two to a put-in. "And the good old boys can still put their johnboats in and catch catfish and spend the night out on the river, secluded, hoot and holler and do what they want to."

Lillington, like many small towns, is struggling to hold its own in a brutal economy. At the edge of town there's a hardware store and a chain grocer. A printing plant and a turnstile manufacturer offer some jobs and shore up the tax base. The small crossroads downtown is composed of small shops and businesses that have nothing to do with the river. A new hospital is in the offing, as is a satellite branch of East Carolina University's dentistry school.

About twelve miles downstream at Erwin, there's a new access point, the Cape Fear River Trail Park, so a good day's run through rapids is now possible without much trouble. "It will pay off down the road—I really feel like the future's very bright for the area," Avrette says.

"It's like somebody said: We're the ham on the sandwich. You've got Raleigh on one end and Fayetteville on the other, and we've got this river."

There's one odd fact about Lillington that I find delightful and seems to reinforce David Avrette's conviction that the river is the key to the town's future. When land across the river from the town center was annexed, the new map located the center of downtown—which used to be the intersection of U.S. 401 and U.S. 421, the main crossroads of the business district—smack in the middle of the river.

Before I head outside to find Dale Ryals at Cape Fear River Adventures, I ask Avrette if he has any last wisdom to share with me about the river. He grins. "Fishing's always better when the water's rising—always," he says softly, his eyes alight. "Unless you're fishing smallmouth bass, and then late fall when the water is dark and still."

I don't have to travel far to find Dale Ryals. She's waiting for me across the parking lot from Howard's, standing on the porch of the colorful shack that houses Cape Fear River Adventures. A trailer loaded with canoes is parked off to one side, and other canoes and kayaks settle on the sandy gravel outside the shack. She waves me inside, grinning. She grins a lot and has an easy, wide-open laugh. You can't hear that laugh and not laugh along with her. She's petite, with bobbing blond-gray curls almost held in place by barrettes, and a face that is animated and young. Maybe because she is so relaxed, so open, so quick to laugh, she seems like someone I've known for years, even though I met her only once, briefly, while scouting the river for our paddle.

Dale grew up in Erwin, a dozen miles downriver, where she still lives. "We always lived *near* the river," she tells me. "We never lived *on* the river. They call them the 'low grounds' down that way because they always flooded. Not every year, but they flooded easily. It was probably about a mile and a half from our house to the river. And as children we did walk down to the river. It was good entertainment—with mom attached, of course."

Like so many people along the river, she grew up fishing and messing around in small boats. She used to rent a canoe occasionally from the fellow who had taken over the canoe business from David Avrette. Then one day she came by to arrange a rental, and the place was closed. She sought out Avrette. "I think at first he thought I was just passing the time of day, a lady asking about canoes. Anyhow, that's how I got started: Asking questions will get you in trouble!" She laughs at the punch line, but clearly the memory is a pleasing one. She says, "It was a pretty October day, one of those wonderful fall days when everything is right with the world, nothing can be wrong on one of those days, and it sounded like a good idea."

Dale was ready for a change. She'd worked for twenty years for the local bank and then worked some more years for the post office. She found she could handle the canoe rental business on the side until she was ready to leave the post office altogether. Three years in, her enthusiasm is as strong as ever.

She tells me, "We have had somebody out there on the water for the last thirty-three months consecutively, so there's always somebody out there." It's not so much a brag about her own business acumen as a testimony to the river's allure to paddlers in every season. She guesses as many as 4,000 paddlers a year go down the river, and many of them pass through her shop.

I tell her about riding the right-hand chute downriver at Buckhorn at the very beginning of our journey.

She laughs big. "You don't want to do that!"

I'm laughing now. "We ran it! It was like the log flume ride at Great Adventure."

The chute is a remnant of the Cape Fear Navigation Company, she says, one of many along the river, wherever rocks cluttered the main channel. "The natural rapids that were there, they canaled out around them, and that's what that is."

"It's a wild ride, I'll say that."

"Yeah!" she says. "You get yourself so committed that you can't turn around."

"Yeah, once you're in it, you're in it."

"There was some guys we dropped off here one morning, and it was raining that particular morning, and I thought, they're going to have a bad day already. I told 'em, 'Go through the garden—y'all don't want to go down that right canal.' Well, lo and behold, they had to—and they come up from Wilmington, they come up every year—one of 'em emailed me when they got back. He said, 'Yeah, I went through it just as soon as you said *not* do it.' But didn't tell me that he turned over at the end of it."

"I guess there are those people that if you say, *don't* do it, they just *have* to do it."

"He was one of 'em. He lived to tell it—that was the good part."

"Well," I say—now that it's dawning on me just how fortunate David Webster and I were to run the chute without dumping—"We went through it right side up. I'm not sure how we did, but we did."

Dale keeps on talking about how tricky the chute is. "And then we had a family that came through, guy had his father, his son, and the wife. She was on a kayak, but the family was in a canoe, and they go over there and they turned over right to begin with too." She shakes her head, laughing. "So no, not a good idear."

"Well, we made it, so I'll chalk that one up to luck."

"Pat yourself on the back!"

I confess that we did dump the canoe at Lanier Falls, above Raven Rock. "We were a little overconfident, hit an underwater rock, and the next thing you know we're in the water floating down the river."

"It's instant! That's what I tell people. They come to me and want to know, 'Am I gonna get wet?' I tell everybody, 'Come prepared to get wet.' They may go out a hundred times and they don't turn over. That hundred and first time, though, then they turn over several times. It's just like walking out there on flat ground, all the sudden one minute you're up, next minute you're on the ground. And there's no earthly reason why you're down there, but you're there. And that's exactly the way it is out there. Cause everything looks perfect, you're lined up, everything's good, but one little thing flips you, just like that."

That's how it is, all right: paddler to swimmer in a flicker of time.

"I had a relative, a cousin. This was an accident looking to happen. He took one of the canoes and he had his wife and two children and two large dogs. The kids are about eight and nine. Tried to get him to take one of the dry boxes with him. 'No, this'll be fine.' He had a cell phone, $500 camera. Down there near Erwin, he turned over. He didn't tell me about it, but somebody else that was out that day come back in and I asked if he saw him down there. They said, 'Yeah, we helped him get everything back in the boat.'" She squeals with laughter. "The camera and the phone was gone. You don't bring your most *valuable* stuff out here, because whatever you bring, the most valuable thing is going to be gone *first* thing."

What she's saying makes perfect sense to me—I've felt the river under me, big and muscular.

The river is so challenging precisely because it is a different river every day, depending on the water level. In fact, it can change drastically in just a few hours—because of the water withheld or released by Jordan Dam. "It can move fast," she says. "With the runoff, it can move quick. A lot of what we do here is education, or getting people to rethink how they view the river. The locals view it one way. And people who come in here view it another way."

What's different now is the relationship between rainfall and river level. She explains, "With the river, it's always been, if it rains, it's going up. But with Jordan Dam in place, it will hold it back. If it's calling for rain in our area, they will hold the water back and take the river down a little bit—that will make up for the flow coming in from the rain. And then if they're going to get a lot and it doesn't look like we're going to get anything, they will let the river rise so that it don't push the lake level up above what they need up there." So if it pours rain in Chatham County or around Kernersville and Greensboro, two days or so later the water will rise at Lillington and make the downstream run to Erwin and beyond quite sporty.

A couple of years back, in February, the winter rains came hard both upstream and down in the same week. "Flood stage is fourteen feet," Dale tells me. "And they left it up at fifteen feet for about eighteen hours before they started bringing it back down. They have no choice—they have to do what they have to do. But it can make problems for people out there on the river."

It's a good example of reexamining what we "know" to be true about the river—a truth that isn't quite so true anymore. "So the thinking that if it rains, don't be in the river, is not necessarily true anymore," Dale says. "We've been very fortunate here—we have a good safety record. To date there have been no accidents of any kind in that respect, which is great, and we're very thankful for it, but we're very cautious about letting the boats go out."

Dale checks the river level at Lillington every morning at 7:15, and if the gauge shows three feet or higher, her boats don't go out. Period. She has seen the river rise nine feet between the morning check and sundown.

"People like to ask us, 'Well, which way would you run this rapid?' And 'Which way would you run that rapid?' And we don't tell people that, cause something could have washed in there since the last time we heard about it. I say, 'You have to make that decision when you're out there. We can't tell you.'" The paddle guides sometimes suggest the most advantageous routes, but not Dale. "You have to make your own decision at the crossroads."

She tells me another tale of paddlers who seemed oblivious to the power of the river. "The first year I was doing it, I was at home because the river was up at nine feet. I got this call from these guys. They said they had stopped here at Howard's and somebody had told them they were stupid to be in the river at that level."

The river hadn't been that high when they'd started out—it had risen dramatically all day long.

"It was six boats from the base"—Fort Bragg—a lot of her customers come from there. "They had come downriver and had been staying overnight and they were going to Elizabethtown. And they wanted to portage around this section here down to the Erwin Bridge. I came up here that day with the van and they were sitting out here with their boats." The boats were so heavily loaded, she shuttled them down the back way to Erwin, driving slow, hauling the trailer. "It rode really well and we got down there and I stopped them at the top. I could have opened the gate and taken them down to the river, but I didn't because I was trying to discourage 'em big time. You could hear the river up at the top, the rapids, and I thought, 'They don't need to be in that river.' It was right at four o'clock in the afternoon and they were headed to Elizabethtown."

The paddling guide reckons the distance from Erwin to Elizabethtown at close to sixty-eight miles.

She continues, "They planned to get there before dark!" and laughs uproariously. "Somebody hadn't thought out this trip too good. But anyway I told them, 'Ya'll might want to go down there and look before you start this.'"

They could have camped out and waited overnight for the river to go down—the local sheriffs wouldn't have hassled them. "They'd rather have 'em up there safe than have the rescue trying to get 'em out of the river later. Anyway they went down there and looked, and about half of them looked undecided about going, but the one that was in charge said, 'We're going.'" She shakes her head. "The last I saw of them, they were putting on their life jackets and I was leaving. I said, 'I don't want to see you on the evening news.'"

What happened to them? I want know. Did they ever call and report in?

"No! They either had a really good time and forgot who I was, or they had a really bad time and didn't want to tell me. I figured the way the river was running, if they could stay up, they probably made it to Elizabethtown by dark!"

Another group of thirty-eight paddlers rented every boat she had and, when she rendezvoused with them at Erwin, found that eight paddlers were missing. They had overshot the take-out by miles and had to haul their boats up a high bluff to a farmer's field, where she could retrieve them.

During her first year of operation, a two-soldier party arranged to rent a canoe, but they would do their own shuttle, doing the Buckhorn–Lillington run with an overnight stay at Raven Rock. "Well, if people ask, you give them all the information they want," Dale says. "Otherwise, you don't try to tell them how to do it. These particular guys, just as they were talking, it seemed that something just wasn't right. They were late. They had gone up to Buckhorn and left one truck. Come back down here, they got the canoe, decided they couldn't get the canoe on the truck they had taken up there. So they turned around and went back to Buckhorn, changed out the truck and brought back the other truck. Then as I heard them talking—they had not asked me anything about how to do the run, which way the river ran or anything—they were planning to put in here and paddle to Buckhorn!"

She can hardly stop laughing over the memory.

"It was like that movie, *National Lampoon Vacation*, it looked like what could go wrong, was going wrong. And bless their hearts, apparently it was something they had to do for their military rating. I thought, now if they're not back here tomorrow at the time they should be—'cause I knew they weren't planning to hang around Raven Rock, all they were gonna do was stay the night and come on in—but bless their hearts, they were in here early. And I was so happy to see that boy! Because I tell you, if they hadn't been in here on time, I would have sent the rescue out for him. They did not know which way the river flowed. They didn't know nothing about paddling. Nothing. It was just amazing!"

She has plenty more stories, of a party consisting of two men and a pregnant woman who got stranded at Raven Rock after dark and called for a pickup. They had come down the river planning to take out at Northington's Ferry, just below Lanier Falls. "They thought there was a ferry that crossed the river there. Well there was—about 1800." This particular crew hauled their boat one and a half miles up the steep trail to the Raven Rock parking lot, a heroic penance for their oversight.

"Things like that just amaze me, that people don't look before they go. They don't do any planning—they just get in the boats and go."

And it's not just paddlers who get in trouble on the river. "There was one guy, it was a summer or two ago, he was down there in one of these older looking ski boats. I was down there putting some canoes in. I heard him coming downriver—oh, he was wide open. I thought, hmm, that don't sound good. Then I thought I heard him cut the motor, and I didn't pay any more attention to him. I thought he was coming in. But lo and behold, late that afternoon, we're out there washing boats and this guy comes up telling us about this guy, he said, 'Have you seen him?' He described him. And I said, 'No. We can go down there and look, but I don't think he's down there.' And I said, 'Describe the boat he was on.'"

It was the ski boat.

"I said, 'Well surely he didn't go on downriver.' Well, he went down to the Wildlife access. And as he was going in, the fire truck was just coming out from down there. The guy was stuck on that rock garden out there in the river. He'd made it through that first little rapid, but when he got to the rock garden, he couldn't get through down there. Some kayaker had called 911 and the Buie's Creek Water Rescue had come down there and got him off the rock." She laughs, still incredulous. "I was surprised he made it that far!"

It's a funny story told in retrospect, but it must have been terrifying for that powerboater to come zooming past the bridge straight into the jaws of a rock garden, to hear the bottom getting ripped apart by the boulders till it was stuck fast in the middle of a roiling rapid.

"That's why I just don't understand people just getting out there and going, not knowing what they're going to run into downstream."

As if on cue, two lanky young men come in, one wearing a tractor cap cocked on his head. They want to take a trip downriver in a johnboat and are seeking advice. "Are there any dams on the river?" they want to know.

Dale takes them over to the map and does a quick tutorial of the rapids, the distances between take-outs and landmarks, the locks and dams, the portages. She says, "I had a neighbor who tried the johnboat thing, and he swam about halfway to Erwin Bridge because he lost his johnboat—pretty well beat it to death going down the river from the Wildlife access towards Erwin."

In that case, maybe they will paddle and tow behind them an inflatable stocked with supplies. She says doubtfully, "I've seen people try that, leave here with one of those coolers in a floating ring trailing behind. When they get to the rapids, they either lose them or they end up inside the boat."

They want to know about the wildlife on the river, and she briefs them on some feral hogs spotted on one stretch, coyotes on another, the alligators way downriver. "I'd keep my eyes peeled. If you see what you think is a log floating down the river, don't go bump into it, because that might not be what it is."

One of the young men says, "I don't want to wake up and have a 'gator in my face."

She reassures him, "Pretty much if you leave them alone, they're going to leave you alone. If you surprise one of 'em, you know—that's why you keep your eyes peeled. You see on TV where the people are out in the Everglades looking at alligators—they're right there. That's a little too close for me, to be *right there*. I like to keep *right there* way over yonder somewhere."

She goes on, "And you definitely want to keep in mind you need dry bags with dry clothing in it, because the time of year you're talking about, the water's still going to be fairly cold, and hypothermia will set in really quick, especially if you get a cool day like this and cold water to go with it."

One of the guys asks, "We would need life jackets, wouldn't we, if the game warden stopped us? But would we need to have 'em on?"

I chime in, "You'll *want* to have 'em on."

Dale agrees. "Yeah, I'd have mine on, period."

She supplies them with the names of Wildlife officers they can contact for more information. They thank her politely and leave—seeming a little overwhelmed by all they'll have to contend with on the river, but also grateful for her guidance,

I tell her, "You just saved them some heartache."

She says, "At least these young guys are sensible enough to be asking questions before they start out."

Outside, the river flows past looking sluggish and low, flat all the way across, not a ripple in sight.

"With the river down low, people don't realize the power of the water. They don't realize how much *force* is there. Even though it's moving very slow, or looks to be, even though it looks very gentle, there's still a lot of power behind that water coming down. And it just amazes me that people don't realize that. But they're not out there every day, and so they don't. It's just a matter of teaching them as to what to look for and what to do."

I'm grateful for my paddling companions, for their wisdom and ability. Dale says, "People don't understand it's not a waterpark out there—you're in nature."

Outside Cape Fear River Adventures, I stand in the cold and look toward the river. Just downstream at the bridge, one of the tall cranes, articulating like a giant insect, lowers a steel form onto the new twin span.

~~~~~~~~~~

In a way, it is odd that Lillington should be so aloof from the river, and probably fitting that the town center now lies in midstream, for the river has figured largely in its history.

The fine highway bridge at Lillington is the descendant of several failed bridges.

Back in 1871, just six years after the guns of the Civil War had gone silent, the first bridge was carried away by flood before it was even finished.

Lillington finally got its bridge in 1901, though not before construction was delayed by the so-called Prohibition Freshet of 1901, which carried away concrete and other building materials. The bridge lasted scarcely seven years before two of its spans were washed away by the great flood of 1908.

The spans were replaced, and the bridge stood up to regular traffic without incident. Apparently, though, it was one of those bridges you closed your eyes to cross, for it was high — twenty-nine feet above mean high water — very narrow, and somewhat rickety.

The bridge would "creak and sway, causing an automobile crossing it to assume the waving motion of a rowboat on the sea," as described by the *Harnett County News*. In 1920, as if to prove the point, a truck crashed through the wooden planking, though not all the way through, and the driver survived. To make the bridge even more tenuous, highway engineers paved it with gravel, adding an enormous static weight to the span without reinforcing the structure. As late as November 1930, the district highway commissioner was claiming the bridge would stand up to another decade of traffic.

But that was like David Webster proclaiming he had never dumped a canoe. The universe deplores such declarations of certainty. Less than a month after the highway commissioner pronounced the bridge solid, on the night of December 13, 1930, the bridge collapsed into the river, taking two cars with it. A third vehicle, a tobacco truck, almost fell into the river, but it stopped just short, teetering over the edge, and the driver was rescued.

A bridge can be a threat of what's across there coming over to your side, or it can be a way out, the open road to everywhere else, until it falls and you're stranded on the wrong side.

Many of the bridges across the Cape Fear River have had similar checkered histories of collapse and washout, fire and deadly accident. A river is either a means of transportation or a barrier to it, and a bridge is a way of crossing that barrier, until it too gives way to gravity and momentum. The current bridge is high and sturdy, steel and concrete, and traffic rushes across it at forty miles an hour oblivious to the little boats passing beneath it.

~~~~~~~~~~~

That Sunday in May, we hike back down the bluff to our canoes and shove off, quickly leaving behind the Lillington bridge. We will eat under way.

On the river again, we encounter two snakes. One is a black slithery fast thing racing across the river. Ethan grabs it out of the water, and it turns out to be a northern black snake, very common and very docile. It immediately crawls up his arm and allows itself to be handled.

If it were a black racer, it would have already bitten him savagely and severely and probably repeatedly—though not poisonously. A cottonmouth, which we have not seen, would of course be worse: aggressive and venomous. Later I spy a black water snake and we leave it alone, content to watch it slink among the shallows on the western bank, curving its six-foot length over exposed tree roots and doing its best to hide from us. I don't want to get too near it, for it too will bite aggressively, though without venom.

All day long we cross ledges, where the water is creased across the entire channel by what in some cases look like (and are) old man-made dams. Beginning in pre-Revolutionary days, several enterprising companies tried to make the river navigable all the way up. Many of the rapids are the result of the wrecks of these dams, the large stones scattered and strewn, some still reaching across the river, broken only in places, presumably by surges of high water, so that often a ledge will have a chute on either side. The stones are hewn into flat, squarish blocks, a dead giveaway that they are man-made. We negotiate them as best we can, alert to the surface roils that betray underwater obstructions.

As before, the Grumman continues to get hung up every so often, but though it means we have to exert ourselves at regular intervals, it's not a big deal. Usually I can nudge the bow off by simply pushing forward with my feet and shifting my weight, never leaving my seat, heaving the boat forward a few inches at a time until the bow is floating free and the stern slews around with the force of the current and we are on our way. The technique is not elegant, but it works, and there's no danger of harming the sturdy Monster.

We settle into a rhythm with the paddling. Ethan has lent me a longer paddle today, and it makes all the difference. I didn't even realize I was paddling with a short stick, but now the difference is clear and mapped straight into the muscle of my arm. With each stroke, the blade bites deeper, so I don't have to work nearly so hard.

THE MIDDLE REACHES

Ethan wrangles a northern black snake (Amy Williamson photo)

I take three or four strokes and then rest a beat, three or four more and rest a beat. I calculate it takes two strokes to move us ten feet, which means that it takes well over a thousand strokes to move the canoe a mile. We will make more than twenty miles today—probably closer to twenty-five—which adds up to more than 26,400 paddle strokes apiece.

Every so often I rest my shoulder. David suggests that our balance is best served if I paddle on the left and he on the right, that when I paddle right I paddle harder or faster, throwing us out of whack. Turns out he is right. I can only figure that it is because either (A) I am right-handed or, more likely, (B) the power of the right stroke is actually created by the left arm, and my left arm is stronger than my right, since I ripped one of the heads of my right bicep in an accident a couple of years ago.

We go through a long fall of rapids, each more challenging than the last, and as the day wears on, Ethan is alertly scouting a suitable camping site. We want to make it past Old Bluff Church, well below Erwin, an old mill town on the east bank.

But we can't find Old Bluff Church.

The paddle guide warns that the historic church is best approached from the land, and that paddlers can then descend 110 vertical feet on steps in the bank to reach the water. But this doesn't help, since we're on the water. We spy thickly forested bluffs, but no stairs.

So we cheat. Since we have rare cell phone service, Amy uses the Google

The elusive Old Bluff Church, 110 vertical feet above the river (author photo)

Maps function of her phone to locate us, and, lo and behold, we have made it to the foot of the stairs—still invisible in the lush undergrowth. If there is a church there, it will have to wait for another day. There does not even seem to be a suitable place to land, no sandbar or mudflat, no grassy bench or creek mouth, just a sheer wall of foliage reaching up from the river.

Long after our paddle, I go in search of Old Bluff Church and find it using my GPS. It turns out to be a gorgeous and austere white meetinghouse, built in 1855 for the Scots congregation of the Presbyterian Church in the upper Cape Fear Valley. At least two earlier meetinghouses once existed on the site, crude log structures, the first dating to 1759. The church stands with its back against the wooded bluff, and spread out in front are acres of graves chronicling two and a half centuries of parishioners' lives. Union soldiers camped here on the eve of the Battle of Averasboro. When I visit, the place is deserted. I discover the path in the woods to the left of the church that leads through thirty or so yards of slope to a steep wooden stairway. The stairs deposit you onto another path, where more stairs await, and finally you are at the river.

But you would never find the stairs from the river—it's just too overgrown.

As we pass below Old Bluff Church, it's apparent that the landscape along the river has changed. High up, the river was broad and relatively shallow, with channels and islands and sandbars at the mouths of the many creeks that feed into it. This far down it has become channelized—a single, reasonably deep channel with high banks thick with trees and foliage, including gargantuan draping bowers of bright poison ivy.

So Ethan is getting a little concerned about finding a suitable site, and about twenty miles down, maybe three miles below Old Bluff Church (or where it is in theory), he pulls over to a rocky island at the head of a chute and a small rock-garden rapids. We all lift ourselves out of the boats and stretch.

"I've been looking out for one of those sandbars like we've been seeing at the mouths of creeks, and I haven't seen one for awhile," he says. "This may be our last opportunity for a really good campsite, and we can hang out and play in the rapids here."

The downside, of course, is that we will have a longer way to go tomorrow. I don't mind. Ethan is the one with a meeting to make. Since he's headmaster, it's sort of important that he be there.

We survey the site, a ledge of rock just above the water level, a low bench of sand. The sound of water rushing through the chute would soothe us right to sleep. It's about the best stopping place we've seen since Lanier Falls, above Raven Rock.

I let the others vote—still in the mood to simply go with the rhythm of the day. It's an odd fact of adventuring that all the planning you do in advance actually allows you the freedom to give in to circumstance, to let the trip unfold rather than be too firmly directed. It's the way I teach writing: Prepare and plan, then give yourself up to it. Abandon the plan whenever a better one presents itself—just don't lose sight of your overall purpose.

So we gather on the rock, and my companions vote to push on, a little bit farther. It's a reluctant vote—all would rather unpack, relax, start a fire, enjoy some hot food.

I don't much mind—in fact, I'm pleased. Now I know for sure we will make Fayetteville tomorrow without a frantic push, just steady paddling.

The light is fading and we're all pretty fatigued after a long day of paddling, tired in our muscles and eyes. I'm hoping we don't have too much farther to go. A couple of miles more, maybe, then blessed rest. It's only once we have paused for a breather that I realize just how hard we have pushed ourselves today, how leaden and sore my arms feel, how wooden-stiff my legs.

It's nearly six o'clock and we've been on the water for more than nine hours, so fatigue is probably a factor in what happens next.

Ethan and Amy shove off and make a perfect, effortless run down the chute, fast and thrilling, as David and I watch.

Now it's our turn. We ought to unload the Grumman as we did at Lanier, run the chute empty, then paddle back through the eddy to the backside of the rock and reload our gear. But we've been running smaller chutes perfectly all day, losing our shyness of white water, and it's getting late, and we're tired and probably a little too relaxed. We board the Green Monster and follow the exact track that Ethan's canoe took, but at the bottom of the sluice an underwater rock rises up from nowhere and we strike it hard.

The canoe slews sideways, broaches, and next thing you know we're both in the water, the canoe is upside-down, and we're being shoved along in a fast, powerful current, holding onto the canoe as best we can.

The water is deep, the current fast. It rushes in my ears, drowning out all other sound.

The river has us. This is Steinbeck's metaphor at its most literal.

I can feel the force of the river grabbing at me, shoving me hard into a rock. A sharp stinging pain burns my hip and thigh, but I'm not cut, only bruised. For a few dizzy moments, we are shooting downriver out of control, and I get that cold feeling in my belly I once got while fording the Gallatin River in Yellowstone Park with a heavy pack and guitar strapped to my back, when the snowmelt current grabbed me and would not let me out of the river. At such moments, you just have to reach inside and settle yourself down, hold it together and simply hang on stubbornly, do the next necessary thing. I did it in the Gallatin, climbed up a high, mud-slick cutbank and out of the clutches of the river, though it took everything I had and a little more.

That all sounds quite heroic, but of course as I'm being swept downriver, I'm cursing loudly, as embarrassed as I am scared.

But David is calm as ever, even laughing, bobbing along downstream, big straw sombrero still cocked on his head. We let the current carry us downstream a hundred yards or so—what choice—and then the current widens and slackens and Ethan and Amy come paddling back toward us and help us wrestle the waterlogged canoe upright and toward a rocky landing site. We pile our gear on the rock. Miraculously, all that's missing is the Chapstick out of my pocket. Even our white plastic trash bag has floated off only a little ways before Amy snags it and hauls it into their boat.

It takes three of us to tip out enough water from the Monster that we can begin bailing without the river filling in more than we are taking out, and after awhile the boat is dry again and we begin reloading our gear. I worry that our sleeping bags will be drenched, making for an uncomfortable night ahead. It seems impossible that they could have been submerged that long in such roiling water and not be sopping.

David remarks, "Well I guess we'll see how good the Ethan method of packing really is!" On his instructions, we both double-sacked our bags in contractor-grade plastic trash bags, about a million-ply thickness.

Soaking wet, we climb aboard the Green Monster and resume our journey into the gloom ahead.

About three miles downstream, with the light failing, we pull up onto a cobble bar, which Ethan suggests might be our last chance for a reasonably comfortable campsite. "We don't want to have to strap ourselves to trees," he says, only half joking. I can hear in his tone a note of worry. He's used to rivers that offer regular campsites, and as the Cape Fear turns coastal, high ground is getting scarce. There's no real paddling trail with campsites, just accidental stopping places. So we'll make the best of it here.

Fine by me. My legs are cramped and stiff, and my belly is grumbling. It will be nice to step onto dry land, relax, and just let the day go down. I'm pretty sure there's a bottle of good Malbec left in our supplies.

A cobble bar is different from a sandbar in one very important way. While both are low and relatively flat, a sandbar is soft to sleep on, ideal really, and a cobble bar is, well, literally a bed of rocks. The place is quite picturesque otherwise, shaded by the first river cypress we have seen all day, a towering tree with a broad overhanging canopy fairly in the middle of the site. Since Ethan and Amy have brought sleeping pads, the stones present no drawback for them. They simply move some of the largest to the side, set up their tent, and floor it with the pads.

Ethan scouts a sandy bench just above the cobble bar. David and I step over and pace it, measuring off the footprint our tent will require. It will do, with a little engineering.

Using our canoe paddles and careful to avoid contact with our hands, we up-root the poison ivy at the edge of the clearing. David is allergic to poison ivy and breaks out badly when exposed. (In the event, he will return home with some on his arm, a nasty rash for a week or so.) Then we remove a few sharp rocks and, again using canoe paddles, level the sand by raking it toward the river.

In this fashion, after twenty minutes or so of crude labor, we create a reasonably level, soft space, pitch the tent, and haul the rest of our gear up to the site. We're not worried about having disturbed the site; a week after we're gone, it will be overgrown again, the level sand rinsed back down the slope by rain.

Our tent, which was been stowed only in its cordura nylon zipper bag, turns out to be unexpectedly dry except for a couple of damp spots, which David mops up with a T-shirt conveniently provided by Amy.

Now comes the moment of truth. The canoe turned upside-down. The sleeping bags were immersed for minutes in cold, moving water. If they are wet, it will mean a miserable and probably sleepless night, not the restful—and much needed—repose we have been looking forward to all day.

I unpack my bag first: It is bone dry. (I note in my journal, "Ethan rocks!")

David's is dry, too. This is as close to a miracle as we could wish for on the river.

Everything in my expensive, expedition-store-bought dry-packs is damp or downright sodden, including my jacket and my spare (previously) dry shirt. But being a belt-and-braces sort of guy, I packed the really important stuff in a second protective layer, supermarket-brand ziplock bags, so wallet and notebooks and first-aid kit are all dry. David learned his lesson from last night and dry-bagged his wallet, so tonight he won't be using our tent as a drying rack for his money.

I gather firewood—there's a lot lying about, busted tree branches, driftwood of all kinds—and lay out a fire ring near the water. On his backpacker camp stove, Ethan cooks another jumbo pot of pasta, and we each wolf down about three pounds.

We are bone-tired, wet, mosquito-bitten, sore, and having the time of our lives. The wine flows freely into absurd plastic cups and bottles.

Before Ethan has time to build a fire, a cool drizzle begins, a slow, fitful precursor to the raging storm that will descend upon us soon and last all night. We gather under the lone river cypress, and for a long time it keeps us dry as a huge umbrella, while we stand or sit on plastic drums drinking wine. Ethan builds a fire closer to the tree. There's no danger of it spreading, not with an increasingly steady rainfall and the river so close (and rising) and a site made of rock and sand for many yards in any direction.

And then the second miracle of the day occurs, this one woman-made. Amy fishes around inside one of the plastic buckets and comes up with a treat she has brought along especially for me, in gratitude for being included in the expedition: a bottle of Glenlivet single malt scotch.

Perfect.

As the fire flares bright and hissing and the rain turns into a steady, drenching downpour, we stand in the gathering darkness sipping single malt scotch and talking, sharing stories of the day. I savor the burn of scotch on my tongue, the warmth it brings to the belly, the calm that floats into the head. "I'm glad we capsized," I say, "especially since we were really in no danger, not really." Capsizing and being carried along by the rushing current allowed me to feel the power of the river in a visceral way, as a personal yet oddly detached force, the way nature can feel.

I admit I had a moment of panic when, clinging to the overturned boat, being rushed along by the current, I tried to touch bottom and couldn't, then quickly lifted my legs up to the surface and rode to the eddy that way. The greatest danger on the river, aside from being pinned on the downstream side of a canoe against a rock or tree, is to have your foot snagged by an underwater crevice, so that you're held down and can't get your head above water. And that didn't even come close to happening. David proved to be cool and unflappable. "David, you were great. The whole time I was cussing, you were laughing."

David says, "Well, it was sort of fun."

Amy says, "It's not an adventure if everything goes smoothly, all according to plan. What fun is that?"

Everybody voices agreement. And of course she has a point — maybe even *the* point of all this.

The difficult moments, the groundings and even capsizes, the out-of-control panic of being swept along by the current, the rainy night watching the water rise as we feel the rain pattering on our shoulders like drumming fingers and sip our precious cups of scotch, all serve as punctuation marks for the trip, transforming it from a trip into an adventure.

All in all it has been a great day, a memorable day, and this is the perfect way for it to end: four intrepid comrades standing around in the rain making toasts.

We begin to see spectacular arcs of lightning across the river, white-orange and blue, and count down until the thunder reverberates. It's getting closer — six miles, three, two, walking its way toward us like artillery fire sighting in. Then, in a gust of sudden wind and a burst of splattering, heavy raindrops, it breaks full on us. Standing under a lone tree is not the best place to be, so reluctantly we scuttle off to our tents.

It's a restless night, with the constant fury of the storm outside invading my dreams. The tent sways in the gusting wind, as if the world is breathing us in and exhaling us, and at some point the tent begins leaking from the uphill side. In the morning we will discover that a runnel has formed on the bank above us and sluices down till it hits the tent, then diverts, leaving a pool of water backed up on the rear of the tent and scoring deep ruts on either side. Beyond that, we remain relatively dry.

In the heart of the night, both David and Ethan stir at various times to check the level of the river and make sure the boats are still there, tethered to the tree.

But about that hour, I am blissfully asleep, rocking in the cradle of the river.

I wake the way you awaken in nature, for no apparent reason, without the blast of an alarm or even the morning voices on the radio. Despite the storm and fatigue, or maybe because of both, my sleep was deep. My body feels sore in that wonderful way that means your muscles have relaxed after long labor and the rest has kneaded itself like a deep tissue massage into your limbs and muscles, leaving you aching and exhilarated.

I peer out into the gray light to hear Ethan already up and moving around. We need an early start to make Fayetteville, a paddle that will stretch our endurance and cover better than twenty-five miles. But I'm game for it. At this point, I can't imagine pulling out of the river early. During the night, the river has risen a whole foot, which is good news for the Monster. It will be a fast day for us, a day with no groundings, no capsizing, just steady paddling, some fun fast water, and a lot more wild country giving way to the inevitable trashy detritus of civilization.

This morning I perform the hardest task of the whole trip: I take my sodden river shirt off the roof of the tent and button it on. This seems like no big deal, but realize I have just emerged from the double dry and cozy cocoon of sleeping bag and tent. The shirt is still soaked and muddy from yesterday's dunking, and further soaked by the rain, which somehow didn't wash the mud out of it as I had hoped. It's a cool, overcast morning with occasional drizzle that will follow us all day long.

So I take a breath and just put it on, feeling the clammy weight of the sleeves on my shoulders and arms, around my belly. The pants are wet, too, but somehow I don't mind that. The wet shirt, though. Ugh.

We strike the tent in good order and pack it away, filthy from sand and sediment carried down on us by the runnel and the rain. We shove off by 6:30, and after a few paddle strokes, I no longer notice the clammy shirt or my own grogginess. We suck down orange juice and munch granola bars and fruit and move swiftly downriver in the glory of a serene morning.

We and the morning birds—herons and ducks, mostly, and some others that flit by too fast to name—have the river all to ourselves, and ahead of us the fog steams off the river in ghostly filigrees, silvering the new light. As the day warms, turtles begin to adorn logs and rocks, always lined up by size, a silly, fussy orderliness that always makes me smile.

We encounter the last patch of fast water on the river just above Fayetteville, where a number of local kayakers are playing, traveling to and fro across the river, upstream and downstream. They seem to belong to the houses and cottages near the river. One of them asks, "You going through them rapids?" Sure, we say, and off we go in a perfect run.

It's a glorious day for paddling, overcast and drizzly, and the rise in the river means that we are hustling along in a deceptively brisk current.

Just above Fayetteville we hear what we think at first is thunder. It grows louder, more insistent, more frequent. But it isn't thunder. We are passing the live-fire range of Fort Bragg, home to an impressive cadre of units, most famously the 82nd Airborne, about 40,000 soldiers in all. It is also home base for the John F. Kennedy Special Warfare Center and School and the Psychological Operations Command. When it opened as Camp Bragg in 1919 (the "camp" designation signaling that it was not yet a permanent army garrison but a transient training facility), it was a proving ground for field artillery units. The remote location made it an ideal place to shoot off cannons.

What we are likely hearing are the concussions of 155-mm howitzer shells, so-called Excalibur rounds that can be calibrated to strike within ten feet of a target twenty-five miles away, a fact that both amazes and terrifies. The large sign on the west bank announces, "The Sound of Freedom."

The sounds of live-fire remind me just how often in history the Cape Fear has been the site of battles and bloodshed.

Fayetteville has a long history as an arsenal. Prior to the Civil War, some 7,000 muskets left over from the War of 1812 were stockpiled in the federal arsenal here. Upon secession, the Confederates promptly seized the arsenal but found that the unrifled weapons had deteriorated so badly that they were more dangerous to the man firing one than to the enemy. When Confederate troops overran Harpers Ferry, they stripped all the machinery from the federal armory there and shipped it to Fayetteville, which then became one of the chief manufacturers of rifled muskets for the Confederacy, producing 10,000 of them. At the height of production, 2,000 men and women worked there.

In March 1865, just two weeks after the fall of Wilmington, General William Tecumseh Sherman invaded North Carolina from the south with 60,000 troops, hardened by fighting and headed for the rail terminus at Goldsboro,

A pencil sketch of the U.S. Arsenal at Fayetteville—note one of four defensive towers (courtesy of the Museum of the Cape Fear Historical Complex, from *Harper's Weekly Journal of Civilization* 9, no. 431 [April 1, 1865])

where he planned to link up with other Union armies coming by train from Wilmington and New Bern. Within days, his army drove the rebels from Fayetteville and occupied the city. A thousand Michigan engineers took sledgehammers to the equipment inside the arsenal and knocked down the walls with battering rams and explosives—a task that took three days. The massive foundation stones trace the grassy rectangular footprint of what's left of the great arsenal, now bisected by N.C. 87.

Then one wing of Sherman's army chased the Confederates across the river to Averasboro, near Taylor's Hole Creek. The war was pretty well decided, but men kept dying anyway. In military parlance, the Battle of Averasboro was a "delaying action," one that cost more than 1,600 men killed, wounded, or missing in action.

A few days later, at Bentonville, another 4,500 men fell in what, in retrospect, was the last gasp of the Confederacy and a fairly pointless battle between woefully mismatched armies. General Joseph E. Johnston had been ordered to stop Sherman's march northward. Johnston had served as the senior Confederate commander at the first major battle of the war, Bull Run. But a year later, he was severely wounded by an artillery shell at the Battle of Seven Pines and spent five months convalescing. In 1864, Jefferson Davis— with whom he was constantly bickering—ordered him to stop Sherman's advance on Atlanta. Instead Johnston conducted a series of defensive withdrawals in order to keep his army from being overwhelmed. Furious, Davis relieved him of command. Now Johnston was back.

He cobbled together a ragged army of veterans from the Army of Tennessee, some coastal artillery units, garrison troops from Savannah and Charleston, regiments from Florida, the Carolinas, and Georgia—whoever was still able to carry a rifle—still only about half the number of men in Sherman's army. Initially, with surprise on their side, the Confederates pushed the Yankees back, but overwhelming numbers and cool strategy carried the day. Johnston's men fought valiantly, but they were just no match for the Yankee juggernaut. Lieutenant General William J. Hardee, who faced Sherman's army at Bentonville, concluded, "I made up my mind that there had been no such army in existence since the days of Julius Caesar."

Sherman went on to Goldsboro, his main objective all along, because from there he could at last resupply his men by railroad—with rations, new uniforms, and even mail. And two other Union generals were converging on Goldsboro, General Alfred H. Terry, bringing up the forces that had just captured Fort Fisher and Wilmington, and General John M. Schofield, whose 21,000 troops were coming in from New Bern. Once combined, the massed army could move north to join Sherman's old comrade Ulysses Grant and checkmate General Robert E. Lee.

Told in summary, the Civil War along the river sounds like a chess game, and from the quiet safety of headquarters it probably seemed just that. But the river country is rugged, boggy, and densely thicketed, a maze of creeks and dirt roads that peter out into swamp, and Sherman's men must have been mightily glad to be shet of it and have firm ground under their feet and fresh grub in their bellies.

The final act of the campaign was played out in the parlor of a farmhouse on the Raleigh–Hillsborough Road, just above present-day Jordan Lake, in the headwaters of the Cape Fear, beginning on April 17, 1865. Generals Sherman and Johnston had never met, though they had fought over the same ground for four years. Sherman took the train from Raleigh, where his troops were now encamped, to Durham Station, then mounted a horse and proceeded up the Hillsborough road with a small escort, looking for Johnston under a flag of truce.

The two generals shook hands while still mounted. Then Johnston suggested they retire to the home of James and Nancy Bennett—sometimes spelled "Bennitt"—a little ways down the road, three and a half miles east of Hillsborough, where Johnston's troops were encamped.

One of the Bennetts' sons, Lorenzo, had gone off to war and died of disease. Their daughter Eliza's husband had also enlisted and died at the front, leaving Eliza widowed with a young son. The Bennetts' second son, Alphonzo, also died during the war, but he left behind no service record, so it is unclear whether he enlisted or simply stayed behind and succumbed to illness.

In any case, all the young men were gone, and the Bennetts would have to work the farm alone from now on. James was pushing sixty, and his wife, Nancy, was sixty-four. They had once been poor sharecroppers but had worked their way up into what was called the "yeoman famer" class, property owners, part of the backbone of the community. But the war had overwhelmed them, robbing them of their children and their modest prosperity. Before long, they would lapse into a sharecropping bargain again, this time leasing out their own farm to tenants.

It intrigues me to wonder what Mrs. Bennett was thinking and feeling when she opened the door to the generals and their retinue. They requested the use of her parlor, which meant that she, her husband, and her daughter were banished to the cookhouse. She did not complain or vent her grief, did not chastise them for the years of slaughter over which they had presided.

Instead, she offered the generals a pitcher of cool buttermilk. Then she led her husband and her widowed daughter to the cookhouse, to wait out the parlay.

The generals' meetings lasted two days. On the morning of the first day, Johnston came prepared to ask amnesty for Confederate president Jefferson Davis and his cabinet, to end the war politically as well as on the battlefield.

Sherman arrived on the scene bearing a telegram. When he was alone with Johnston, he unfolded it: President Abraham Lincoln had been assassinated. This complicated negotiations. Now Davis was possibly implicated in the assassination plot. Sherman insinuated that Johnston should alert Davis to flee

The Bennett farmhouse near Durham where Sherman accepted
the surrender of the last Confederate army (author photo)

fast, in case Sherman's amnesty did not prove protection enough from Federal authorities.

Lee had already surrendered the 26,000 men under his command in Virginia, but Sherman didn't want to have to beat each army separately. He offered generous terms for a surrender by all the armies in the Carolinas, Georgia, and Florida. Johnston understood he could not defeat Sherman's army; the best he could do was to disband his men into guerilla units, which would guarantee a generation of bloodshed and reprisal. He agreed.

But Washington did not. The secretary of war and the new president, Andrew Johnson—a native of Raleigh—accused Sherman of overstepping his bounds. He was relieved of command, and General Grant was ordered to Raleigh to enforce a proper surrender. But Grant gave his old friend one last chance, and Sherman met with Johnston a third time at the Bennett farmstead, where he offered Johnston essentially the same terms Lee had gotten from Grant at Appomattox.

Jefferson Davis ordered Johnston not to accept the terms, to disband the infantry into the countryside and escape with the cavalry to escort Davis south. But Johnston, to his everlasting credit, disobeyed the order. On April 26, 1865, in the largest surrender of the war, he surrendered almost 90,000 Confederate soldiers in four states and effectively ended the Civil War.

Two different generals on two warring sides—Grant and Johnston—had disobeyed their respective presidents in order to stop the bloodletting. Remarkable—I don't know of another moment like it in history.

In any case, at both ends of the Cape Fear River, momentous events had occurred: the greatest naval bombardment in history at Fort Fisher (which still lies downriver in our story) and the largest surrender of the war in Durham County.

And in between, Fayetteville, the arsenal of the Confederacy.

So a war that had cost more than 750,000 dead was finally laid to rest with a few signatures scribbled on pieces of paper at a farmhouse located some twenty-seven miles north of Mermaid Point.

Past the Sound of Freedom now, we're approaching Fayetteville in a moderate current. The country on both banks of the river is still wild and overgrown.

Amy remarks, "Look how clean the river is still—no trash, no debris. And we can't be very far from Fayetteville." That can only be true because it is inaccessible to roads and people. There is something surreal in her observation, the juxtaposition of a large slice of real estate devoted to maximizing our national ability to wreak death and destruction on an enemy, and the pristine nature of much of that real estate.

But that surreal juxtaposition of lethal power and serenity seems fitting in this place. In Fayetteville, not long ago, I had my most surreal experience in years. My wife and family drove up from Wilmington to see a special art exhibit: a limited-edition folio of Lewis Carroll's *Alice in Wonderland* illustrated by Salvador Dali. We spent an hour or so admiring the lush pages of fanciful drawings about the wild adventures of a little girl who falls down the rabbit hole into a weird, nonsensical world of bizarre contradictions. Then we took the kids on a short walk literally across the street to the Airborne and Special Operations Museum. The exhibits were captivating: life-sized paratroopers descending from the vaulted ceilings, artifacts of every war in history, Jeeps and weapons and rolls of honor.

But what grabbed my imagination was something called the Pitch, Roll, and Yaw Vista-Dome Motion Simulator. You file into a small theater and hold on tight for a trip seen through the eyes of an airborne trooper parachuting out of a plane, riding in a Humvee, and operating a tank. As the museum promises, "The Pitch, Roll, and Yaw Vista-Dome Motion Simulator adds another dimension by physically moving a specially designed seating area up to 18 degrees in concert with the film. Suddenly a larger than life film of airborne and special operations becomes almost real. The 24-seat simulator provides visitors with an extreme taste of what the Army's finest are trained to do."

The sensation is uncannily real—your body *feels* the buffet and swerve and shock of movement. Dali would have loved it: art that simulates war, or perhaps war simulating art, in a completely harmless experience.

The live-fire range is not so harmless. Anyplace where you work with high explosives is dangerous ground. In March 2011, an Excalibur round apparently detonated inside the barrel of a howitzer and sent seven soldiers to the hospital with lacerations and shrapnel wounds. The sound of freedom is a reminder of a lethal business.

In fact, long before the Civil War, Fayetteville found itself at the center of conflicts. It was still called Cross Creek on June 29, 1775, when a band of fifty-five Patriots met in Lewis Barge's tavern at the corner of present-day Bow and Person Streets. They were gathered at the instigation of Robert Rowan, a prominent legislator who also held several other offices and would go on to become an officer in the militia during the American Revolution. Rowan, like his cohort, was incensed by the British attacks on Lexington and Concord, Massachusetts, on April 19. Following his lead, they drafted and signed a resolve to resist such military aggression, which they called the Cumberland Association. It read in part,

> We, therefore, the subscribers of Cumberland County, holding ourselves bound by that most sacred of all obligations, the duty of good citizens towards an injured Country, and thoroughly convinced that under our distressed circumstances we shall be justified before you in resisting force by force; do unite ourselves under every tie of religion and honour, and associate as a band in her defence against every foe; hereby solemnly engaging, that whenever our Continental or Provincial Councils shall decree it necessary, we will go forth and be ready to sacrifice our lives and fortunes to secure her freedom and safety.

The wedge of grass near the tavern, formed by the sharp intersection of Person and Bow Streets, came to be known as Liberty Point. Today it is a small park with a stone monument to the audacious spirit of Rowan and company. Their rather modestly titled, inflammatory document has become known in popular usage as the Liberty Point Resolves, or even the Liberty Point Declaration of Independence, though it stops short of advocating a full break with Great Britain and anticipates some kind of constitutional reconciliation.

In the same year, Flora MacDonald showed up in Cross Creek with her husband, Allan. Flora was famous—or notorious, depending on your political bent—for helping Bonnie Prince Charlie escape the wrath of the British after the slaughter of the Scottish clans at Culloden.

Flora was living on Benbecula, an island in the Outer Hebrides. She arranged for the prince to travel with her disguised as her spinning maid, Betty Burke, under the safe passage of her clan. Later she was arrested for aiding in the prince's escape and was imprisoned for a time in the Tower of London. She emigrated to America with her husband. Samuel Johnson described her as "a woman of soft features, gentle manners, kind soul and elegant presence." In any case, she and her husband are credited with uniting the Scots in the Cross Creek–Campbellton area and goading them on toward Wilmington, where they would eventually land in a hard fight at Moore's Creek near the Black River.

Fayetteville's role in the Revolution was not confined to the Cumberland Association or the rallying of Highland clans to attack the Patriots downriver. When all the shooting was done, the North Carolina Constitutional Convention convened in Fayetteville on November 16, 1789. After a full week of haggling, the convention ratified the U.S. Constitution by a vote of 195–77 and proposed eight amendments, dealing with a shopping list of concerns ranging from the duration of a soldier's enlistment to the manner of election of senators and congressmen.

Until the state had a bona fide capital, during the period from 1774 to 1789, the General Assembly met in Fayetteville. During the same year that the U.S. Constitution was ratified by the convention, the General Assembly granted a charter to the University of North Carolina, to be located at New Hope Chapel Hill. UNC thus became the first *public* university in the United States.

The settlement of Cross Creek–Campbellton had already been renamed Fayetteville in honor of the Marquis de Lafayette, who commanded troops in the fight against the British in the South. Lafayette visited Fayetteville in 1825 to a hero's welcome as part of his grand triumphal tour of the new nation he had helped to bring into being.

It was not the last time the city would reinvent itself. On May 29, 1831, the Great Fire of Fayetteville consumed the state house, 125 mercantile establishments, a number of churches, and more than 600 homes.

And on August 27, 1908, in one of its cyclical rampages, the Cape Fear descended upon Fayetteville in a torrent, completely inundating the city of 12,000. It was the same flood that washed away two spans of the Lillington Bridge upriver. For two days the water rose, leaving 3,000 residents homeless, fully one-quarter of the population.

The hulk of a barge at its last mooring near Fayetteville (Amy Williamson photo)

But the river is far from flood as we paddle past the sound of freedom toward the city that three times has been named an "All-America City," whose motto is "History, Heroes & A Hometown Feeling." A derelict barge looms into view on the west bank, its hull canted toward the river. It's still at its last mooring, though the hull is open to the river, and through the rust you can spot broken branches and machinery. On its slanting deck, someone has very neatly painted in Day-Glo orange block letters, TPOT.

When the railroad bridge and then the I-95/U.S. 301 bridge loom into view before noon, we're flabbergasted. By one o'clock we're passing under the double bridges. First N.C. 24/210 and then Person Street and the Riverside Sports Center ramp, and it's clear we'll have plenty of time to make the Wildlife ramp on Old Route 87.

From the river, you'd never know you were passing through a major southern city of fifty-eight square miles and more than 200,000 people, the sixth-largest city in the state. Just as from the city, you'd hardly know the Cape Fear River was running dark and powerful past your door. Only the bridges, and the lone ramp at Riverside, betray the secret.

More than a bait-and-tackle shop, Riverside is just what it sounds like, a large tract of land right on the river. It includes a steep two-lane boat launch ($5 per boat), a picnic area, a restaurant, two large World War II–era Quonset huts for storage, lots of parking, and a large open-air amphitheater. The covered stage backs up to the river, and the ten grassy tiers in three angled sections look right down onto the river behind the stage.

On a later visit to Riverside, I meet a large man in a ballcap named Dwight Vinson, a Chapel Hill native who moved to Fayetteville a long time ago. For a time he lived near Lock and Dam #3 just south of the city, where he fished and hunted regularly. "Every city on a river has a riverwalk," he says. "We don't have one here. There's all that land across the river, but they've never done anything with it. It doesn't make any sense to me."

It's hard to argue with him. The west side of the river is all green, yet it's almost impossible to get to from the land. It seems like an opportunity waiting for a visionary who can reclaim Fayetteville's place on the river. But I guess this only bears out David Avrette's point: The river was for so long a thing to be feared, not enjoyed, that it may take awhile for a new generation to feel safe cozying up to its banks.

Tucked up under the concrete shade of the eastern abutments of the N.C. 24/210 bridge is a camp that looks more like a big open-air living room: three overstuffed recliners, side tables, a mattress, assorted other chairs, a red shopping cart. Just downriver at the Person Street bridge, on the opposite shore, is sited another camp, a small village, really, of three tents, folding tables, coolers, and even a wooden dresser. No one seems to be home, but the camp trash spills in a plume down the sheer clay cutbank to the water. Clearly the camp has been there awhile.

It turns out that the camps are indeed permanent residences for the homeless, though they might argue that since they live reasonably comfortably, protected from downpours and hammering sun, they do have a home, albeit an unconventional one on public property. Apparently Fayetteville had a large homeless population that took over a swatch of woods off Ramsey Street, where the Veterans' Administration hospital is located, and created a veritable tent city, till the authorities cleared them out.

Beyond the camp, what at first appears to be a kite trapped in a tree turns out to be a POW/MIA flag flying over a derelict sailboat without a mast tethered to trees a little ways downriver. There's lots of trash in the water. We have made a habit of plucking out the odd plastic bottle or wrapper during our trip, but we could fill several dumpsters with the junk and trash on this stretch of the river.

Along this section, we pass many outflows, some picturesque natural-looking falls, some pipes. One emits a horrific chemical odor. The only people we spot seem as derelict as the broken barges and disused barge landings, old

Semipermanent homeless camp under the highway bridge at Fayetteville (Amy Williamson photo)

cabled-together bunches of gray pilings called "dolphins" flanking high platforms.

On the banks, we can see very little but thick foliage, but behind that we hear the continuous hum and roar of heavy industry and from time to time get a glimpse of a smokestack, a metal roof, a steel tank. At one point, incongruously, like some colonial relic from the Mosquito Coast rising out of the jungle, we spy a thirty-yard slice of railroad track perched on trestles fifty feet above the riverbank. On the rails sits a rusty old steam-powered crane. Was it once used for unloading barges? One of these days, I can't help but imagine, one of those rusty joints is going to give way, and several tons of corroded metal are going to come hurtling into the river.

The riverfront feels abandoned, as if whatever industry was once located here just took off, leaving behind machinery, barges, docks, sheds. The thicket of kudzu and poison ivy is reclaiming the ground with a vengeance.

We pass a derelict barge on which some wit has written TITANIC, a rusting hulk leaking heaven knows what manner of heavy metals and chemicals into the river. A reminder that until only a couple of decades ago, barges still plied the waters between Wilmington and Fayetteville. Some of the earliest dredging projects in the nineteenth century were undertaken to allow service to the large cotton mills at Fayetteville.

In an age before diesel tugboats and barges, shallow-draft steamboats carried the products of the mills down to Wilmington. The first steamboat on the river above Wilmington was the *Henrietta*, built by James Seawell on his plantation near Fayetteville and launched in April 1818. From the 1830s onward, a fleet of steamers regularly carried passengers and freight back and forth between Fayetteville and the Wilmington waterfront: the *North State*, the *D. Murchison*, the *Governor Worth*, the *Cotton Plant*, the *Zephyr*, the *Fanny Lutterloh*, the *Black River*, the *Flora Macdonald*, the *John Dawson*, the original *Henrietta*, and dozens of others.

These vessels were smaller and had a shallower draught than the palatial Mississippi riverboats, but they were nonetheless the emblem of a colorful era when Fayetteville had its sights firmly on the river, when the river was the main highway for travelers, businessmen, mercantile supplies, and industrial goods.

Captains made their names at the helms of fast vessels, as did river pilots like Dan Buxton, an African American legend from Fayetteville who plied the river for half a century.

J. H. Myover, in *A Short History of Cumberland County*, published in 1905, characterizes the mercantile class during the heyday of steamboats on the Cape Fear: "The oldest inhabitants still look back on those times as the 'good old days' of Fayetteville. The merchants were not the progressive men of the 20th century; they were conservative and cautious and honest as the day, with their word as bond. They made money slowly, but they lived simply, and gradually accumulated modest fortunes."

Fayetteville enjoys another minor distinction, one that delights baseball trivia fans. On March 7, 1914, Babe Ruth hit his first home run in professional league play in Fayetteville. He had signed with the minor league Baltimore Orioles in the International League. The Orioles held their monthlong spring training in Fayetteville, an easy train ride from Baltimore. The game was an intra-squad contest among Orioles, divided into Sparrows and Buzzards. The Babe was—of course—a Buzzard.

As we paddle the last mile to the pull-out, a couple roars by in a powerboat that nearly swamps us with its wake, then continues blithely up-river. This is a sign that the river is now reliably deep enough for boats with motors, and our paddling idyll will soon come to a close.

As we draw nearer to the Wildlife ramp south of the city, we spy a camp on the east bank. Just like the homeless village under the bridge upriver, this fishing camp seems fairly permanent, including not just tent but awnings, an outdoor kitchen with a gas grill, and an array of coolers and furniture. We drift toward the east bank to confer with an old man and a much younger woman. The woman is energetically slapping a fish onto the ground; then she produces a cleaver and begins to hack at it. We keep a safe distance, conversing with her long enough to learn she is engaged in the St. Jude Hospital fishing tournament—the same as the very first fisherman we spied on the river just below Buckhorn Dam. Then we push back out into the current.

At last there is the Wildlife ramp. It is 2:55 P.M., so we arrive exactly five minutes ahead of our scheduled time. I am elated—more than sixty miles of river, rapids, capsizes, thunderstorms, distance, and here we are. Ethan needs to get on his way by 4:00 P.M., so I told our drivers to be here at 3:00.

We beach the boats, and then it starts to rain. Before long, we are drenched by a hammering downpour. At the foot of the ramp, a guy in a two-man inflatable boat sets off in the driving rain to ferry supplies across the river to the couple at the fish camp. We wait patiently in the rain, but our drivers have gotten lost, and they do not arrive until nearly 4:30. From the moment the bow of the first canoe touched the foot of the ramp, the skies opened and it has rained steadily. Now as the trucks appear, splashing toward us down the muddy road, the rain stops as suddenly as pulling a switch.

The pull-out on Highway 87 marks the end of the middle river for us. David Webster and I will return in a couple of days and continue alone in a johnboat to Wilmington. We haul out the canoe and kayak and strap them to David's Jeep and Ethan's car and light out for home. Ethan will just make his meeting. David and I take our two drivers for a celebratory fast-food feast. Turns out we're all famished.

We still have more than 120 miles to go to reach Wilmington harbor, a mileage greater than the actual distance between cities because of all the loops and turns of the river, and another 35 after that into the rough waters of the Cape Fear estuary to reach the actual Cape Fear on Bald Head, formerly Smith's, Island, and to reach the sea buoy marking the true end of the Cape Fear channel.

That will wait for another day, for a boat with a motor, for a good night's sleep and some dry clothes.

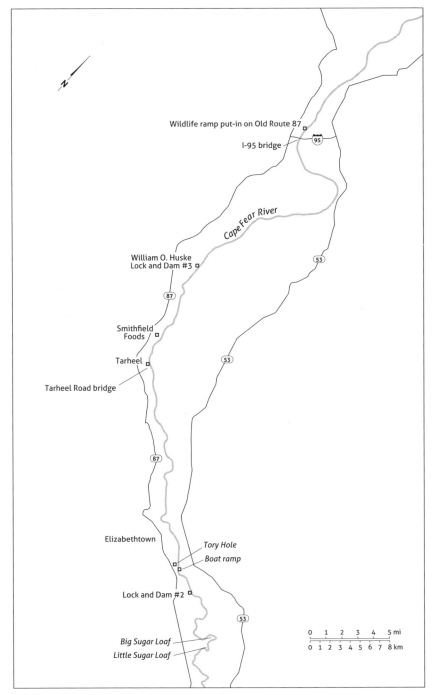

Wildlife ramp put-in on Old Route 87

I-95 bridge

Cape Fear River

William O. Huske
Lock and Dam #3

Smithfield
Foods

Tarheel

Tarheel Road bridge

Elizabethtown

Tory Hole

Boat ramp

Lock and Dam #2

Big Sugar Loaf

Little Sugar Loaf

0 1 2 3 4 5 mi

0 1 2 3 4 5 6 7 8 km

The Lower Reaches: Fayetteville to Wilmington

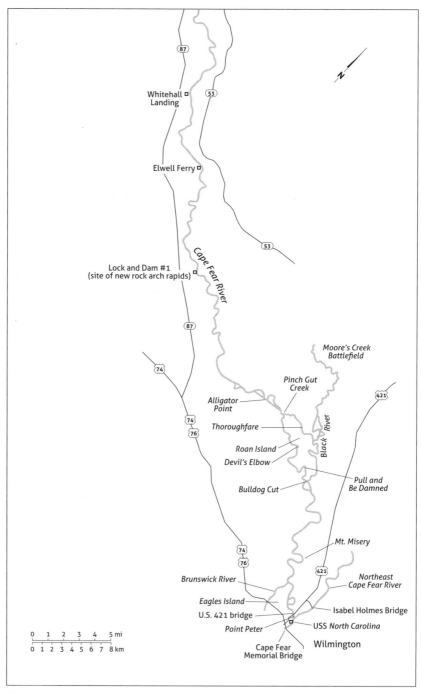

**The Lower Reaches: Fayetteville to Wilmington
(continued)**

David Webster and I launch our johnboat at the Wildlife ramp at Old Route 87, just to make sure we will have a continuous trip and cover all of the river. I don't know why this is so important to me, but there is a kind of implicit integrity in covering every yard of the downstream flow.

We have arranged to borrow the sixteen-foot johnboat *Sea Whip* from the UNC Wilmington Center for Marine Science Research. We were to have a center-console bateau with a steering wheel, much more comfortable for the long haul; but at the last minute it blew an engine, and so we are assigned an olive-drab aluminum skiff with a thirty-horse four-stroke engine that can make it fly, steered by its tiller arm. It's a functional boat, wide and with a large bow platform for working. The seat is a flat piece of aluminum, so we always sit on soft boat cushions. Even then, your hand tends to go numb after a period of steering the tiller, which is also the throttle arm, and which requires a certain amount of steady exertion to keep up to speed.

We get a later start than planned today. We're due at Lock #3 at 10:00 or so, at the next lock around noon, and at Lock #1 by 3:00 P.M. But these are loose times (time on the river always seems so) that should allow us ample leeway to loiter along the way to observe anything of interest.

So I back the truck and trailer down the long ramp, and David shoves off aboard *Sea Whip* and promptly disappears around the tree-lined bend. Motor trouble. He drifts about, the engine starting and stalling. He beaches the boat at the ramp, and I climb aboard to help diagnose the problem. Eventually we discover that the cooling port ("pee-hole") is clogged and manage to unclog it, and from that moment on the motor hums us along efficiently and, for all our speed, quietly.

The litter from Fayetteville begins to lessen and finally disappears from the river. The only access now seems to be from private fish camps, occasional home-built ramps, some quite elaborate, and walking paths which culminate usually in a clearing with a lawn chair or two and maybe a fishing rod holder. Sometimes there's a fire ring, a cooler for bait and beer, or a more elaborate rack for holding multiple rods. This is evidence of local access for people who probably know the river well, or at least their little stretch of it, though none of them is fishing today.

A mile downriver we pass under the I-95 bridge. This is a landmark, in the sense that the interstate more or less defines the boundary between the coastal plain and the Piedmont. From now on, the landscape and the watercourses will change in dramatic ways.

For starters, the white water is gone. The unbroken current is mostly an artificial effect caused by the creation of the dams downstream. From here on the river is no longer a completely natural watershed defined by gravity. You could argue that the entire river is a bit unnatural, given Jordan Dam's position at the headwaters, and Buckhorn Dam just below Mermaid Point. But sixty-odd miles of distance have given gravity the edge after all, and so as we discovered, there is plenty of white water between Buckhorn and the pooling channel at Fayetteville. From now on, though, the river will run wide and fairly deep, dredged and channeled, the severest oxbows long since straightened out by the Army Corps of Engineers, though many are still navigable in small boats. Seen from the air, the brown meanders and oxbows create a lovely recursive pattern of loops and whorls.

From Fayetteville on down, the river is backed up behind William O. Huske Lock and Dam #3, the first of three sets of locks and dams on the river as we head downstream. I've called ahead and spoken to Phil Edge, who has arranged for lockmasters to be on hand to lock us through as we pass on down the river. The Huske lock was built in 1935 to finish the navigation channel from Navassa to Fayetteville, 111 river miles apart. The channel is 8 feet deep, but in summer drought it can be lower. The chamber itself is 40 feet wide by 300 feet long—big enough to accommodate a tug-and-barge combo, though the last one passed through years ago.

All three locks are built according to an ingeniously simple design. Each is basically a rectangular well with sidewalls twenty feet high and double doors at either end. Both sets of doors close into a V facing upstream. Once the chamber is full and the doors must be opened upstream, the pressure provided by the now deep water inside the lock is fairly matched with the depth of water flowing in, so it does not take a great deal of force to open the steel doors. The lockmaster walks out onto a catwalk above the doors and turns a great wheel, which is geared to provide the leverage to swing the heavy doors. To lower the water level for boats headed downstream, the lockmaster closes the upstream doors and pumps water out of the lock until the level matches the downstream level.

David Webster inside a lock aboard *Sea Whip* (author photo)

All the locks are built into the right or west bank of the river, providing consistency, and each has a canoe pull-out upstream so paddlers can portage the lock and dam and put in downstream at the public ramp to continue their journey.

For our little johnboat, the lock chamber is a giant tub, and as the great doors are wheeled closed upstream and the water goes down, you can smell the dampness of the concrete walls and watch the spiders in the spaces behind the ladder rungs recessed into the walls. It takes about half an hour to fill the lock with 1.8 million gallons of river water, then drain it, lowering us nine feet from thirty-two feet above sea level to twenty-three feet. The water drains in a loud cataract from the opening lockgates.

Once again, the trip takes us.

It's odd, in a way, since the river is at once so completely there, so concrete and forceful, and yet so ephemeral. This becomes clear as we wait in the lock and watch it drain away, disappearing beneath our hull.

What is the river?

Not the water—that is gone by the end of any day, spilled profligately into the ocean. That would be like defining I-95 by its traffic, which at any given point along the route changes by the second. A river is a container of sorts, containing water along with all the animals, fishes, and birds that move through it and locate themselves within it for a day or a lifetime. But it's also a dynamic engine of movement, a progenitor of plant and animal life, a habitat that is always in motion, a flow of water and the air above it, a place that just won't keep still.

The lockmasters are nearing the end of the American or white shad run, during which, for a couple of weeks each spring, they fill the locks and raise the water level, then open the upstream doors so the fish can get out. Otherwise the dams would prevent them and other anadromous fish—fish that swim from the ocean up the river to spawn—from procreating. Many have argued for years that the Army Corps of Engineers ought to just blow up the dams and let the live river through.

Shad, striped bass, and long-nosed gar aren't the only big fish in the river. In 1994, anglers pulled in a sixty-nine-pound flathead catfish and a seventy-eight-and-a-half-pound Arkansas blue catfish, both state- and world-record catches. Both species are nonnative, though the flathead was introduced deliberately decades ago and proved all too adaptable to the Cape Fear.

We continue downstream beyond the lock, preceded by clouds of water striders that boil about in oddly organized swarms, buoyed by the surface tension, always maneuvering en masse to avoid the sharp prow of the powerboat. The very surface tension that allows them to walk on water traps heavier bugs and bees that have had the misfortune to venture too close to the water, and the striders overwhelm them with their front appendages and feast on the poor creatures. Flights of bright-colored dragonflies flit around our boat, electric blue and green, catching the light.

Alongside the boat a mating pair of Louisiana waterthrushes paces us. Whenever you see two birds flying together in nature, odds are good they're a mating pair. The thrushes, six and a half inches long, olive brown on top and streaked white on their undersides, fly low over the water and disappear after a few hundred yards, their places taken up by a new pair, and another yet, all the way down the river to Wilmington, escorting us on our way. Like most birds, waterthrushes mate for life, though they are not averse to a little opportunistic coitus with strange birds—so-called extra-pair copulation. They don't hold it against each other, male or female, and simply enrich their gene pool.

The banks are planted with sycamore and green ash, which has furrowed gray bark and a compound leaf like a pecan tree. There's not much cypress yet. Upriver on our cobble bar we spotted our first river cypress, and we won't see bald cypress till we get lower down in the coastal meander.

We're also seeing wild mistletoe, black willow, and the ubiquitous oversized garlands of poison ivy.

Black willow deserves a word. It grows in stands low down along the river, bright green against the darker foliage of conifers and oaks. Its bendy trunks stand out black against the bright green backdrop, and the effect is of an Impressionist painting. I find them among the most beautiful trees on the river.

At times the river closes into a channel not fifty or sixty yards wide. This is baffling. You'd think it would just keep widening toward the sea, but instead it widens and constricts by turns. At one point below Lock #3, we drop the anchor and play out all thirty-five feet of anchor rode and don't hit bottom, so in that stretch at least the river may be nearly as deep as the shipping channel way down below Wilmington, now dredged to a depth of forty-two feet.

The river has risen at least two feet above where it was when we started out in canoes, after several days of bountiful rain in the Piedmont, and the water is gushing into the mainstem from a network of fifty miles of tributaries above Buckhorn Dam. All that mass of water. The river is roughly 200 miles long and the average width is probably 200 yards. Think of how much water volume it takes to raise more than 15,000 acres of river even one inch, let alone two feet.

We're adding to our list of birds now as well: red-eyed vireos, more Carolina wrens, catbirds, and Louisiana thrashers. Ospreys become more frequent. I've always thought of them as saltwater birds, since I am used to seeing them nesting on the day-mark platforms in shipping channels and soaring above the Intracoastal Waterway with fish in their talons. But David informs me that they are equally at home in any body of water. They just need a nice high platform on which to nest.

Sometimes they will share a nest with bald eagles, digging a cubby near the base of the nest while the eagles occupy the high open bowl. "Kind of like basement tenants," David explains. I think of the aerial dogfight we witnessed below Raven Rock between an osprey and a bald eagle, and it's hard to imagine a very congenial landlord-tenant relationship.

Every so often, just for the pure joy of it, we kill the engine and drift along in the lethargic muddy current, listening to the amazing stillness. There's not an airplane motor or a highway noise, no factory or buzz of high-tension wires, no human voices or barking dogs. Just the ripple of the water and the occasional splash of a jumping fish or a yellow-bellied slider dropping off a downed tree. The fluffing of the wind, the racket of birdcalls.

Glorious. Almost unimaginable in our world.

Anybody who hasn't heard that stillness should drift on down the river till the noise stops, hold his or her breath, and just listen.

We spy five turtles on a log and sneak up on them so they don't plop into the water until we are right up on them. We drift along in two knots of current. We could be a hundred miles from civilization. Out here on the river today, it sounds like the seventeenth century.

All too soon, we're back under power and approaching the Tar Heel Road bridge, being overflown by a Cooper's hawk. The sun glances off his russet underbelly, and when he turns, the slate-gray of his wings cuts a dark silhouette. In each of the many shady creeks we pass, a great blue heron stands patiently fishing from the banks.

The creek mouths look like deep Vs in the bank as seen from the water, always angled downstream. Usually they are crisscrossed with fallen trees or branches driven down by ice or wind or age, so that it would not really be possible to navigate back into them, even in a canoe, let alone a johnboat.

But when you approach from the water, they look cavelike and mysterious, each one a cut gouged in the steep bank, full of sand and mud and rocks and gently bubbling water and eddy pools where fish lurk. You peer in and the bright day becomes twilit, the shade inviting. The gray light seems to have density, like water or mist. You strain to see as far back as you can, but you can't see far beyond where the heron is standing stock still, either oblivious to you or doing its best to make itself invisible.

It's inviting—each time, you're tempted to land the boat, step out, and wade back into the creek, into the cool shade and that mysterious, provocative light.

But if you do, the odds are that you will sink to your knees or even thighs in glutinous boot-sucking mud, a slush of silt and clay and sand that will instantly remind you of quicksand, though at some point you will stop sinking and start extricating yourself and, if you're lucky, your shoes.

Tar Heel's economy relies on Smithfield Packing, which operates an enormous plant just off N.C. 87. Each day, more than 30,000 hogs are slaughtered and processed by 5,000 workers. That's 8 million per year, more or less. This is the terminal point in the factory hog farm operation in eastern North Carolina, of which more later when we get downriver.

Below Tar Heel we start to see Spanish moss garlanding the limbs of trees, one more hint that we are heading toward the black water of the coastal meander.

David is amazed at the silt load today, after all the days of rain. The particles of dirt are suspended in the water column like coffee grounds, that thick and distinct. It reminds me of what a friend of mine, writer Ron Hansen, used to say about the Missouri River, a boundary of his native Nebraska: "Too thick to drink, too thin to plow."

The silt accumulates in big, dark, chocolate-looking blooms visible on the surface, darker even than the dark water around it, as if emitted by a boiling vortex underwater. At first we mistake the blooms for shallow bottom, the kind we scraped over in that old Grumman, but here we are in deep water, dense with soil.

Below Tar Heel we come across more private docks, some very well camouflaged houses tucked into the dense foliage above the river, and more private boat ramps.

We pass a falling-in bulkhead on the east bank, flanked by large mooring dolphins, trees growing through the rotting wood that are no older than twenty-five or thirty years. David says, "That's history right there—going away."

Nature is reclaiming—or has already reclaimed—all the old steamboat landings, where the captains would put in to load heaps of firewood for their boats' boilers and local travelers would board and disembark. All kinds of goods were loaded or off-loaded. Now the last of the wooden infrastructure is rotting away, fading out like old photographs.

At Elizabethtown, dark blue and buff barn swallows swarm erratically under a concrete Highway 701 bridge. At least they look erratic, but in fact they are chasing and eating insects in flight. They will not nest under metal bridges. Their method of nest building is to attach a mud "cup" to the protected concrete underbelly of the bridge.

Elizabethtown, like so many other towns, has largely turned its back on the river. Yet it came into being in 1773 *because* of the river. Near the site of the current bridge, Isaac Jones operated a ferry. When the town was laid out on Jones's 100-acre tract, the first order of business was to set aside acreage for a public boat landing, to take advantage of the river as the main highway for the shipment of farm products to the coast and finished goods upriver into Bladen County.

Jones was already operating a tannery, a bark house, and a mill. The new town was laid out in 120 half-acre lots costing 40 shillings each, about $277 in today's currency.

Late in the American Revolution, the area around Elizabeth Town (as it was then written) became a hotbed of Tory activity. An organized band of 300–400 local Tories had been raiding their neighbors' property with impunity and carrying the loot for sale downriver. They were led by Colonel John Slingby and Colonel David Godden, described by combatants as "bold, daring and reckless, ready to risk everything to put down the Whigs."

Downriver, Wilmington was by this time occupied by British troops under

Lord Charles Cornwallis, and upriver, Cross Creek was controlled by Tories. "The state of the county was deplorable," writes John H. Wheeler in his 1851 *Historical Sketches of North Carolina*. "The Tories had overrun every portion; their opponents had been driven out of the county, their homes ravaged, and houses burned. About 60 had taken refuge in Duplin; hungry, naked, and homeless, exasperated to madness, they resolved to drive the Tories from their posts or die in the attempt."

The Whig leaders, Colonels Thomas Robeson Jr. and Thomas Brown, concocted a plan of deception and entrapment. A correspondent to the *Wilmington Chronicle* who interviewed some of the survivors wrote in 1844, "Colonel Brown and his brave men marched fifty miles through a wilderness subsisting on jerked beef and scanty bread" before reaching the Cape Fear River. They sent Sallie Salter, daughter of one of the prominent families in town, into the Tory camp under the pretense of selling fresh eggs. Actually, she was there to spy on the Tories. She reported back their number and defenses.

In the predawn darkness of August 27, 1781, Robeson, Brown, and their sixty men stripped off their clothes and crossed the river, which was neck deep. They held their muskets by the muzzles, the firelocks high above their heads. On the Elizabethtown side, they fanned out and attacked the Tory fort from several directions at once, calling out the names of known Patriot commanders, ordering phantom units to join the attack.

Another correspondent, who signed himself simply "Y.Z.," elaborated on the effect of the ruse for the *Raleigh Independent*: "The *ruse re guerre* was carried on until the Whig band was multiplied into ten or eleven companies. It succeeded in making an impression on the garrison that it was attacked by a body of one thousand strong led by experienced officers." He heard the tale recounted by Colonel Brown himself while they were both passengers aboard a packet sailing between Smithville (Southport) and Wilmington.

Early in the battle, both Tory commanders were killed, amplifying the panic. The Tories fell back on the river, fleeing into a deep ravine now known as Tory Hole. There, they were trapped. Patriots fired down on them until they surrendered, confiscated their goods and property, and banished them from the area.

Like an earlier battle downriver at Moore's Creek, it was a small engagement by comparison with Saratoga or Yorktown, yet it was both symbolically meaningful and practically useful in keeping the British from truly controlling North Carolina. And the entire course of the battle was shaped by the fact of the river. First, it provided a refuge for the Patriots, a barrier to hide on the other side of. And because the Patriots were across the river, the Tories falsely assumed they were safely out of their reach. The Tories had to make it across the river at some risk, and then the Patriots trapped the retreating Tories against the river to complete their rout.

～～～～～～

Tory Hole is now a shady park with a picnic shelter and hiking trails, but no camping facilities—though years ago I camped out in the shelter with a video crew that was shooting a documentary of the river for public television, but we had special permission.

We spot it as we motor past because it's right under the Highway 701 bridge and adjacent to the Wildlife boat ramp. But other than the boat ramp, you could spend all day in Elizabethtown and never even know the town is on the river. There's no river walk, no public dock, not even a restaurant with a river view. To me, that's unfathomable. The river is relaxing, mesmerizing, a moving panorama that shifts colors and moods constantly with the hour, the weather, the season. It's one of the best tourist assets a town can have, and it's free. You don't have to build it, just create a spot from which to see it. Up on the high banks away from the river, the town goes about its business.

So we motor slowly past Elizabethtown, on our way to the sea.

Below Elizabethtown, at Lock and Dam #2, we wait with a line tied to a piling at the approach for the doors to open. A team of Wildlife officers puts in a small boat just below the dam and motors slowly upstream, edging as close to the dam as they dare, the bow of their little johnboat invisible under the cascade of white water over the dam—just beyond the boil line. They tell us later they are monitoring striped bass, the next species that will be locked through upriver. Their report is terse and to the point: "Not many out there." They haul out their boat at the ramp downstream from the lock.

We enter the lock and the drill is the same. It's somewhat smaller than Lock #3, just 200 feet long, but still cavernous to us as the water rushes out into the river below, and we descend nine feet in about ten minutes to fourteen feet above sea level.

A few miles below the lock, we pass cautiously under the cables of the Elwell two-car ferry, one of the last three remaining inland ferries in the state. (The others are the Sans Souci on the Cashie River and Parker's Ferry on the Meherrin River.) The cables are supposed to be dropped to the river bottom when the ferry is not running, but occasionally they remain strung across the river at approximately the height to take a boater's head off. The gasoline-powered, two-car ferry was started in 1905 by brothers John Roland Russ and Walter Hayes Russ and connects N.C. 87 at Carvers Creek with N.C. 53 at Kelly.

The Elwell Ferry, one of just three inland ferries left in North Carolina (author photo)

On March 1, 1942, gasoline fumes in the bilge ignited and blew up the little ferry. Walter Russ, the operator, was blasted out of the boat and clung to the cable.

As his niece Kay Russ Andress relates in an online archive site,

> My grandaddy and Uncle Walter had built and put the ferry in about 35 years before but Uncle Walter was the one who ran it. When the ferry blew Uncle Walter was found clinging to the cable that crosses the river by Woodrow Norris. Woodrow could not swim but somehow he got in the river and brought Uncle Walter in. He did not know how he had done it. My grandaddy got to Uncle Walter just before he died there on the river-bank. He said to granddaddy "John, it looks like it has come home to us." Then he died. Grandaddy always thought Uncle Walter thought the ferry was bombed. I can just remember how obsessed everyone was with the war.

It's doubtful the Nazis were targeting the Elwell Ferry, but the sudden pyrotechnic violence of the accident must have come as a horrifying shock to those who witnessed it, a routine ferry run of a few hundred yards ending in fatal disaster.

We cruise downriver, alone in the verdure of the tangled banks, and the river begins meandering, flattening and twisting in recursive loops, forming oxbows and false channels, keeping us alert to follow the main channel, where we can be sure of good water. Soon enough we arrive at Lock #1 at Riegel-wood, which will drop us another eleven feet.

The lockmaster at Lock #1 is a young woman of average build, and she has no trouble managing the machinery. She says, "We'll be here at the lock another week or so to lock through the striped bass." She has to shout above the rush of water draining out of the lock, then opens the gates and waves us on our journey.

~~~~~~

In the coming months, engineers will begin a massive project to help spawning fish make it upstream: shad, salmon, striped bass, and the endangered short-nosed sturgeon. Currently, for about two months every spring, three times each weekday, the lockmasters lock through the fish as if they were an upriver-bound vessel. As Frank Yelverton explained it to me, about 50 to 60 percent of striped bass and shad use the locks, but the sturgeon generally don't go near them. Frank is a planner with the U.S. Army Corps of Engineers, which has cooperated with a number of other federal and state agencies to make this project happen.

The Corps had to blast downriver in order to deepen the shipping channel by four feet for a stretch of about thirty miles. The rock in the riverbed is five times as hard as the concrete in the average driveway, so blasting was the only way to get it out of there. But blasting is, obviously, deeply disturbing to the sturgeon. So after some wrangling with Cape Fear River Watch and U.S. Fish and Wildlife, the Corps struck a deal whereby it was allowed to blast out the deeper ship channel if it could figure out a way to create a fish passage for the sturgeon here at Lock and Dam #1.

Engineers considered removing the dam altogether, but that was impractical: The intake pipe for the City of Wilmington water supply is located just upriver of the lock and relies on the deep water backed up behind the dam. After years of meetings and a good deal of haggling, $12 million was allocated for the ingenious solution the engineers had long wanted: an artificial "rock arch" rapids.

It's a technology pioneered by Luther Aadland, the program consultant for the Minnesota Department of Natural Resources' Stream Habitat Program, who has embedded such rapids on watercourses in Minnesota and elsewhere in the upper Midwest. Basically, the Corps is placing hundreds of tons of rocks in the channel between the lock and the east bank, a distance of about 270 feet. The rocks continue downstream for about 250 feet, falling at a 4 percent grade, about 10 vertical feet from the top to the bottom of the rapids.

The rapids are designed to provide "resting pools" for spawning fish. Large rocks are laid in parallel lines, called "vanes," across the riverbed, stairstepping down the river. Inside each step are deep pools ringed by smaller rocks.

When it's finished, it will seem like a natural rapids to the fish, who will climb it like any other rapids. It will have the added virtue of stabilizing the dam. Everybody will benefit: fish, the engineers who maintain the dam, the quarter of a million people who rely on the Wilmington water supply intake, and even recreational kayakers.

And fishermen most of all. The whole cost could be recouped in a few years by a rejuvenated shad fishery. Here at the lock site, near East Arcadia, the shad used to choke the river in the spring, often around Easter. Blacks and whites would gather at the river in fish camps and work the shad nets for the duration of the run, sometimes for commercial profit. It was a time of socializing and gorging on fresh fish—shad don't keep well.

During antebellum days, it was customary for slaves to celebrate a holiday on the day *after*, when they were treated to leftover food. Thus evolved the custom in the African American community of eating shad on Blue Monday, the day after Easter. In recent years the custom has been revived, and now every year, local families and visitors gather for the Cape Fear Shad Festival—a day of fishing, music, reunions, and cookouts on the river.

The new rock arch rapids will only add to the allure of the festival. It's one of those simple, elegant solutions that actually make the river more vibrant and natural—despite all the engineering involved—and I wish more such solutions could be found for the other vexing problems that face the river.

I revisit Lock and Dam #1 on an August morning when the work is well under way. A huge staging area has been laid out above the dam, complete with a portable site office, acres of massive boulders, and an earthen dock for the front-end loaders to wrestle the boulders onto the trucks.

From the bluff overlooking the lock, near the lockmaster's office, I watch the flatbed tractor-trailers crawl down the incline to the staging area beside the lock. The boulders they carry are so massive that each trailer can accommodate only four or five to a load. From my perch above, they look like the toy Tonka trucks we played with as boys, loading them with the rocks lining my mother's garden, gigantically out of scale compared to the trucks.

Down below, another front-end loader lifts the boulders one by one from the trailer. Each is spray-painted with a number indicating its longest dimension in feet, so it can be fitted into the vanes in the most advantageous position: 3.4, 4.7, 5.6, 6.5. The design calls for the rocks to be four to six feet long, but the figure is approximate. Just as important, the Corps will reject rocks with fissures or cracks.

Semitrucks are loaded with the massive boulders to construct
a rock arch rapids at Lock and Dam #1 (author photo)

Out on the river, a barge is snugged to the side of the lock, another staging
area. A giant yellow crane lifts the rocks into position, its high articulating
arm resembling a robotic insect from a science fiction movie. The whir and
grinding of engines drifts up to me, the steady clatter of heavy engineering.
Two bucket shovels work at the periphery of the project, and men in bright
yellow hard hats and vests crawl over the structure, which takes shape before
my eyes.

And I'm not the only one watching.

A fellow drives up in a pickup truck and parks at the edge of the bluff,
shuts off the engine, and pulls out his lunch. I saunter over to talk to him, lean
in his open window. He's a genial guy wearing cargo shorts and no shirt, tan
from lots of time outdoors, his white hair tousled. He resembles the actor who
played the father in *The Waltons* on TV. His name is Alan Long, and he's retired
after forty-five years as a pipefitter with Federal Paper and then its successor,
International Paper. Since the project began, he's come here every day to enjoy his lunch and check on the progress of the fish passage. Today he's brought
a container of shrimp and a salad.

He lives just down the road, has lived in the area all his life with time out
for service in Vietnam. As a young man, he used to canoe the river from Buckhorn Dam to Lock #1 every December—he liked being on the river in the

crisp, cold weather. He's also fished this part of the river since he was a boy. Alan is a big fan of the fish passage. Like other fishermen I've talked to on the river, he doesn't really believe the Corps' claim that 50 to 60 percent of shad and stripers make it upriver through the locks each spring. Once this passage is finished, though, he believes the fish will spawn in record numbers and the fishing will improve markedly.

He remembers a time before the Corps locked through spawning fish, how bad the fishing was. "We used to come out here in the '50s and fish all night, right at the foot of the dam, with a net, and if we caught four fish, we'd brag about it," he says. "All night long, *four fish*." The old-timers, he tells me, used to fish with homemade bow nets fashioned from weeping willow branches, worked from the front of the boat, the bag of the net facing upstream. "They caught plenty of shad then, before the locks. The locks destroyed the fishing."

Then in the early 1960s, the Army Corps of Engineers started a program of locking through the spawning fish. Alan remembers the big shad run of 1968. "When I was in Vietnam, they wrote me and told me, you won't believe the shad that are in the river!"

Alan loves fishing the river. His biggest catch to date was a twenty-eight-pound striped bass. He remembers the legendary river fishermen, guys like Ed Bigford and Hack Mathis, a commercial fisherman who once held the record for the biggest catfish caught on the Cape Fear: nine and a half pounds. That's puny by today's standards, but there's a reason, as Alan explains: "They stocked these big catfish in the sixties, and they ruined this river. Ruined it. What I mean is, they aren't good table fish. Not very good eating at all. And they ate everything. The channel cat is the only native catfish that survived."

He's referring to nonnative species such as the Arkansas blue and the flathead. In 2005, a fisherman from Fayetteville hauled in a seventy-eight-and-a-half-pound flathead above Lock and Dam #3. The flathead measured fifty-two inches long with a girth of thirty-nine inches. His fish beat the previous record of sixty-nine pounds, set in 1994. Hundred-pound catfish are said to lurk in the deepest pools of the river.

Alan also has vivid memories of the tugboats that used to haul barges through the locks; indeed, the locks were built to make it possible for them to run the river between Fayetteville and Wilmington. The International Paper tugboat was named *Southern Craft*. It would chug up to the company's wood yard at Elizabethtown and bring down one barge at a time to Riegelwood. There a string of barges would be assembled and pulled down the Intracoastal Waterway to Georgetown, South Carolina.

The tugs that hauled oil barges back and forth to Fayetteville in the 1950s and 1960s included *Huck Finn*, *Tom Sawyer*, *Rebel*, and (of course) *Damn Yankee*. But those tugs are long gone, and the barges with them. A pipeline now does the work of the barges. So the locks are mainly used now for pleasure boats and the occasional excursion boat. Once the fish passage is complete, we'll have the best of both worlds: a navigable channel made possible by locks and a natural route for spawning fish.

Through his binoculars, Alan watches the crane lift another huge rock into place. He says, "Hey, you want to try these?" He hands me the binoculars. I put them to my eyes and the river is suddenly close. I gaze at foaming water already spilling through the big rocks. It's a gorgeous sight, refreshing and alive, and I can almost feel the river slewing around our canoe as we thread our way down among the rocks and feel the slap of cold water on our faces.

Alan says, in the hopeful tone of a boy wishing for a new bike for Christmas. "I just hope they let us fish right there in the rapids. That would be some fishing."

In March 2012, for the first time in more than a hundred years, a striped bass—tagged months earlier—swam up the rapids below Dam #1 and leaped across it into the spawning pool upriver.

Still chugging along in our trusty *Sea Whip*, now clear of the roiling dam and the eddy pool below it, David and I join the lethargic current again and cut the engine. The boat slowly slews around so that we drift backward, and in this manner we enjoy a lunch of sandwiches and soft drinks.

On the east bank we discover a delightful sandy beach, one that would have made a perfect campsite with room for half a dozen tents, easy beaching of the boats, and a soft sleep in deep sand. We ground the boat and step ashore. Immediately David says, "Look at that!" He points out a turtle crawl: the symmetrical flipper trail of a female yellow slider shinnying up the beach to lay her eggs. Crossing the turtle crawl are raccoon tracks, which we've seen in many places along the river, along with piles of broken *corbicula* shells that they have apparently incorporated into their not very fussy diet. But there's no excavation—the turtle nest seems undisturbed.

He knows how turtles behave—he's studied them for decades. He walks the beach and discovers five more turtle crawls, all undisturbed, despite the heavy traffic of raccoons, deer, and birds. He points out each track he comes across. "There's raccoon," he says, totally absorbed in the hieroglyphics of movement across sand. "There's more raccoon. There you can see her dragging her flippers. There's a crow." Crows will excavate a nest as quickly as raccoons.

Carefully, he tracks one crawl across the beach in a waggling path. "She was looking for just the right spot," he explains. And he finds it, a small indentation in the sand. Carefully, he scoops away a few handfuls of sand and reveals a small clutch of turtle eggs. We won't move them or turn them, since that would kill the embryos. We just look, and then David gently covers them again with sand and spreads some detritus over the spot to camouflage it from predators.

Turtle eggs, hidden in plain sight. Someday they'll be lined up on logs, littlest to biggest. It's a nice thought, worth the trip.

Below Lock #1 we spot an American swallow-tailed kite, even among soaring birds considered one of the most graceful and eye-catching, with its long black forked tail and black wings and white underbelly. It swoops and dips and for about five minutes treats us to an aerobatic show, crying *keep keep keep*! Farmers were long in the habit of shooting the swallow-tailed kite for a varmint, in the mistaken belief that it preyed upon their chickens, and they nearly wiped it out as a species. But in fact the swallowtail feeds mainly on insects and mice, so it is their ally. For unexplained reasons, the kite has recovered, and sightings are now more common in the Southeast.

But it's not that common on the Cape Fear. So it remains probably the single most gratifying bird sighting of our little trip: a beautiful creature, back from the brink of extinction, cavorting in the sky seemingly for the sheer joy of it.

I know, I know—this is shameless anthropomorphizing.

Probably the kite is hunting, or scouting for a likely hunting ground, or doing some other practical, respectable animal survival thing. But it's not true that in nature all animals do only functional things, activities with a serious purpose. All you have to do is note the number of otter slides along the river to understand that we haven't always got the answer about why an animal does anything. Animals are stubbornly enigmatic about their motives.

As we make our way downriver, we do indeed spot otter slides—muddy tracks fifteen or twenty feet long, always flanked by another route by which the otters can climb back up to the top of the slide, and usually near an otter house. Here the otters do not make their houses by damming a stream with a structure under which they can safely den. On the river, they pile up their sticks against the bank, in slow water, behind a downed tree or in an eddy.

And why do they slide? Just for the hell of it. The fun. It does not get them food or mates or clean them of parasites. Yet they will slide down the muddy sluice again and again, cavorting in the water and then scrambling back up the trail to the top so they can slide down again.

They mate in water and eat fish and are active night and day all year long, these three-and-a-half-foot-long critters. But when they slide, by all accounts, they are just playing.

The surface of the river has turned glossy, like a dark caramel glaze. It reminds me of the mirror blackness of the Black River, which comes in just downstream. David and I won't explore the Black on this trip, but it's a significant—not to say hauntingly beautiful—element of the Cape Fear River basin. So before we motor past it and come in range of Wilmington, I can't resist detouring into that captivating and disorienting stretch of the Black called the Three Sisters.

In fact, it's not so much a detour as a treasure hunt that will bring us back to the main stream of the Cape Fear.

~~~~~~~~

The water of the Black River looks exactly like its name—dark as Guinness Stout. The Black forms out of the Great Coharie, the Little Coharie, and Six Runs Creek up in Sampson County, then collects the South River before joining the Cape Fear.

My guides on the Black on an overcast April day are Virginia Holman, a writer colleague in my department, and her husband, Curry Guinn, a professor of computer science. Both are avid paddlers, but Virginia, by her own admission, caught the paddling fever. She'd rather be moving across water in her sleek Explorer sea-kayak than doing almost anything else.

They moved down to the coast from Durham a few years back so Curry could join the faculty at UNC Wilmington. Virginia went out on a guided kayak adventure and fell in love with the freedom and physical joy of navigating waters of all kinds—creeks and rivers, the Intracoastal Waterway, even the ocean. She and Curry have circumnavigated Bald Head Island, a venture challenging both for its distance and for the rambunctious waves and wind.

Shortly after moving to the coast, Virginia went away for a few days to a professional conference right around her birthday. She returned hoping her husband was going to surprise her with her very own boat. "I figured it would be on the roof of the car when he came to pick me up at the airport," she tells me. But, alas, the car was kayak-less. It was only when she got home that her young son insisted she go into the bedroom. There on the bed, stretching practically from wall to wall, perched her first kayak.

Virginia is dark-haired, quiet, organized, and by her own description shy—the kind of person who does a lot of alert watching and listening. Like Curry, she is slim and fit, hefts her own boat on and off the roof rack without any obvious strain, and gives me a useful lesson in how best to get in and out of a

Curry Guinn and Virginia Holman, guides to the Black River
and Methuselah (author photo)

kayak so as not to overturn it: Straddle it and use your arms to steady the boat
behind you, sit down and then tuck in your legs. To get out gracefully, just repeat the process in reverse. I've been floundering in and out of my kayak for
months now, and I'm grateful for the lesson.

We put in just before 9:00 A.M. at Henry's landing, a private access point
off Route 210 that costs $5 per boat. It's a beautiful, quiet, cool morning. Under
overcast skies, with nary a breeze to be had, the surface of the Black River is
an obsidian mirror, a hard reflection of the banks, trees, and sky. It's almost a
surprise to see a bow wave rippling the image as my kayak slides off first and
I feel the river moving under me.

The Black is special for lots of reasons.

One, of course, is its color, an extreme liquor of tannins—the same ingredient that gives tea its color, but oh so much darker. The tannin leaches out of
decaying trees, especially bald cypress. From the banks the river does indeed
look black, but up close in certain lights it glows with a delicious red cast.
And if you look directly overboard, you can see all the way to the bottom,
like peering through smoked glass. It's also one of the cleanest rivers in North
Carolina—it runs relatively (and deceptively) fast through a giant natural fil-

ter, the Three Sisters Swamp. It's so clean that in 1994 the state declared it an Outstanding Resource Water, a designation reserved for only the most pristine streams and rivers.

There's very little human activity along the Black, one of the reasons it is so pristine. In six hours of paddling, we come across just one item of trash, a freshly discarded beer can bobbing in the wake of a fishing skiff headed upriver. About 8,000 acres of the most valuable land on the eastern bank makes up Cone's Folly, a timber and game preserve, a legacy of the Cone Mills textile family. The land includes a variety of rich habitat: streamhead pocosin, pine savanna, and mesic pine flatwoods—that is, flat, poorly drained pine forest that remains moderately moist rather than inundated by swamp.

Because Cone's Folly remains undeveloped except for a house and some outbuildings, it is home to healthy populations of white-tailed deer, black bear, wild turkey, otter, mink, and red-cockaded woodpeckers. Bachman's sparrow, also known as the pine-woods sparrow, dull-colored and increasingly rare, also nests there. Eleven rare plants grow there, including two-flowered bladderwort, also called floating bladderwort, one of just two populations in North Carolina. Just as the native Venus flytrap devours flying insects, the bladderwort traps and digests small aquatic creatures.

The story goes that back in the Depression, Ben Cone, the owner of Cone Mills in Greensboro, wanted to buy the tract for a hunting getaway. It was owned by a bank, which had foreclosed on the property and, for whatever reason, refused Cone's offer to purchase. Cone then bought the bank, acquired title to the property, and promptly sold off the bank.

Much of the Three Sisters Swamp is held in trust by the Nature Conservancy, and more tracts are being negotiated. The Three Sisters Swamp is so named because the main river channel threads off into three narrow, twisting channels in the swamp. The channels eventually rejoin the main river, which runs into the Cape Fear fourteen miles above Wilmington.

And what really makes the Black River so remarkable is the natural treasure that lives inside the Three Sisters, the treasure we're after on this paddle: a stand of old-growth bald cypress, hundreds of giant—and ancient—trees. Two geoscientists from the University of Arkansas, Malcolm Cleaveland and David Stahle, surveyed the forest in 1985–86. Specifically, they extracted core samples from seventy-five trees and analyzed the rings, looking for evidence of drought (narrow rings) and rainy years (wide rings).

In the process, of course, they were able to date the trees.

What they found was astonishing: The oldest tree they cored turned out to be at least 1,700 years old. In the lore of paddlers, it's known as Methuselah.

Paul Ferguson, the dean of paddlers in this part of the state, chronicled his search for the elusive ancient tree in "Searching for Methuselah." Cleaveland and Stahle marked each tree they analyzed with a metal tag. Methuselah was awarded BLK69. But the tags seem to be long gone: rusted off, taken by souvenir hunters, or simply ejected by the trees themselves during growth spurts.

It is a swamp, after all, and man-made objects tend to corrode, rot, and disappear—Nature's little magic trick.

So the location of the certified oldest tree in the eastern United States remains elusive. Ferguson claims to have found it, finally, with help from the original researchers. But Methuselah may not even be the oldest tree in the Three Sisters. Cleaveland and Stahle pointed out that they found many trees that, by size and root system, appeared even older; but these had fallen victim to core rot, and so their innermost rings were gone. They felt certain that some of the cypress trees were more than 2,000 years old.

Think about that. Wood from one of those trees could have been used to fashion the cross of Jesus.

The Black was a busy river in the nineteenth century. Cypress logs were hollowed, by a combination of hewing and burning, into canoes to carry pitch and tar from the pine forests downriver. Lumbermen floated whole rafts of cypress logs to market. So how did these fortunate old-growth monsters survive? We can only speculate that they were just too hard to get to. And there were plenty of deadfall logs to be had for the taking, so the labor of cutting the great trees and manhandling them through the swamp might have been, financially at least, a losing proposition. Good news for us, all these generations later.

Whatever saved them, they are still standing as we maneuver our kayaks into an ever-narrowing channel. As the obvious route disappears into a maze of choices, we beach our boats on a peat bar so Virginia and Curry can get their bearings. Curry scouts a possible portage but, after several hundred yards of tramping through soggy wilderness, finds nothing but meadow and more woods.

That's the thing about the Sisters—indeed, about the Black River generally: Its appearance and navigability change drastically with the amount of rainfall in a given season, even a given week. A passage that was dry ten days ago might now be a flooded chute. An open channel last week might now be a tangle of logs and sandbars, more a trail than a channel. The water changes the appearance of the landscape in subtle and dramatic ways. When the Black is in true flow, it overruns its banks.

"When that happens," Virginia warns, "you can't find the river. Then it's *really* dangerous."

"Yeah," Curry adds, "there's no place to take out."

They talk awhile about what looks familiar or strange, landmarks they recognize from the last trip, but for a long while they can't quite get their bearings—or at least they get two very different bearings to follow toward the mainstem. I'm not much worried. We've got plenty of daylight left, and the swamp is not extensive. Proceeding in any direction will eventually get us either to a big channel or to dry land that opens on a road.

Also, my watch has a reliable compass.

"Follow the water" is Curry's mantra.

His logic is simple: Sooner or later, the swamp has to drain back into the main channel of the river. There's just no place else it can go, since water can't run uphill. And if it stopped, it would simply pool into a deeper and deeper lake. Clearly it's draining somewhere downstream.

We take a chance on the right fork, which sluices with a robust current through an obstacle course of logs, low-hanging branches, sandbars, and cypress knees. The only danger is that at some point the tangled foliage will make it impassable for boats, but in that case we can backtrack, assuming we're not hopelessly tangled and stuck.

We proceed a few hundred yards, and soon the narrow channel opens into true swamp, shallow, thickly forested, budding with cypress knees—upright conical wooden stalagmites that protrude three and four feet out of the water, sharp as teeth on top. They are part of the root systems of the big cypress trees, ringing them like a defensive palisade. It is claimed that they help the root system draw oxygen from the air, but like so many things in nature that we assume are settled questions, the exact function of cypress knees still causes lively debate among scientists. They remain a picturesque mystery.

I like that. It's always humbling to have to say, "I don't know." And it is useful, too. Such an admission of doubt forces us to pay closer attention to facts, to what we actually observe in nature, rather than what we assume to be true. The truth may turn out be counterintuitive.

When it comes to how we've treated the river, how it has survived all the certainties that it could be channeled and dammed, its banks clear-cut and rid of pesky predatory birds, mammals, and Indians, we could all benefit by an occasional bow to mystery, the admission that our certainty is often fleeting, truer knowledge descending like a hammer-blow on what the last generation "knew" for sure.

So we don't know exactly why we find cypress knees ringing these venerable, gargantuan trees. But whatever else they do in nature, the cypress knees create a fairly impenetrable barrier to small boats.

Following Curry's lead, we climb out of our kayaks and haul them by their bowstraps through the swamp, joking about Humphrey Bogart and *The African Queen*—the classic movie in which he is forced to trudge through a swamp, maddened by mosquitoes, hauling his ancient boat by hand, while Katharine Hepburn perches imperiously at the helm urging him on. Once out of the water, he discovers that his body is covered by leeches, and all at once our manly hero is undone, frantically clawing at his flesh and yelling, "Get 'em off me!"

Our travail is not nearly so dramatic—or traumatic. The bottom is sandy, good footing except for an occasional hole that soaks me up to the waist. Soon enough—no more than a quarter of a mile in—we find a good channel of live flowing water, and we hop aboard our boats and paddle toward daylight and the big river channel.

There's just one problem: We've missed the goliath trees we came to see.

But that's okay—now that we have our true bearings, we reenter the swamp, paddling upstream, and soon are floating among the giant trees, sliding through a watery forest that seems to rise up right out of a fantasy movie.

For the next hour or more, we slip in an out among the great trees, threading between cypress knees to touch the soft, mossy bark of the oldest trees east of the Mississippi. Many of them are hollowed out, gray sculptures that twist and curl out of the swamp floor and rise in straight, limbless trunks fifty or sixty feet into the air before breaking out into a canopy. Around them the swamp is lush with pop ash, willow, water oak, water tupelo, and sweet bay magnolia. On small hummocks flare the bright green spreads of southern lady and cinnamon ferns.

Virginia spies one great hollow tree and follows a lead between cypress knees and under low-hanging branches of water oaks to reach it, and I follow. We take turns actually paddling inside the tree, which swallows the front half of my boat and envelops me in cool shade. I back out among knees that rise higher than my head. I tap one of them with my paddle, and it gives off a soft, deep *tunk*, like a drum.

The light is otherworldly, shadow laced by shafts of sunlight. The water now takes on the reddish cast and is transparent all the way to the bottom. The tree trunks are silvery gray, mottled by dark green moss. Above us, through breaks in the canopy, the sky looms overcast, broken by blue as clouds scud fast across the bowl of heaven.

We are just an hour or so from a city, only a mile or so from the nearest paved highway, yet we're about as far off the grid as it is possible to go. There is no cell phone coverage back here, no way in or out except by small boat. We hear no noise made by humans—no car engine, no rattle of air conditioning, no radio or TV, no outboard motor. Just the humming buzz of insects, the gentle splash of paddles, the soft glide of the boat through the still water, and the music of birds.

From time to time a bright yellow prothonotary warbler flits across our vision. Unlike most warblers, which nest in brush, this canarylike variation settles in holes in trees. It's mating season, and the sharp call of *chip chip* alternates with the song *sweet-sweet-sweet-sweet*. We've heard but not seen a persistent barred owl—*Hoo-hoo! Hoo-aw!* It's a sharp call, almost a bark, guaranteed to make you jump.

One sound startles us all at once: frantic splashing and thumping of hooves. Two deer have spotted us and bounded off, thrashing through the water, crashing through the brush in their flight away from us, for in this part of the world, *we* are their most dangerous predator.

We pass trees of all sorts that have been girdled by beavers—they strip the bark expertly low down on the trunk, and eventually the tree dies and falls, providing them with material for dams and lodges. We see many ancient cypress trees, each one an individual shape, roots twined in a signature pattern, boles bulging from the trunks in patterns that create a unique face for each one. The large hollow tree we paddle inside of has an interior protrusion that looks for all the world like the head of a large alligator.

Almost certainly we have seen Methuselah, but there's no way to tell for sure. Its location is a closely guarded secret, lest some enterprising vandal discover it. I don't care—it's enough that old Methuselah is out there, hidden in plain sight among a forest of its ancient cousins, bearing up into its third millennium.

That's treasure enough for me.

7

About eighteen miles above Wilmington, on a tributary of the Black (and therefore of the Cape Fear), a replica wooden bridge across Widow Elizabeth Moore's Creek commemorates an important battle of the American Revolution, fought at daybreak on February 27, 1776. It was not a battle that ever found its way into the history books I studied in grammar school, not like Concord or Lexington, Saratoga or Yorktown. Yet, for a couple of reasons, it was important far out of proportion to the number of troops who fought there. First, early in the war, it was one of the only Patriot victories in a long string of defeats.

Second, it helped foil a grand scheme of the British to stamp out the rebellion in the South and split the colonies, which would almost surely lead to their surrender.

Sir Henry Clinton, in command of a fleet of more than thirty warships and transports, had sailed up the Cape Fear to aid Royal Governor Josiah Martin. Martin believed that the Piedmont was swarming with loyal Tories, and that if he could just incite them to rise up against their radical cousins on the coast, he could easily pacify the Carolinas. Then the British and their Tory allies could move up into Virginia and press the Continental Army from both north and south.

And with the help of the MacDonalds, he succeeded at least in inspiring a band of Scots in Cross Creek and Campbellton (both now combined into Fayetteville) to organize into a regiment and march on Wilmington.

Moore's Creek flows into the Black River. It might be more accurate to say that it disappears into the Black, a maze of twisting channels with no easy take-out. If you paddle Moore's Creek, you start at the battlefield and paddle five or six miles, then retrace your route back to the battlefield. It's a deep creek with sheer banks. The Scots Tories, led by General Donald MacDonald, found the Patriots at Moore's Creek.

The stage for the battle had been set days before as a series of maneuvers by the Scots to get into position to attack the Colonial militia, and of the Colonials, under Richard Caswell and Alexander Lillington, to get the drop on the British. The Colonials succeeded. About a thousand of them waited across Moore's Creek. They had removed the planks from the bridge and greased the stringers, making it a difficult crossing for the Scots. Mac-Donald fell ill, so Lieutenant Colonel Donald MacLeod led the charge. His men carried Claymores, large heavy swords more suited to medieval tournaments than a battle in which your opponent's weapon could drop you from a hundred yards away.

"King George and broadswords!" they shouted three times into the dawn mist and gamely splashed across the deep creek into the mouth of massed musket fire and small cannon shot.

According to Colonel James Moore, who was in overall command of the various Colonial units engaged, "The loss of the enemy in this action, from the best accounts we have been able to learn, is about thirty killed and wounded, but as numbers of them must have fallen into the creek, besides many more that were carried off, I suppose their loss may be estimated at about fifty." Eight hundred fifty more were captured. Captain MacLeod made it almost to the Colonials' breastworks and fell dead with "upward of twenty balls in his body."

Just as important for the Colonials' war chest, they captured 1,500 muskets, 350 shotguns, 150 swords and dirks, 2 medicine chests, 13 wagons and teams, and a cache of gold. With all that firepower, it is a mystery why the brave Scots relied on swords, which they never got close enough to use.

The bloody defeat marked the end of British ambitions to subdue North Carolina until a second invasion five years later. Cornwallis, Clinton's battle-field commander, took out his fury on General Robert Howe, a Patriot who had already served the Continental Army in a variety of campaigns before returning to his home on the Cape Fear at Sunny Point. Cornwallis and a force of about 900 soldiers landed at Howe's plantation and burned it. Then Cornwallis, his boss Sir Henry Clinton, and all British troops in the Cape Fear region sailed away to try their hand at capturing Charleston.

They took with them Martin, the last royal governor of North Carolina. The new governor was Richard Caswell, one of the Patriot heroes of Moore's Creek.

The Scots had organized at Cross Creek/Campbellton for their march on Wilmington—one reason, perhaps, that the state legislature so readily changed the name of the place to Fayetteville in 1784, in honor of the Marquis de Lafayette, the passionate French general who became as dear as a son to George Washington during the hard days of the American Revolution.

For many years, skeptical critics claimed that the Battle of Moore's Creek did not occur on the site of the park. But in 2012, a team of professional and volunteer archaeologists excavated a portion of the site. Dr. Chris Fonvielle, a historian colleague of mine at UNCW, reported, "During the course

Reenactors stage the surrender of the Scots Tories to Colonel Caswell's Patriots at Moore's Creek (author photo)

of the weekend we excavated about two dozen lead musket and rifle balls, a British penny dated 1738, and a King George III and Queen Charlotte of Mecklenburg-Strelitz coronation button. The British monarchs were married in 1761, only fifteen years before the Battle of Moores Creek Bridge."

So X marks the spot, all right.

Moore's Creek reminds us of just how formidable an obstacle even a narrow watercourse can be, if someone is determined to keep you from crossing it.

Back on the river below the Black in our little *Sea Whip*, David Webster and I skirt a series of islands—Birds Cove, Thorofare, D, Cross Way, Raccoon, Roan. Everything along the river was named long ago, for purposes of navigation. Generations before there were decent roads into the interior, the river was a busy highway, one reason it was referred to in early accounts simply as the Thoroughfare.

Well into the twentieth century, steamboats carried passengers as far upriver as Fayetteville and brought down timber, crops, cotton, turpentine, tar, and products from the mills at Fayetteville to be shipped out of the port. The 125-mile stretch between Fayetteville and Wilmington was home to 110 steamboat landings, some as close as a quarter of a mile apart, making a trip on the river a leisurely affair of stops and starts, more like a ride on a local commuter train than on a hard-charging express. Going downstream with the current at a stately eight knots per hour, the early boats could make Wilmington in six days.

The landings were named for the families who owned the riverside land, local creeks, prominent characters, conspicuous landmarks onshore, towns, plantations, and features of the river. From Fayetteville on down, they included Sandy's Landing, Blockers Steps, Old Ferry, Mutton Landing, Willis's Creek, Prospect Hall, Lucy Robeson, Tarheel, Brickyard, Elizabethtown, Big and Little Sugar Loaf, King's Bluff, Black Rock, Narrow Gap, Neil's Eddy, Raccoon Bluff, Mount Misery, and Navassa Works.

Steamboats on the Cape Fear were not the floating palaces of the Mississippi; they were smaller and cruder. The earliest steamers were called "flats" and, as their name implies, were flat-bottomed boats with two decks and shallow drafts. The passengers occupied the upper deck, and the lower was loaded with all manner of cargo, from cotton bales and barrels of tar and turpentine to sheep and cattle. Later boats were larger and more sophisticated, often featuring entertainment and sit-down dining with the captain.

One of the first vessels was built on James Seawell's plantation above what was then called Campbellton and launched in 1818. He named it for his daughter, Henrietta. The name survives today on the third boat to bear her name, moored at the Wilmington waterfront—alas, powered by internal combustion engines, not steam boilers.

The fleet included *Alice, Thelma, John Dawson, R. E. Lee, Cape Fear, Maj. Wm. Barnett, Nellie Hart, Juniper, Scottish Chief,* and *Southerner.*

Many of the landings were just muddy clearings beside the river near the sites of plantations or dirt roads, where cargo could be staged. Passengers boarded and deckhands ferried cargoes across wooden gangplanks extended from the bow of the boat. Some landings had rudimentary docks, or wooden stairs leading up from the river. In order to transport heavy cargoes of turpentine or tar, oxen or mules were harnessed to the upended barrel, which had wooden axles hammered into both ends, and the barrel was pulled along a "rolling road" to the landing. Deckhands sawed off the axles so the barrel could be loaded upright.

Elizabethtown had a primitive landing on a steep bluff. Passengers would routinely hire a local African American strongman to carry them on his back to and from the boat. He was known as the "human elevator." When he wasn't piggy-backing white passengers, he made his living catching fish.

One of the more elaborate was Whitehall Landing, just off present-day

Route 87 above Elwell's Ferry, at approximately the halfway point between Wilmington and Fayetteville. The landing itself was sited on Whitehall's riverside plantation and was the eastern terminus of the Whitehall Road, which originated twenty-three miles west of the river at the plantation of General Hugh Waddell, near present-day Whiteville. Waddell gained fame for his exploits with the Patriot cause during the Revolution. Whitehall Road was a well-maintained thoroughfare on which to transport plantation products, especially large volumes of cotton and turpentine, to market via the river. Whitehall Landing took on the character of a town, with its own sawmill, turpentine still, stores, blacksmith shop, and post office.

Whitehall became infamous for a disaster that occurred there at 11 o'clock on the night of February 16, 1858: The steamer *Magnolia*, tied to the wharf, "exploded her boilers, scattering wreck and death on every hand!" in the words of a correspondent to the *Fayetteville Observer* the following day. He goes on, "From all the information which I could gather in the hurry and confusion incident to this accident, it appears that the boat had been running under unusual pressure of steam, which was not permitted to escape after she was stopped to deliver a passenger and a few articles of freight."

So great was the explosion that it was heard nine miles away,

> shaking, jarring and blowing into a million of atoms the hull, apparel and machinery of the boat, and hurling for hundreds of feet on every side human bodies, fragments of iron, wood and clothing, strewing and lining the shore so completely with particles of the wreck that one could scarcely have escaped unhurt had he been standing a hundred feet away on any side. . . . The boiler, weighing two or three thousand pounds, was blown *at least three hundred feet* over a store-house some 30 or 40 feet high, striking in its flight and breaking a stick of ton-timber 16 inches square, upsetting two others, and cutting off two trees at least eight inches through! Bolts and bars of iron were cast as mere playthings from its giant blast. The tree-tops round about are hung full of great sheets of the deck, and articles of clothing flutter from the branches as though they had been vomited from her boiling cauldron and hung there to dry. A portion of a door, with the lock attached, was found at least *six hundred feet* from the wreck! The hull of the boat is torn to fragments, and presents the idea of a huge mastodonic skeleton exhumed, with its big ribs alone remaining to outline its form!

Captain John Stedman and an unknown number of others—probably more than twenty in all—died in the blast. Many of the missing passengers were never found, so presumably they were literally blown to bits.

One odd detail conveys the spirit of communal feeling of the time. A buckskin purse containing $122 in gold—an enormous sum at that time—was found hanging from the limb of a tree, and the man who found it, rather than merely pocketing his windfall, took out an advertisement in the *Wilmington Journal* to induce the owner to claim it.

But with so much traffic on the river in those days, the occasional accident was probably inevitable. Other steamboats suffered boiler explosions as well, including the *Evergreen* and the *Fanny Lutterloh*. Seawell's first sidewheel steamer, *Henrietta*, plied the river until 1865, when it was the oldest steamboat still in service in the United States. On its final voyage, passing Dram Tree south of Wilmington, it suffered the simultaneous explosion of all three boilers and sank. The *A. P. Hurt* foundered in a gale in 1923 while tied to the wharf at the foot of Orange Street in Wilmington, overwhelmed by waves that broke over its low deck. Others burned or came to grief on sandbars.

Sometimes the river froze so solid that traffic halted, waiting for a thaw.

From James Seawell's first *Henrietta* until the early twentieth century, more than fifty boats cruised the river. Early each morning, the Wilmington boat would arrive at Fayetteville, signaling its approach with a series of blasts on its steam whistle. As soon as it had docked and off-loaded its upriver cargo, stevedores began loading it for the return trip and passengers swarmed aboard.

But the steamboats are only ghosts now, and the river from Elizabethtown on down feels abandoned, a forgotten thoroughfare, undiscovered as a secret. The brown current moves sluggishly toward the sea around myriad bends. Most of the old landings between towns are just names on a map, overgrown with thick foliage. You have to listen hard to hear the distant echo of a steam whistle, the *chuff-chuffing* of the engine driving the big paddlewheel, the clatter of drays hauling bales of cotton, the clamor of voices giving commands, calling out greetings, telling stories.

In those days the Cape Fear was alive with human traffic. Now, ironically, it feels wilder but also disconnected from the commerce of the towns and people along its route. It has ceased to be a crucial transportation route and now is merely picturesque. Yet for us it is indeed a thoroughfare into the storied past of the region, a watery corridor of natural wonders and a kind of routine splendor.

The day is getting on to late afternoon, and David and I, bounding along in our johnboat, are wind-chapped and sunburned. We press on.

At Riegelwood, site of the large International Paper pulp mill, we begin seeing both bald and river cypress. The saltwater intrusion caused by the deep dredging of the river channel from the sea to Navassa has killed off many of the cypress, and they stand tall and stark, gray and pocked with holes drilled by various woodpeckers and enlarged for nesting by woodducks and other creatures. Their crowns provide perfect nesting platforms for ospreys: higher than anything else around, with unobstructed views in every direction.

The habitat along both sides of the river is now turning swampy, with red maple, tupelo gum, pond pines (short needles, small cones, the exact opposite of the longleaf pine), tree branches laced with Spanish moss.

We pass Alligator Point and Pinch Gut Creek, then two hairpin turns, Devil's Elbow and Pull and Be Damned. Bulldog Cut traverses a natural ox-bow. Soon enough we come out into a wide, open stretch of river, not hemmed in by trees but by pink wild swamp rose, white spider, burr-reed, alligator weed, and other river grasses: prime alligator habitat.

I spy a fox squirrel scampering up the vertical trunk of a big oak and hiding in the crotch of a high branch. We cut the engine and drift toward the bank, training our binoculars on the motionless squirrel. It's an uncommon critter around here, quite large compared with the common backyard gray squirrel—almost two feet long nose to tail. In fact, I mistook it for a raccoon at first, the shape was so big and dark. It leaps from branch to branch and finally disappears, even from our powerful binoculars.

Off to our left, just beyond a buffer of trees, lies Sutton Lake, a cooling reservoir for the Progress Energy coal-fired plant above Wilmington, with its twin orange-striped smokestacks poking up from the flat horizon. Soon those smokestacks will be obsolete, the entire plant converted to a much-cleaner-burning natural gas—a great boon for the river.

The plant is built on the site of old Mount Misery, a twenty-five-foot-high sandhill bluff on the east bank. The origin of the name is obscure, but the story goes that recalcitrant slaves were sent to work there as punishment. The land was hard to cultivate and barren, opening a world of misery for laborers. At one time it was also the site of one of the many ferries across the Cape Fear.

The railroad bridge at Navassa is swung open. Shortly after the Civil War, when a railroad bridge was built across the river, Navassa became the site of the Navassa Guano Factory, a fertilizer manufacturer that imported guano from Navassa Island off Jamaica. Over time, it was joined by three other fertilizer factories, and by the mid-twentieth century they collectively employed 4,000 workers. The fertilizer concerns are defunct now, and the town has shrunk back to about 1,800, though some of the original factory buildings remain.

We come out of one last narrow, double-curving channel and spy above the low underbrush of the east bank the PPD Building, the tallest on the Wilmington waterfront, looming over the landscape.

Over the trees to our right rises another incongruous sight, at least for a couple of boaters who have not seen another vessel for many miles and are emerging from a wild river: the towering steel superstructure of a capital warship, the USS *North Carolina*, the true dreadnought on the river. It dwarfs anything else afloat beyond the state port, with a length of 728′ ⅝″ (the official dimensions are exact). Think of it as stretching more than two long city blocks.

The last journey of old BB 55 (the official navy designation) was fittingly dramatic.

A flotilla of tugboats muscled the battleship into its final berth on Eagles Island back in 1961, with an audience watching from grandstands onshore. At one point, the ship appeared to be stuck hard aground in the middle of the river, blocking the entire channel. But somehow, with a last combined effort, the laboring tugs nudged it off the bottom. The last violent encounter of the ship's storied career lives on in local lore. As the stern swung across the current, it bashed into the Fergus Ark, a floating restaurant moored at the foot of Princess Street, where the old shipping warehouses used to stand. The concussion rattled the Ark but did not sink it, and for the remaining years of operation it featured a plaque in the vestibule reminding diners that in the entire history of the U.S. Navy, the Fergus Ark was the only restaurant ever to have survived a collision with a warship.

We pass under the U.S. 421 highway bridge and pass Point Peter, long known as Negro Head Point, on our right, at the confluence of the Cape Fear and the Northeast Cape Fear. (It was Negro Head Road that crossed Moore's Creek Bridge.) The land between the two rivers once was part of a plantation owned by Roger Moore. After the Revolution, he sold off a 3,000-acre tract identified as Negro Head Point to Peter Mallet and Arthur Magill, who in turn sold his half to Mallet. Hence Point Peter.

As with many of the names on the river, the origin of "Negro Head Point" is the subject of speculation and argument. The 1939 *WPA Guide to the Old North State* recounts the tale of a slave uprising in 1831, the same year that Nat Turner's band murdered more than fifty whites in the Virginia tidewater country. Dave Morisy, a slave, "was incarcerated for fomenting a plot in which insurgent slaves were to murder all the white people between Kenansville and Wilmington." Morisy and fifteen others were arrested. Morisy and David Hicks, a black preacher, were convicted as ringleaders. They were hanged and then beheaded, their heads stuck on poles at the junction of the Cape Fear

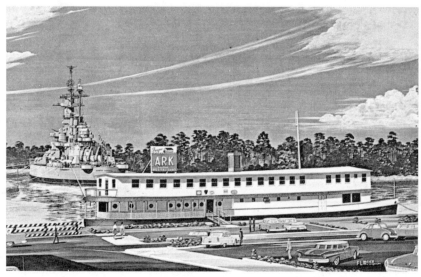

A vintage postcard of the Fergus Ark floating restaurant, which survived a collision
with the USS *North Carolina* (courtesy of the Historical Society of the Lower Cape Fear)

and the Northeast Cape Fear, and slaves were paraded past to "gaze upon
them" and see firsthand the terrible fate of rebellious slaves.

But the point was already so named back in colonial days, so the story
doesn't quite pan out. Now Point Peter/Negro Head Point is home to a nautical salvage yard where tugs nudge up against the bank and the hulks of
derelict boats lie open to the river, along with rusty boilers and unidentifiable heavy machinery. We throttle back as we enter the harbor, and soon we
are abreast of the great battleship, and the lovely waterfront of Wilmington
opens on our left.

It's breezing up, whitecaps in the harbor, wind bristling up the long straight
channel against the outrushing tide, piling up the water in short, scalloped
ridges crowned by whitecaps.

Eagles Island derives its name from a less mysterious source having nothing to do with raptors, though it appears on early maps as "Cranes Island" or
"Buzzard Island": Two of its early settlers, Joseph and Richard Eagles, arrived
there in 1725.

The *Captain John N. Maffitt* is tied up at the USS *North Carolina* park,
having ferried visitors to the ship. It's an old navy tender, named for a captain
of Confederate blockade-runners and ironclads who began his career on the
USS *Constitution*. He wasn't a Wilmington native—he was born at sea—but
he died here, and Wilmington has claimed him.

THE LOWER REACHES

In a career that lasted just about seven years—a little longer than twice the time it took to build the vessel, the USS *North Carolina*, the "Showboat," as it was called, earned fifteen battle stars in every major campaign in the Pacific. It's famous as the first battleship to steam into Pearl Harbor after the devastating surprise attack by the Japanese. For the soldiers and sailors massed onshore to watch its magisterial arrival into the wreckage of the harbor, it served as a massive, armored symbol of hope and a promise of victory, the very incarnation of U.S. sea power returning to the Pacific.

At any given time, USS *North Carolina* was home to more than 2,300 officers, enlisted men, and marines. It was torpedoed, and on six different occasions the Japanese claimed to have sunk it. Ten of the crew were killed in action, and another sixty-seven were wounded. But the ship lasted out the war and was mothballed, scheduled for the breaker's yard finally in 1958. North Carolinians started a campaign called SOS—"Save Our Ship" after the famous Morse code distress call. More than 700,000 schoolkids contributed $25,000 worth of nickels and dimes. Against all odds, SOS raised enough money to bring the ship up the Cape Fear River on October 2, 1961, to its final muddy berth, where it is guarded by an old, sluggish alligator named Charlie, who apparently has mated. The youngster that hangs around with him now was christened "Clyde" after the *Wilmington Star News* conducted a naming contest.

So as David Webster and I turn into the harbor at Wilmington, we are slowly passing the great stern of the ship that was once considered the most fearsome single weapon in the world, the fifth in a line of warships bearing its name, one of them a Confederate ironclad built right on the Wilmington waterfront—and not very well, it turned out—by Berry & Brothers in 1863. The sixth is a nuclear attack submarine, recently commissioned on the Cape Fear River.

Entering the Wilmington harbor is like arriving all at once in civilization. We feel the ghost of that excitement the early settlers must have felt returning from the wild interior, at last coming around the bend to open water and the bright busyness of a city on the make. There's a lot to take in, so we linger awhile in both present and past before resuming our journey downriver.

~~~~~~~

Bouty Baldridge, the first river keeper on the Cape Fear, explained to me once why he thought Wilmington survived when so many other settlements along the lower river gave up or were overwhelmed in those early years of colonization. We were patrolling the river and had just run up to the Black. It was a chilly day in early spring. The sky was bottle-blue, the water flecked with whitecaps, and in our open runabout we felt the damp chill through our thin jackets.

"Captain's Creek is why Wilmington made it and Brunswick Town did not," he said. "The stream runs all year with freshwater." Sea captains used to fill their casks there—now the spring runs underground at Second Street between Cape Fear Community College and the Coast Line Convention Center, all that remains of the great railroad enterprise that served Wilmington in its heyday.

Like the river itself, Wilmington was known by a variety of names in its early days: New Carthage, New Liverpool, New Town, and Newton. The city originated in 1731 with a dual grant of 640 acres each to John Maultsby and John Watson by Royal Governor George Burrington. In a low, flood-prone country, it was high ground. They intended to set up a trading operation at the confluence of the Northeast Cape Fear and the Thoroughfare. Within a year, others had joined them, and within two years, an enterprising settler named James Wimble laid out a plan for a settlement he called New Carthage. In addition to his mercantile interests, Wimble was a surveyor, a seafarer, and a ship builder.

But the new residents called the town New Liverpool.

Meanwhile, downriver, the inhabitants of Brunswick Town (the old town) simply referred to it as New Town or Newton. In 1739, at the request of residents, the General Assembly finally settled the matter of names and designated it Wilmington, after Spencer Compton, Earl of Wilmington, one of the original Lords Proprietors and a patron of then–royal governor Gabriel Johnston. Compton served a brief, undistinguished tenure as prime minister of Great Britain and never actually visited America, let alone the city that bears his name.

Here in 1765, patriotic citizens took exception to the Stamp Act, by which the British Parliament hoped to raise money to pay the cost of the expensive war they had just fought in America against the French and allied Indians. Five hundred citizens assembled on October 19, hanged the tax man in effigy, then burned the effigy in a bonfire fueled by barrels of tar.

The *North Carolina Gazette*, a Wilmington newspaper, continues the story:

> On Thursday, the 31st of the same month, in the evening, a great number of people assembled again, and produced an effigy of Liberty, which they put in a coffin and marched in solemn procession with it to the churchyard, a drum in mourning beating before them, and the town bell, muffled, ringing a doleful knell at the same time; but before they committed the

body to the ground, they thought it advisable to feel its pulse, and, finding some remains of life, they returned back to a bonfire ready prepared, placed the effigy before it in a large two-armed chair, and concluded the evening with great rejoicings on finding that Liberty had still an existence in the colonies.

And, the chronicler was careful to add, "not the least injury was offered to any person."

Things almost got out of hand two weeks later when the tax man, William Houston, showed up in person, rather than as merely an effigy. The crowd marched on his house, waving flags and beating drums, and demanded to know whether he would enforce the law. He responded that he "should be very sorry to execute any office disagreeable to the people of this province." A politic answer, but not good enough for a boisterous crowd that had been ramping up its zeal for almost a month. They demanded and got his resignation.

At this gesture, the mood turned giddy: "They then placed the stamp master in an armchair, carried him around the courthouse, giving at every corner three loud huzzahs, and finally set him down at the door of his lodging, formed a circle around him, and gave three cheers. They then escorted him into the house, where were prepared the best liquors, and treated him very genteelly. In the evening a large bonfire was made and no person appeared on the streets without having 'Liberty' in large letters on his hat."

You have to hand it to that crowd—each demonstration showed more imagination than the last, and they turned the whole thing into a party, complete with a sense of humor. Not like those hooligans up in Boston throwing tea into the harbor and blaming it on the Indians—though like Boston, Wilmington owed its existence to a deepwater harbor, and the river that carried ships to it from the sea. How fortunate that deep water was adjacent to the highest ground along the east bank for all the miles up from Bald Head.

Nevertheless, Wilmington has always had a complicated relationship to the river, for both prosperity and destruction floated up its reliable channel.

The river brought settlement and commerce, but it also brought invasion: first by the Spanish, who sacked Brunswick Town in 1747. Then came the British in 1776. They burned Brunswick Town, which was mostly deserted by then anyhow, the inhabitants having fled in advance of the marauding Redcoats, putting the town out of business for good. Five years later, the British returned to occupy Wilmington.

In 1862, a blockade-runner named the *Kate* brought yellow fever up the river to the city and laid it low; about a third of the inhabitants evacuated. One result was the increase in slaves who bolted from their absent masters' households, many of them using the river as a conduit to the United States Navy fleet blockading offshore. Ironically, the river claimed the *Kate*. Just about the time the yellow fever epidemic was being killed off by cold weather, in November 1862, the ship ran aground at Bonnet's Creek just above Southport and broke apart.

At the close of the Civil War, the Yankees overcame Fort Fisher and brought their gunboats upriver to meet their advancing troops.

In the twentieth century, Wilmington moved its port downriver to the site of the World War II shipbuilding works and otherwise turned its back on the river. In those days, it was a railroad town. At one time, multiple railroads converged in Wilmington, most prominently the Atlantic Coast Line. A trolley line transported tourists to the beach, and a short line ran up and down the beach. The boast was that you could board a train anywhere in the United States and, using only rail transport, step off onto the sugary sands of Wrightsville Beach.

Then, in a single blow, the commercial life of Wilmington was virtually shut down. In 1960, the Atlantic Coast Line Railroad moved its headquarters to Jacksonville, Florida—and transferred 300 employees and their families. The era of the railroad shut like a door closing. Most of the Atlantic Coast Line buildings were razed. And the city lost its identity for awhile.

It's hard to imagine, but the two signature institutions that give the city its identity now were not even on the horizon yet: the battleship USS *North Carolina* and the University of North Carolina Wilmington. The former is now the iconic image that appears in virtually every panoramic photograph of the harbor and is among the most visited attractions in the state. The latter, formerly a small, county-supported junior college, has stamped itself indelibly on the intellectual and cultural life of the city and, of course, has become a huge economic driver as well.

It's no accident that UNCW biologists have played a huge role on the river. For the past fifteen years, the UNCW Lower Cape Fear River Program has been monitoring the river at thirty-six sites, recording levels of dissolved oxygen vital for fish and clean water.

When I arrived in Wilmington in 1989, the waterfront was largely an unsightly combination of derelict buildings, weedy parking lots, tank farms, bulk loading docks, the Coast Guard dock, and a handful of restaurants. Water Street along the river was a runway for prostitutes, and drug dealers haunted the alleys. It was a fairly unsavory neighborhood after dark.

Now the riverfront has been revitalized in a major way. The derelict warehouses have been either torn down or remade into condos and retail businesses. Galleries and restaurants have opened in ground floor spaces that used to be shops, banks, factories, and even private homes.

Most significantly, Wilmington has once again embraced the river, thanks to a nonprofit group called Wilmington Downtown, Inc. The one-mile Riverwalk now carries pedestrians from Chandler's Wharf on the south end to the Hilton Hotel on the north. The plan is to link the Memorial Bridge at Dram Tree Park, the southernmost end of the Wilmington waterfront, to the Isabel Holmes Bridge, which crosses the Northeast Cape Fear at the northernmost end.

Plaques affixed to the railings recount historical and environmental information. The Riverwalk is well-lit, with comfortable benches and even a dedicated night patrolman. All it lacks is public art. Meanwhile, transient slips receive cruisers who come up the river from the Intracoastal Waterway or the ocean fairway. A new convention center faces squarely on the river. The Chamber of Commerce looks out on the river. Water taxis chug back and forth between the cityside and the battleship. The catamaran cruise boat *Wilmington* ferries small groups up the Black, down to the estuary, or just around the harbor. All that's missing is a fleet of tall ships anchored off the cotton wharves, as they were in James Sprunt's heyday.

But every so often we get a glimpse of the great age of sail when a tall ship moors at the foot of Market Street or at the state port: the Coast Guard barque *Eagle*; the HMS *Rose*, famous for its movie role as HMS *Surprise* in *Master and Commander: The Far Side of the World*; the *Pride of Baltimore II*, an 1812-era topsail schooner whose topgallant masts are so high they had to be swayed down so they could pass under the Cape Fear Memorial Bridge—a problem that the shipmasters of Sprunt's day never faced, for in their day there was no bridge, just the river.

The *Pride* happened to be skippered by a former student of mine, a sailor by the name of Jamie Trost who used to work the foredeck of my thirty-two-foot sloop during Saturday regattas off Myrtle Beach. He turned the tables on me, recruited me for a voyage down the coast to Jacksonville, Florida, under his command, and so I gladly shipped out one May morning and sailed under the Cape Fear Memorial Bridge, down the fairway beyond Southport, and out to sea. Along the way I got to helm the graceful, powerful ship through an entire night watch ending at midnight while we busted along in a rising gale and the rest of the crew laid aloft to take in sail. It was the greatest sleigh ride of my nautical life—and it reminded me of what used to be commonplace in Sprunt's day, when young skippers ran the channel with valuable cargoes and, with young adventurers like Sprunt aboard, made fast passages from Wilmington to ports all over the world.

One of the most famous ship captains was, of course, the aforementioned John Newland Maffitt. Maffitt was born on a windjammer at sea, en route to New York. His parents were part of the great emigration from Ireland. He joined the U.S. Navy in 1832 when he was just thirteen years old and served on a variety of ships, including the USS *Constitution*, for which Paul Revere forged many of the fittings. But it was the Coastal Survey that brought him to Wilmington.

For three and a half years, Lieutenant Maffitt lived at Garrison House at Fort Johnston, at the mouth of the river in Smithville—now Southport. One of his party was John Pembroke Jones, who went on to serve as executive officer aboard the *Merrimac* during its historic battle with the *Monitor* and to command the ironclad CSS *Raleigh*.

In those days, of course, Maffitt and company had no recourse to GPS or satellite photos. They had to spend months on the river taking soundings. They took bearings off three fixed points at a time to establish the precise locations of channels and cuts. They made their map the hard way and published it in 1853. As described by the National Oceanic and Atmospheric Administration, "The sounding boats had six oarsmen, a coxswain to steer, two officers to observe horizontal sextant angles between fixed signals on shore to position the boat, two leadsmen, and an officer for recording angles and soundings."

Maffitt's legacy lives on in Wilmington in the namesake tender that ferries tourists around the harbor, and at his grave in Oakdale Cemetery. A living apostle of his legacy is Robert D. Maffitt, his great-grandson, who provided me a copy of the map his great-grandfather drew with such meticulous care. I met him aboard the *Wilmington* on a day cruise on which I was guiding a tour of landmarks along the river. It was an unseasonably bright and sunny November day, the river breeze sun-warmed and pleasant, and he spent his time at the open stern.

Bob Maffitt is a powerfully built, genial fellow with a grizzled gray beard and a strong handshake. His clear baritone voice carries a bit of New Jersey in it, betraying his origins. He found his way back to the Cape Fear only in late adulthood. Now he puts on a facsimile of his great-grandfather's uniform and educates visitors about his ancestor's role, not just in the war, but in reliably charting the lower Cape Fear River—his signature accomplishment. Bob Maffitt speaks of both the river and his great-grandfather with affection. "If he came back today, I think it would really surprise him, the way people have fallen in love with the river, how many people have written books about it, including his good friend James Sprunt. It would shock him."

Like his great-grandfather, Bob Maffitt is a trained survey engineer. He settled in Wilmington just about a decade ago, surveying house lots. But his avocation is the lore of his great-grandfather. And that is all mixed up with the history of the river.

He says, "The thrill I get is that it amazes people—and to think that my great-grandfather charted this whole river and allowed boats to get up. He really started something." Maffitt's original map remains remarkably accurate, allowing for the intentional dredging that has gone on since.

Just a few years after he completed the survey, John Maffitt resigned from the U.S. Navy and put his hard-earned hydrographic knowledge to work outfoxing the Yankee blockade ships, slipping in and out of the Cape Fear roads like a shadow on moonless nights in cargo vessels such as the *Cecile*, the *Nassau*, and the *Lillian*—whose officers included a teenaged purser named James Sprunt. Later Maffitt took command of the *Florida*, an armed raider resembling its famous cousin, the *Alabama*, on which Maffitt's son served. The *Florida* captured twenty-three vessels in just eight months at sea, and Maffitt became infamous among the flag officers of the U.S. Navy.

"They wanted him bad," his great-grandson says with undisguised admiration. "They wanted him for piracy." Since the Federal government did not recognize the legitimacy of the Confederate government, all crews and captains of Confederate raiders were deemed to be privateers, subject to hanging.

Nobody in nineteenth-century photographs smiles, especially not military officers. They typically evince a ramrod pose for the camera, their countenances stoic and grim, eyes staring and fixed—one reason so many of them look a touch insane. But Maffitt's portrait betrays the ghost of a smile on his lips. His broad Irish nose and bemused eyes under thick brows make you think that mischief is on his mind. He looks devilish and handsome, with his unruly shock of thick, dark hair, a guy you would stand to a drink just to hear his outrageous stories.

"He was Irish, crazy damn Irish, and he had a sense of humor," Bob Maffitt tells me, shaking his head. "Every woman was in love with him. Women are *still* in love with him." He leans in confidentially. "You want to know a secret?" I'm game. So he says, "My great-grandfather was the real Rhett Butler."

Which I can believe, though Rhett Butler was something of a scoundrel who took a long time declaring his loyalty, and he was famously ungentlemanly. Maffitt, by contrast, was a gentleman who placed a premium on honor, as he told the *Illustrated London News*: "We treat prisoners of war with the greatest respect. Most of those we have captured have spoken well of us. To be sure we have met with some ungrateful rascals; but you meet with those the world over."

His exploits were colorful and full of derring-do: evading six Yankee pursuers out of Mobile, running the Frying Pan Shoals and over the bar of New Inlet on a stormy night black as the inside of your pocket, joining the British navy to avoid arrest by U.S. agents in a foreign port. And Bob tells me the topper. "People always want to hear the glamour, the battle. When he had the *Florida*, they loaded it with cargo from Cuba, and he was going to Mobile. The Yankees knew he was going to Mobile and they were waiting for him. They put thirty-seven holes in her. He had yellow fever. He ordered his men to tie him to the mast and he gave orders and he got to Mobile."

Me: "You think that's really true?"

"Oh, yeah!"

Bob Maffitt regards the river with the enthusiasm of a kid, and it's hard to listen to him for even a little while and not catch it. "I would like to see the river stay just like it is. No large ports." He talks of the hush of the river, of its beauty. Of how it feels to go upriver just around the bend and find yourself in a wilderness. He says, "One of the things I like about the river is that you can go up the river and be back in the 1800s."

And of course, that is just about when all the traffic started.

～～～～～

One man who is trying to bring river traffic back to the Cape Fear is Doug Springer, captain of the *Wilmington*, a forty-six-foot motor catamaran that can accommodate forty-nine passengers on its jaunts up and down the river—serving up cocktails, jazz and bluegrass music, and narrated lessons in history and the environment. It was on his boat that I met Bob Maffitt.

Springer is lean and weathered, his blond hair and moustache tinged with gray, with the steady, alert eyes of a waterman under a sun-creased brow shaded by the visor of a khaki ballcap. We're lounging on canvas studio chairs on the deck of his boat, the clear side-panels buttoned down to ward off a brisk northerly wind. Even tied to the dock alongside the Wilmington Riverwalk, the vessel undulates with the passage of wind-driven rollers under its narrow twin hulls.

Doug earned a degree in marine technology at Cape Fear Technical Institute (now Cape Fear Community College) right on the river, then went to work in the Gulf of Mexico and on the waterways of South Carolina. After a stint in the air force as a computer specialist and other indoor jobs, he "retired" to a house on the river in 2004. He had long dreamed of living on the water, of tying up his boat at a private dock at the foot of his lawn, and for a long time he assumed that meant the ocean side. The he discovered a house for sale on the Cape Fear. The owner showed it to him and his wife during a day that poured rain.

"That's the kind of day I call a 'river day,'" he says and smiles.

They fell in love with the house and the view. "I used to say, the first thing I see in the morning is the river, and the last thing I see at night is the river," he tells me. "I just love the water. The very first time my dad gave me the oars to the rowboat, I rowed across the river and wouldn't come back. They had to come get me."

He jumped into the Cape Fear with both feet. He succeeded Bouty Baldridge as river keeper, performing double duty as executive director of River Watch, the organization that keeps the river keeper in business. "Some people are born to be a river keeper," he says. "Bouty was. I wasn't."

But he had other instincts—for organizing, marketing, and fundraising. River Watch was in danger of losing its headquarters, and funding was precarious. But Cape Fear River Watch had one key asset: a legacy of credibility. Baldridge was known for his integrity and his absolute commitment to the stewardship of the river, and so despite its shoestring budget, River Watch had a seat at the table when big issues came up in government and industry that would affect the river. So, among other accomplishments, River Watch was able to play a key role in nudging the Army Corps of Engineers toward the rock arch rapids solution at Lock and Dam #1.

Doug's strategy was simple: "If you could get all the stakeholders to support one solution, then we'd have a better chance of getting funding." Meeting followed meeting, then passionate argument resolved into a plan of action.

Doug succeeded in building a sound financial foundation under River Watch and drew support from across the community. In his words, "There are three legs to the stool: Education, Action, and Advocacy." He handed over the river keeper job to Kemp Burdette, who had been recruited and groomed through a "rainmaker" grant sponsored by the Z. Smith Reynolds Foundation. Rainmakers are young individuals chosen for their ability to recruit new members and find resources—money and local partners—to address each of those three legs.

In those days, Doug ran a thirty-six-foot Willard Trawler, the *Lorelei*. "One day I looked at the dock and I said, '*Lorelei*, you've been lazy. We're going to put you to work.'" He started running charters, six passengers at a time. He wanted a bigger boat. So with his wife, Diane Upton, and two partners, all of them investing their life's savings, he founded Wilmington Water Tours. It was the first business to be granted a license to operate from the new Riverwalk.

"Our business model was to get involved with the community," he explains. "It wasn't about money. That's how we would measure our success after our first year."

Doug has a vision for the river that begins in a certain sense of incredulity. When he says, "Not only is this river the most unrecognized and underutilized river in North Carolina, it is also an economic opportunity," he is echoing what we noticed coming down the river: the missing traffic, the sense that the river is mostly cruised only by the ghosts of long-dead steamboat captains and explorers venturing up the flat dark water in shallops as far as they can go before bottoming out.

"People used to make their living on the river," he says. "They can make their living on the river again."

Which is why he started Wilmington Water Tours, to show how the river could once again energize the economic and cultural life of the city. "The only leadership I've ever seen that worked is leadership by example," he explains.

If the river was to enter the lives of the people who live beside it, they would have to encounter it as more than a name on a highway map. "You've got to have somebody physically experience it to become attached to it." You can watch a river from a bridge or a bank and see only a finite slice of it, or you can leave the shore and move on its current, on a boat like Doug's.

His boat is designed to go upriver, where the bottom shallows and a deep V-hull might come to grief on submerged rocks or wedge onto a hidden sandbar. And beyond that, he has a vision and the practical genius, just maybe, to see that vision come true. For instance, he sees a kayak trail from Wilmington halfway to Elizabethtown, with campsites and safe access points. He'd like to see twelve miles of the Northeast Cape Fear designated a "scenic river" and thereby enjoy enhanced protection from heavy development.

His vision can seem grandiose at first blush, but it's axiomatic that one way to solve a thorny problem is to make it bigger. So on Eagles Island, Doug envisions a maritime village and a boardwalk across the marshy shoreline divided into three segments, each covering 100 years of history, each featuring historic signage and displays paid for and maintained by a different private sponsor—preferably from among the large companies that make their homes on the river: heavy industry, banks, creative firms.

As he talks about it, gesturing across the wind-scalloped river to the wild, lush tangle of Eagles Island, I can just about picture it: tourist crowds streaming down from the battleship, stepping onto the boardwalk for a passage through the rest of the history of the Cape Fear—Indians, explorers, Redcoats, Confederates, Yankees, steamboats, Liberty Ships, scientists, and all the rest.

Some of Doug's vision is already coming true through a different agency, the Eagles Island Coalition. Seventeen organizations have signed on to a plan to preserve and manage the 2,100-acre island. The coalition has mapped a matrix of four waterway trails through the marshes and channels that thread through the northern part of the island. And that trail map is just the beginning of a larger plan to promote ecotourism, culture, and history on the island—exactly what Doug says will draw people to the river.

"It's an opportunity to create a whole economy at very little cost," he says. It all seems so vividly real—like it's already been accomplished—that it's hard to disagree.

The economy he conjures is a kind of ecohistorical tourism, a concept I find inspiring. All down the river, I've been struck by how entangled are politics, war, and commerce—*history* in broad strokes—with the environment of the river. The plantation economy emerged because of the very nature of the river country, so why not another kind of economy equally endemic to the place?

Doug points out that five years ago, he counted just ten osprey nests on the river above Wilmington, each with a single nestling. This season he has counted twenty nests—and each is home to three young ospreys. People love watching ospreys. They're acrobatic, majestic, just so damned *big*. When one swoops into your vision, you really can't take your eyes off it. And the nestlings are equally enthralling, poking their open beaks into the air to receive the food that the parent has just retrieved. The osprey nests, the ospreys themselves, are a resource that people will pay to see.

But of course one of the things we've done to the river over the years is dredge it for shipping (more later on this), and the resultant saltwater intrusion—carried by tides running as far above the city as Lock and Dam #1 now—has killed off the cypress in which the ospreys nest. The dead trees will stand for a long time—until a storm knocks them down. This past season something like one in five trees on that stretch of the river was knocked down by storms.

But Doug is not one to bow to mere circumstance. Some people have suggested that one or another environmental group, or the county, or whoever, erect nesting platforms for the big birds. The Coast Guard and others already do this in ship channels as a practical matter, since if they don't create a platform above a daymark or a weather array, the ospreys will simply nest on the thing itself.

Doug wants to go one better. "Let's not just build platforms," he says, with obvious excitement, "but *art* on the river. Who else has done that?" And once again, as he speaks, I can see it, interpretive pieces that both blend in with the austere gray cypress and green river grass and also stand out as something new and pleasing, human-crafted forms that define the riverside as something we have collectively decided to value. I don't know exactly what they would look like, even what color they would be — the shapes keep transmogrifying in my mind's eye. But the idea is captivating, a new way of thinking about an old problem, a chance, in fact, to turn a problem into an opportunity.

For too many of us, the river is invisible — that's the problem. It just doesn't figure into the way we make our livelihood, the way we travel to work and socialize. Not like in the old days, when the river was the only practical highway, not just for people but for goods. So the solution for Doug is to make it visible. "The river is an amazing teacher," he counsels, "if you really watch and you really look."

He likes to tell school groups that if they take away only one fact from his guided tour of the river, it's a simple one: "It's your river. Learn from it. Take care of it."

So recently, as he tied up at the dock after a trip with thirty fifth-graders, he asked if anyone had any final questions. A girl raised her hand. "We have something we want to say to you," she announced. The kids stood up and declared, in unison, "It's our river!"

Doug says, "They got it."

So far, in just a year and a half of running excursions on their larger boat, Doug and his partners have gotten more than 10,000 people out onto the river, many for repeat voyages, so his plan is working out. At this rate, in just a few years, he'll have taken enough voters onto the river to sway any election in the county.

There's a darker history to Wilmington, also connected with Eagles Island. Here in the early days of the nineteenth century, runaway slaves hid out in the tangled swamp of the boggy island.

The island was such a thicket of swamp and pestilence that it became a hideout for "maroons," runaway black slaves who banded together in hidden communities, sometimes for months, even years on end, often governed by a wily and resourceful leader. The most famous of these was the General of the

Swamps. A party of bounty hunters went after his band in 1795, killing the General and scattering his followers.

In 1898, the island gave up its ghosts to the city itself, and the only documented coup d'etat in American history took place just three city blocks off the river on November 10. One of the most notorious racial battles in American history played out in the coup of 1898, during which white supremacists targeted Wilmington to roll back Reconstruction. In the violence, an untold number of blacks were killed—at least sixteen and as many as several hundred. Some of the bodies were hidden in cellars and buried secretly to avoid reprisals to the families by the killers.

Now I find the river of this story carrying me back to my adopted hometown and to that other, darker story that played out on the river and captured my imagination when I first arrived in Wilmington more than two decades ago.

In 1898, Wilmington was the political and economic center of North Carolina. It was the largest cotton exporter in the world. Its population of 25,000 included some 17,000 blacks—among them a large, sophisticated, well-to-do, politically active middle class. The collector of customs, a black man named John Dancy, earned a larger salary than the governor.

The city government had recently fallen out of the hands of Democrats and into the hands of so-called Fusionists: a "fusion" of black and white Republicans (the party of Lincoln) and Populist farmers, who felt exploited by big business, which, among other things, fixed railroad tariffs at exorbitant rates.

Following an election campaign for state and New Hanover County offices—a campaign strategically and relentlessly based on white supremacy—violence erupted in Wilmington. The violence was partly accidental and partly orchestrated and planned by at least two secret groups of Wilmington businessmen. One group, the Secret Nine, was led by Hugh MacRae. The other, called Group Six, was led by Colonel Walker Taylor.

They did not leave minutes of their meetings.

There was purchased for the guarantee of "civil order" some kind of machine gun—probably one of the Gatling guns manufactured for the army in Cuba. There came to be other machine guns in town, along with an undetermined number of small howitzers and hundreds of Winchester repeating rifles. Seven local military or paramilitary groups vied for control over events, and all of them took part in the violence.

A white mob marched on a newspaper that billed itself as "the only daily Afro-American newspaper in the country," the *Daily Record*. The mob burned the newspaper. The editor, Alex Manly, disappeared from Wilmington under a sentence of death—delivered by Alfred Moore Waddell, an ex-Confederate colonel who was, by all accounts, a spellbinding orator, who took charge of the mob.

The purported reason for the attack on Manly was an editorial that had appeared in the *Record*, a rebuttal to the speech delivered by Rebecca Latimer Felton, wife of a Georgia congressman, on the subject of lynching. She claimed that the biggest danger to white farmwives in the South was being raped by "black brutes."

She exhorted her audience, "When there is not enough religion in the pulpit to organize a crusade against sin; nor justice in the court house to promptly punish crime; nor manhood enough in the nation to put a sheltering arm about innocence and virtue—if it needs lynching to protect woman's dearest possession from the ravening human beasts—then I say lynch, a thousand times a week if necessary."

~~~~~~~~~~

The *Record* editorial claimed that sometimes white women were attracted to black men. That sometimes white men didn't take very good care of their women in the first place. The editorial ran in August 1898, a full year after Felton's speech, and went largely unnoticed—until it was picked up by the white newspaper, the *Messenger*, which ran it on the front page every day until election day next to a new report of an alleged black atrocity.

The night before election day, Colonel Waddell delivered a "sizzling" oratory from the stage of Thalian Hall. "If you see the negro out voting," he said, "tell him to go home. If he won't go, shoot him down in his tracks."

White supremacist Democrats took the county and state elections by a landslide—and apparently by means of widespread fraud, threat, and intimidation. We can do the math and determine this: In some precincts, many more people voted than were actually registered. In one precinct, Democrats were reported to have knocked over the kerosene lanterns, throwing the place into darkness, and then made off with the ballot box.

The day after election day, November 9, 1898, at a mass meeting of whites at the courthouse, a White Declaration of Independence was read and signed by more than 400 leading citizens. An ultimatum was issued to a so-called Committee of Colored Citizens. An answer was demanded by early the next morning. When no answer arrived by the deadline, a mob led by Waddell marched on the *Record*.

Between November 10 and November 13, people were killed. Most of them died by gunfire in the streets, some in front of firing squads. Many others were beaten, arrested, or driven from town.

All the dead were black.

Waddell declared that his followers would take political power back from blacks if they had to "choke the Cape Fear River with the carcasses of our enemies." By many accounts his cadre did just that: Wagonloads of bodies were reported dumped into the river at the height of the violence, though many historians dismiss such reports as mere legend, inspired (they surmise) by Waddell's fiery speech.

Democratic white supremacists took power at gunpoint and banished the former aldermen and mayor. A list was drawn up of "undesirables": A few whites and nearly every prominent black politician, businessman, and professional man in town were on it. They were rounded up at bayonet point and forced onto trains out of town.

The Wilmington Light Infantry, a local militia company that had missed the Cuban war and was spoiling for a fight, led the violence. "The Light Infantry squad has much to answer for," wrote one contemporary eyewitness to that organization's killing spree in the black community: "They shot down right and left in a most unlawful way, killing one man who was simply standing at a corner waiting to get back to his work." They were the ones who conducted the firing squads.

The lawyer and later judge who went to the statehouse as a direct result of the coup, George Rountree, crafted an ingenious piece of legislation, usually referred to as the Grandfather Clause. If your grandfather had voted prior to 1861, then you were allowed to vote. If not, you had to pass a literacy test and pay a poll tax. It was so ingenious that it was widely copied throughout the South, and it kept blacks from voting or holding office in significant numbers until 1965, when it was overturned by the federal Voting Rights Act.

I learned all this shortly after moving to Wilmington. I'd heard stories of a "riot," but nobody seemed to know what had really happened. I immersed myself in the Wilson Library at UNC Chapel Hill and pored through other archives at East Carolina University, Duke University, the Lower Cape Fear Historical Society, various public libraries, and even the Aberdeen Proving Ground Museum up in Maryland, where I got to play with a real Gatling gun of the type used by the white supremacists. I found out a lot, but there was also a lot that could never definitively be proven.

For example, we don't know whether Alex Manly, the editor, even wrote the incendiary editorial. It really wasn't his style. Up to that point, he had been a fairly mild guy. His most trenchant editorials called for more bicycle paths so poor black mill workers could save a dime on the streetcar.

We don't know whether Alex Manly was even in Wilmington during those crucial days.

We don't know exactly how many people were driven out of town or, except in a few cases, who they were. Census records do indicate that about a year later, some 1,000 fewer people resided in New Hanover County.

We don't know what became of their property, although we know some of them had considerable property—including bank accounts, business inventories, and real estate. But at least as far as the transfer of real estate goes, some fairly motivated professional historians have tried to track down whether any skullduggery occurred and so far have been unable to verify that any land was stolen.

We don't know who fired the first shot.

We don't know how many people were killed—at least 16, say the coroner's reports; as many as 400, claims one contemporary African American clergyman who witnessed the violence.

We don't know, except in the most superficial way, why all those people did the things they did—and that is what a writer is most passionately interested in: the why. The crucial human mystery at the center of the event.

The more I learned about the story, the more I wanted to learn, and when I discovered that the flashpoint for the violence was a writer, Alex Manly, I was hooked: Knowing what I knew, I had no choice but to write it into a book, to try to answer the crucial question of *why*. And so my book, *Cape Fear Rising*, became not a history but a novel, a chance to imagine my way into the minds and motives of those long-dead actors as they inflicted such great violence on the city that is my home.

Oddly enough, the white men who led the uprising had never suppressed the story: Several of them, including Waddell and Rountree, left behind extensive memoirs. The Wilmington Light Infantry convened a special reunion years after the event just to trade war stories for a stenographer. A black clergyman, J. Allen Kirk, left behind a pamphlet. MacRae wrote straightforwardly of his views on race. Other contemporary witnesses left letters and speeches and telegrams.

The story as I came to know it and write it had a scope and a breadth far beyond Wilmington, far beyond even race. It was a story of the failure of democracy because the people crucial to the community—its leaders—didn't trust it. It was at its heart the story of a community coming apart at the seams for a few terrifying days. Civilization, in any meaningful sense of that word, ceased to operate in Wilmington during those crucial days in November 1898, when the city suffered under martial law, vigilante mobs roamed the streets unchecked by police, and all bets were off. Nobody was safe.

There was nobody in charge anymore. Evil was loose in the streets.

If CNN had been around then, we would have seen video footage that looked like scenes from those chaotic third-world countries we are always sending peacekeeping troops into. We would have seen thousands of black refugees huddled in the cold rain out in the swamps along Smith's Creek, in railroad culverts and cemeteries: babies squalling, wounded men bleeding, sullen faces staring out in fear and anger. We would have seen bodies contorted by violent death deliberately left lying on the streets as a warning to other "rabble-rousers." We would have seen armed squads of white teenaged boys searching black men and women at checkpoints around the perimeter of the downtown, and murderous mobs of drunken, armed "Red Shirts," the equivalent of Klansmen, killing without penalty.

We would have heard window glass breaking, men shouting, and the continuous crackle of gunfire. And the towering blaze at Alex Manly's doomed newspaper would have burned itself into our imaginations so vividly we could smell the pitch pine and taste the acrid chemical smoke.

Who were these people? What did they have to gain? What in God's name made them do the things they did? They were not evil villains—they were mostly family men, deacons in their churches, well-respected, beloved fathers and husbands.

So why were they roaming the streets, shooting down innocent people, subverting democracy?

It would be easier if they were villains, because then we could dismiss them. We're not like that, we could say—as we say it of every real villain history offers us. But we can't get off quite so easily.

Waddell, who led the uprising, was a brave officer and a charmer of young women. Rountree, who wrote the Grandfather Clause, even his enemies agreed, was a fair and honest man, and he later helped get a black man appointed to a judgeship in Washington. William Rand Kenan, who had charge of the Gatling gun, was known for his integrity, upright character, and physical bravery. Colonel Walker Taylor, who had military command of Wilmington once martial law was declared, is best known for his work with underprivileged boys in the Boys Brigade, the forerunner of the Brigade Boys and Girls Club.

These men were—are—uncomfortably like us. They had their good points; in fact, you could argue that for some of them their actions in the uprising were way out of character—good or bad. Inexplicable. In an extraordinary situation, they did things nobody—least of all they themselves—ever expected them to do.

During the violence, for example, Dr. Silas Wright, the ousted mayor, a man known for his inability to act decisively, suddenly became a hero, riding to and fro at great personal risk to try to stop the shooting. Rountree, a man of law and reason, suddenly found himself walking the streets with a Winchester in his hand—feeling, as he later reported in his own words, "like a damn fool."

In some important way, the writer of public events becomes a surrogate conscience for the community. So I needed to grapple with the moral problem they faced, the moral problem that is at the center of the story: When everyone around you is doing wrong, at what point must you, the individual, take responsibility? At what point must you act to stop it?

And how can you act when those people all around you are the people you most respect, who most matter to you, with whom you will have to go on living for a lifetime in a small place? And how can you then not act?

Which version of the story will you choose to listen to?

It seems significant to me that the story of the 1898 uprising is itself a story of stories: The conflict was first played out in newspaper stories; then in dueling sermons from the pulpits of white and black churches; then in adversarial speeches—most famously, Waddell's bloody ultimatum delivered from the stage of Thalian Hall to a packed house; later still in written ultimatums and declarations that are full of narrative detail and more stories; and finally in Waddell's published version and the other, mostly unpublished memoirs of the event.

And the target of all the uproar was an author, Alex Manly, who was telling stories the white community didn't want to hear.

Which story will we ultimately choose to live by? Which version will make us examine our political and racial and humane conscience? Which will best define us? Which will be our most useful warning against next time?

Which will be only a self-serving excuse that lets us all off the hook?

It seems to me no accident that the racial violence played out in this river city, a city whose earliest commerce from the days of King Roger Moore and Brunswick Town was founded on slave labor, and whose Civil War identity was "the last open port of the Confederacy," keeping an army in the field to defend an economic and ethical system based on the subjugation of one race by another.

In some ways, the coup of 1898 feels almost like an inevitable consequence of that legacy, the last tragic act inspired by the plantation culture of the river, which survived the Civil War and, one might argue, continues in some quarters today.

Whenever a developer along the river names another tract of upscale houses Such-and-Such "Plantation," I cringe. Sometimes the name reclaims the name of an actual plantation, and the intent is to honor the historic place name. Other times the name is simply quaint. But the term "plantation" carries a loaded legacy, a complicated etymology that is less about pure descriptive definition than about connotation and bloody history.

The story of 1898 runs under Wilmington's social and political life like the tunnels that run down Market Street to the river—or used to. Invisible, but running underneath every act of our daily community life. Burrowed into the core of our civic identity, if you will.

The tunnels used to run from Sixth Street west to the river, branching in several directions, with entrances in many of the mansions, churches, and other significant buildings along the route. Most have been closed off, or they caved in when workers installed water mains or other utilities.

While researching the story of 1898, I explored one stretch of tunnel accessible from the old Wilmington Light Infantry Armory. It had masonry walls and an arched ceiling, too low to stand fully upright in, but high enough to allow movement in a sort of crouch. Historians have argued for years about why they were built: for smuggling and bootlegging, to aid escaping slaves on the Underground Railroad, or simply for drainage. The answer seems, disappointingly, to be the latter—they were just storm sewers, dating back to at least 1745. The town site of Wilmington was contoured among sandy hills threaded by washes and small streams, and the tunnels were built to channel the water that coursed among the lots during rainstorms.

But of course Oakdale Cemetery was built as a final resting place for the dead—not a haven for living refugees, as it became on the night of November 10, 1898, as people crouched among the tombstones, sheltering from the incessant rain beneath the bowers of dogwoods. We find new uses for old spaces, uses which their original builders never intended, and subterranean tunnels are no exception.

Intriguingly, the old residence of royal governors at Brunswick Town, called Russelborough, was connected to the river by a similar arched brick tunnel. That would argue for an escape route, not just a sewer.

The tunnel I explored was well preserved and dry, an intriguing hollow passageway into the past of a vibrant and sometimes troubled city.

8

Near the southern end of the Wilmington waterfront, just below the shops and restaurants of Chandler's Wharf, visible atop a long, sloping hill, David and I in our little *Sea Whip* pass a stately white riverfront mansion.

The great house was built on the site of the first colonial customshouse, back around 1825, by Edward B. Dudley, the first popularly elected governor of North Carolina. Dudley was a prime mover in establishing the city as a railroad hub. He invested the princely sum of $25,000—more than half a million dollars in today's currency—in the Wilmington and Weldon Railroad, which covered the incredible span of 161.5 miles and owned exactly twelve locomotives, all named after counties in eastern North Carolina. The Wilmington and Weldon would eventually play a crucial role in supplying Robert E. Lee's troops during the Civil War.

The Dudley mansion has a storied past.

In 1848, Daniel Webster visited. A few years later, when Dudley's daughter married a young lieutenant stationed downriver at Fort Caswell, two of the groomsmen standing uniformed in the dining room were fellow lieutenants Abner Doubleday and William Tecumseh Sherman. One is credited (probably a little too generously) with inventing the modern game of baseball, which became a popular way for Civil War troops to while away the days waiting for their generals to send them out to be slaughtered. The other made his final 425-mile march through the state and accepted the surrender of the Army of Tennessee at the Bennett Place.

But the most famous tenant of the house was undoubtedly James Sprunt, a legendary figure in Wilmington. Born in Glasgow, Scotland, in 1846, he was brought to Wilmington by his parents, Alexander and Jane, in 1854. By the time the Civil War engulfed the South, he was just fifteen, but on his own initiative he had studied a night-school course in navigation (with a mentor identified only as Captain Levy) and signed on with a blockade-runner—one of those fast, sidewheeler steamers with shallow draughts that slipped into the river at night through channels too shoal and shifty for the deep-draught blockading U.S. Navy cruisers to follow.

He shipped on the *Lilian*, skippered by our old friend Captain John N. Maffitt. Like a storybook hero, he was shipwrecked, rescued, captured, imprisoned for a time at Fort Macon on the Bogue Banks, then escaped and went to sea again.

After the war, his legend really began to take shape—and is all the more remarkable because it is apparently all true.

During his travels, he had traded molasses for twenty-four bales of cotton, which he sent to Wilmington for safekeeping. When the Yankees arrived, they promptly torched a dozen of them. Seven more were stolen, leaving Sprunt with just five. He sold them for cash and invested first in naval stores: turpentine and pitch available from local plantations. He made his first deal with a Mr. G. C. MacDougall—seven casks of turpentine on account—and thus was born the enterprise that would become Alexander Sprunt and Son.

When forests no longer yielded enough local product, Sprunt expanded into cotton.

In partnership with his father, Alexander, James Sprunt, still not yet twenty years old, parlayed his first profits into a cotton-export business that traded with more than fifty agents throughout Europe.

In short order, Sprunts was the largest exporter of cotton on the planet. In 1907–9, for example, Sprunt's firm exported more than half a million bales of cotton valued at more than $30 million—about $740 million in today's dollars.

James Sprunt made enough to buy a spacious home on the river, the Governor Dudley mansion on Front Street. In 1904, he purchased Orton Plantation downriver as a gift to his wife, Luola. The seller was her father, Kenneth M. Murchison, who had restored the main house.

At the Dudley mansion, his houseguests included William Jennings Bryan ("You shall not crucify mankind on a cross of gold!"); William Howard Taft (who so disappointed his predecessor and champion, Theodore Roosevelt, that TR ran against him on the ballot for the Bull Moose Party); and Woodrow Wilson ("a war to end all wars"). Woodrow Wilson's father, Rev. Joseph R. Wilson, was the pastor of Sprunt's church, the First Presbyterian, and a family friend.

James Sprunt was a handsome, well-built man with piercing eyes who could handle himself outdoors and was at home on the water. He was often seen cruising aboard his sleek motor yacht *Luola*. He wore a thick moustache in the manner of the day and dressed in high-collared shirts and dark wool suits. As a young man he was known for his bright red hair. In later years, his thick hair and moustache turned silver, giving him the air of a distinguished patriarch, which he admittedly was.

In 1882, Sprunt suffered an accident that would have sent a lesser man into early retirement. He was driving his sister Jeanie, Mrs. J. A. Holmes, to Mason-boro Sound in a horse cart, probably along the old Shell Road that was paved with crushed oyster shell and ran along the course followed by present-day Wrightsville Avenue. The horse bolted, and Jeanie was thrown clear but not seriously injured. As his niece Jane D. Wood recounts in "Data about James Sprunt, LL.D.," "James Sprunt got his foot entangled in the buckling of the reins, and in the accident that followed his foot was crushed." He was too badly injured to move, and he was taken to a nearby house and laid on the kitchen table. Doctors were summoned. By the light of a kerosene lantern, they amputated his foot. Blood poisoning set in, and his convalescence was long and painful.

Later he traveled north to be fitted with an artificial foot, presumably by Dr. William Baer of Baltimore, of which more in a moment. From that time on, Sprunt relied on his walking stick. But he hardly slowed down.

And he had a new appreciation for those born with deformed limbs or who lived in constant pain as a result of accidents. His own horrific accident inspired him to become the champion of "crippled" kids in the mill district, many of them the children of his own workers. He arranged for them to travel to Baltimore for extensive rehabilitation with Dr. Baer, and meanwhile he funded local hospitals, built several churches, and served as both British vice consul and Imperial German consul for Wilmington. These latter posts were not honorifics; remember, at that period, Wilmington was the wealthiest city in the state and the most significant international port between Charleston and Norfolk.

One of the churches Sprunt built was St. Andrew's Presbyterian, a neo-Gothic structure that fell on hard times and was derelict by the time Hurricane Fran hit in 1996. During the storm, the roof caved in and most of the interior was wrecked. The City of Wilmington stepped in, shored up the walls with steel beams, and reroofed the church. It's a stunning architectural landmark connecting two eras, a concert and wedding venue now known as the Brooklyn Arts Center.

Some fifteen years after Sprunt lost his foot, when he had sufficient resources, his niece recounts, he and his wife, Luola Murchison Sprunt, founded Delgado Hill, "with a view to eliminating, by operating, the cases of curvature of the spine, club-foot, and other disabling infirmities."

At the height of the violence in Wilmington in 1898, as a cadre of white supremacists staged a bloody racial coup, Sprunt was caught in the middle. A mob of white vigilantes, armed to the teeth with Winchester repeating rifles and some kind of machine gun, showed up at the gates of Sprunt's Champion Compress to attack his workers. Most skilled mill workers were African Americans, for a variety of reasons, and many of the unskilled, unemployed white men who made up the mob were seeking payback for what they saw as a raw deal. Sprunt and his younger brother William, now a partner in the business, pledged their word that the black workers would be safe from the mob.

Wood recalls the fatal tension hanging in the air:

In time of riot, passions easily ride the saddle. A company of hot headed men under violent leadership, estimating all negroes alike, and declared against any group of them assembling in any place, trained a machine gun on the crowds of negroes at the compress and ordered them to run. . . . The machine guns were meant for use and not for threats.

At that moment when it was evident that it would be discharged, James Sprunt had himself hoisted upon one of the big uncompressed cotton bales and said, "Shoot if you will, but make me the victim!"

The pledge of safety to the negroes was redeemed. The white men were brought to their senses by this unexpected turn of event, and ignorant of course of the pledge that the Sprunts had given the men, the action of James Sprunt led to the ugly calumny that the Sprunts were protecting their own interests in protecting the negroes. Be that as it may, the spell was broken and the compress negroes were permitted to go in peace and were unmolested through the whole time of terror.

While his workers waited, Sprunt sent envoys into the black community to inquire after the welfare of the men's families. The envoys brought back word that, though the black newspaper had been burned and several people had been shot, the men's families were safe.

Sprunt then let them go home—and more importantly, he provided signed passes to guarantee safe passage through the vigilante checkpoints. No single action of his life was probably more humane or demonstrated more convincingly the power of his personal reputation: The black workers trusted him, and the white vigilantes would honor his orders.

You can be skeptical of the account by Sprunt's niece of his heroic stand against the mob, whether his pronouncement was quite so eloquent and brave. To our more jaded ears, it sounds too much like the slaveholder's "defense" of his property. And we have no way of knowing at this late date how much the incident has been exaggerated into legend—or whether it is quite literally true.

But the fact is that Sprunt's workers remained loyal and kept his compress operating while, for example, Hugh MacRae's Wilmington Cotton Mills emptied out and shut down. Sprunt had been brave all his life, from the time he shipped out on a blockade-runner, and during his life he showed continual deep empathy for those in his charge. So there is no reason to suppose the story isn't true, at least in its broad outlines.

He may well have supported the white supremacist platform in spirit; we'll never know, though the prime movers were all his friends and peers, and he later wrote of Colonel Waddell with great admiration, praising his efforts as an amateur historian. But his actions clearly set him apart from the many wealthy whites who led the violence or quietly orchestrated it behind the scenes—or, perhaps worst of all, stood by and let it happen without interference.

Probably mixed into his motives were the instincts of a savvy, hardheaded businessman who didn't want to be closed down. Whenever I investigate a historical figure, almost without exception, the deeper I research, the more complex the figure becomes. I doubt that any of us has ever acted purely out of a single motive. So empathy, honor, self-interest, a sense of law and order, and a paternalistic racism all might have entered the equation, and I don't presume to judge motive, only to applaud the action.

In any event, Sprunt was not content to simply be a wealthy businessman-philanthropist who had also been a war hero and now was a different kind of hero. Instead of resting on his considerable laurels, he set out to chronicle the history of Wilmington and the region, as much out of local pride as from the zeal of a historian, and he did a remarkably thorough and commendable job of it. He did not rely on stories and folktales—although he collected them voraciously—but tracked down primary sources and amassed an original library that would be the envy of any special collections librarian in the country.

Out of this work came a sheaf of important works, most notably *Chronicles of the Cape Fear River, 1660–1916*, as fascinating and complete an account as we are ever likely to see of the complex historical beginnings of white settlement on the Cape Fear: all the abortive expeditions, failed colonies, shady land deals, Indian wars, royal interference, and national and civil feuding that culminated in the city and region as they existed by the time of World War I.

He did, however, leave out the events of November 1898.

In 1915, the University of North Carolina conferred upon him the honorary degree of doctor of laws, recognizing his writings and "his personal excellence and merit." Sprunt also endowed a fund at UNC to support the publication of historical monographs.

Then, as if all that weren't enough, he helped to engineer a spectacle that, in some ways, served as his crowning achievement and offers a clear portrait of the man whose grasp of both life and history was panoramic, grand, larger than life—and, unfortunately, conveniently missing the less flattering episodes of local history.

He arranged for the staging of an outdoor drama on the riverfront lawn of his mansion at Front and Ann Streets. The full name of the pageant, as it was later published without irony, is instructive:

### A Pageant of the Lower Cape Fear
DESIGNED BY THE LITERATURE DEPARTMENT OF THE
NORTH CAROLINA SOROSIS
TO REVIEW THE HEROIC TRADITIONS OF THE LOWER CAPE FEAR AS AN
INCENTIVE TO THE ACHIEVEMENT OF A MORE GLORIOUS FUTURE.

This outdoor drama was based on his *Chronicles* and was performed four times during June 7–9, 1921. The *Wilmington Morning Star* for June 7, 1921, reported, "On Wednesday evening a portion of the seats will be reserved for negroes, so that they may see history reenacted."

Five writers, using the product of fifteen researchers, all coordinated by a professor of dramatic arts from UNC Chapel Hill, Frederick H. Koch, under the auspices of the local chapter of North Carolina Sorosis, produced the monumental performance. Five hundred "citizen players" acted the roles. In addition to a small naval and Coast Guard flotilla of ships and airplanes that were moored in the river for the occasion, a replica of the blockade-runner *Lilian* and a full-sized pirate ship (standing in for Blackbeard's *Queen Anne's Revenge*) were employed in the show, which was dedicated to "James Sprunt, A Loyal Son Of The Cape Fear Whose Efforts Have Preserved Our Glorious Traditions To Posterity."

This rather florid tribute is nonetheless accurate, for it is hard to find anyone who has ever done more to unlock the history of the lower river and present it to new generations—though the pageant, like his writings, betrays his fatal flaw as a historian: He selectively leaves out events that show his homeplace in a less than glowing light.

Still, his love of the river was genuine. Sprunt didn't just happen to live on the river—he was passionate about it. As a child he sailed on it, swam in it, rowed across it, and whiled away idle hours counting the ships anchored in the harbor below his window. As a young man, he ran the Yankee blockade through New Inlet under the guns of Fort Fisher. As a successful businessman, he was fond of entertaining on his sleek motor yacht *Luola*.

One of the proudest achievements of a life packed with remarkable achievements was to be elected a member of the Board of Navigation and Pilotage when he was in his early forties. This fulfilled an ambition he'd had since those boyhood sessions with Captain Levy, learning navigation, carried through his service on blockade-runners. The man he escaped Fort Macon with was a Cape Fear River pilot, J. W. "Jim Billy" Craig. Now Spunt belonged to that elite fraternity of rivermen.

Indeed, he begins *Chronicles* with a valentine to the river of his boyhood: "From early youth I have loved the Cape Fear River, the ships and sailors which it bears upon its bosom. As a boy I delighted to wander along the wharves where the sailing ships were moored with their graceful spars and rigging in relief against the sky-line, with men aloft whose uncouth cries and unknown tongues inspired me with a longing for the sea, which I afterwards followed, and the faraway countries whence they had come."

Sprunt was a larger-than-life figure whose career spanned the heyday of Wilmington as a peacetime harbor, a wartime arsenal, and a commercial powerhouse. But his heart was always in another era, when he could watch "white sails glistening in morning light."

Writing on the eve of America's entry into the Great War, he expressed his affection for those days before the Civil War launched him on his adventures: "Memory lingers with a certain endearment upon the daily activities of the harbor in that far-gone day, when the course of life was more attuned to the placid flow of the river than in this rushing, jarring time."

The pageant was a celebration of that golden past, a kind of public memorial expressing exactly the kind of nostalgia Sprunt himself felt. But it was also a reminder that a new era had arrived on the heels of victory in modern war and the lucrative shipbuilding enterprise it had brought to the city. The Navy Department sent a submarine chaser and two seaplanes, which were anchored on the Cape Fear just behind the pageant stage. The crews and a visiting admiral (Rear Admiral Edwin A. Anderson) were feted at a dance given in their honor at a reception at the American Legion hall following the performance Wednesday evening, "which should be finished by not later than 10:30 o'clock."

The pageant was front-page news for two days running, and on the third it showed up on page 12 as the pageant committee congratulated itself on having made such a financial and community success.

"Pageant an Inspiring Spectacle for Great Crowd Witnessing It" read the headline on June 8, lauding the performance venue:

> The pageant had for its setting the back gardens of Dr. James Sprunt's home on South Front Street—and a more appropriate place could not have been found in the Cape Fear country. A touch here and a touch there and the placing of seats, and the result was a real amphitheater. In the background the Cape Fear river, with its waters glistening from electric illumination, held in its lap craft of a long gone day and of 1921, all of which had a part in the exhibition. In midstream were anchored, brightly lighted by the Coast Guard cutter *Seminole*, the United States naval sub-chaser 201, and two modern seaplanes, silent reminders that now, as always in the past, America is as mighty with fighting power as she is fond of peace.

The stage, flanked by transplanted pine trees, was set beside the river. An orchestra provided musical accompaniment—"America," "The Star-Spangled Banner," "Dixie," and assorted songs. During one segment featuring antebellum plantation life, called "Confederate Wilmington," the young bridegroom, Bob Harrison, takes the stage with his bride, accompanied by his faithful slave Scipio. "There was an old-fashioned reel dance, with music of the period by fiddlers; then songs by a negro quartet—real honest-to-goodness negro melodies."

It's hard not to cringe a little at the casual racism of both the script itself and the coverage of it in the local newspaper. And yet the pageant is fascinating, an honest-to-goodness *event*.

The nuptial festivities are interrupted by a call to arms—secession! All the other men at the wedding are called up to their respective companies. Though his commanding officer, Colonel Cantwell, wants to excuse him from duty, Bob declares, "I am going."

Colonel Cantwell protests, "But your bride . . . ."

His bride, Agnes Harrison, chimes in on cue, "I would not keep him from such a glorious adventure."

Bob is so worked up that he has forgotten all about their honeymoon: "That's the way to talk! We'll lick the damned Yankees before the watermelons get ripe, eh, Scipio?"

Scipio, forlorn, implores him, "Take me, Marse Bob."

Bob Harrison (slapping him on the back): "Of course I will. Do you suppose I am going to black my own boots?"

It's hard not to wonder how such smug, belittling lines played for the Wednesday night "negroes" in the reserved seats, there to be edified by this spectacle of local history.

In the time-lapse drama required by a two-hour pageant covering some 300 years (about two and a half years per minute), Marse Bob is left for dead on the battlefield—presumably in 1865, when the war came to Wilmington in the form of the armada assaulting Fort Fisher and Sherman's army marching on Goldsboro. He is rescued—of course he is—by southern women, "and great was the rejoicing, especially to the faithful Scipio." Overlooked is the inconvenient fact that Marse Bob has been fighting to keep faithful Scipio—and all his brethren singing the "real honest-to-goodness negro melodies"—a slave.

My favorite moment of unintended comic relief occurs when General Braxton Bragg, in command of the Department of North Carolina, is informed that Fort Fisher is under siege by the Federal fleet. He is confident the fort can hold out, that it is invulnerable (after all, it was known as the Sevastopol of the Confederacy for good reason). But he is pressed: "What if it should fall?"

His answer: "Good-bye, Wilmington."

Bragg has a famous army base named after him, the one we canoed past listening to the Sound of Freedom erupting on the live-firing range, but in Wilmington he is remembered as the dithering general who abandoned the city to its fate when he could have rallied reinforcements to its defense and stopped the Yankees cold in an untenable position between river and sea. He was by all accounts a man whose career was a chronicle of failures and lost battles, but each one seemed to catapult him to a higher post. Had he not been a close friend of Jefferson Davis and brother of Thomas Bragg, who was governor until the eve of war and later became the attorney general of the Confederacy, maybe he wouldn't have been given quite so many chances to lose the war.

Episode 3, "The Fall of Fort Fisher," ends Part 3, "Confederate Wilmington." In the final lines, a courier delivers the devastating—alliterative—news: "Fort Fisher has fallen, sir."

Bragg replies, "Fisher fallen? Well then, Wilmington, goodbye!"

The pageant then unaccountably skips ahead to 1917, as if nothing has happened in the half-century since the fall of the fort and the Great War: no emancipation, no occupation by U.S. troops, no Reconstruction, no cotton-exporting powerhouse, no racial coup in 1898, which means also no heroic, unarmed James Sprunt standing down a machine-gun-toting mob on behalf of his black workers.

Probably the lacuna—at least of the 1898 violence—was calculated. The cast committee included the one man who was implicated in the massacre up to his eyeballs: Colonel Waddell. He led the white supremacist mob that burned Alex Manly's *Daily Record* and started the mayhem, and he was then installed at gunpoint as the new mayor of the city.

The *Star* notes that many of the 500-odd actors portrayed their own ancestors. "King" Roger Moore was played by Mr. Roger Moore, and Maurice Moore by Mr. Maurice Moore, and so on. A Wednesday matinee was scheduled for all the schoolchildren of the city and county. The pageant was hailed, probably accurately, as the biggest event ever staged in North Carolina (excepting battles), and, unable to resist a bit of civic boosterism, the *Star* bragged that "the city has obtained more advertising than from any other single event and will continue to gain such advertisement."

It's easy to make light of the sentimental hyperbole, the rampant boosterism, the nativist racism, and the smug Christian self-righteousness of such a production, yet part of me wishes we could bring it back. Revised, surely, to reflect a more truthful, unvarnished view of the hideous and dehumanizing institution of slavery and the brutal extermination of the Cape Fear Indians. And revised also to take some of the romance out of ruthless piracy and the heartbreakingly avoidable bloodbath of the Civil War. And maybe we ought to put back in that lost, turbulent fifty years and the white supremacist coup that remained an open secret for so many generations.

But there is something undeniably appealing to me about a concerted civic effort to capture that which unites us in spirit and history and bonds us to our patch of geography, celebrating the virtues of loyalty and endurance, hard work and cooperation, a community vision that seeks to redress wrongs and cultivate civic duty and humane action—and the ambition to fulfill that vision with imperfect gifts in an imperfect world. Once in awhile we need to be un-ironic, sincere rather than merely clever, and maybe just a little bit corny.

All that deserves an epic play, performed in public. And by all means, let us stage a matinee for the schoolkids.

The saddest part of the whole pageant is the ending, in which the players watch a parade of great ships entering the port of Wilmington, a "glorious future" that only partly came true, for the city and its port never really recovered from the racial troubles at the turn of the twentieth century that brought trade and business to a breathless halt during three awful days of bloody violence.

And when the Atlantic Coast Line Railroad, which had been leaving piecemeal for years, finally moved out, the city suffered a blow from which it would take decades to recover. Today, Wilmingtonians have to travel to Wilson to catch a passenger train anywhere.

The city that had once been at the nexus of national and even world trade settled into an uneasy role as a tourist destination. Ironically, after Sprunt, the most prominent owner of the Dudley mansion was Henry Walters, who was a driving force in establishing the Atlantic Coast Line Railroad to begin with, helping make Wilmington a transshipment point to the world.

In a strange closing of the circle, the great commercial shipping fortunes began and ended with that lovely, majestic house on the river.

So David and I pass slowly along the riverfront of Wilmington, cruising through its history and toward its future in our feisty little *Sea Whip*. We are caught in its current, in more ways than one, and also in its past, the flooding tide shoving against the downriver flow, stalling it, till it turns at last.

It would be nice to pull up at Chandler's Wharf and have a cold beer at Elijah's restaurant to celebrate our homecoming. Ordinarily, we could do that, then take the boat out at the Castle Street ramp, also called Dram Tree Park. The park is named for the fabled bald cypress that once stood on a miniature island just offshore of Sunset Park. It lasted from colonial times until the 1940s, when a workman unaware of the tree's significance cut it down.

Legend has it that the "Dram Tree" was the landmark where inbound captains toasted the voyage with a celebratory round of grog for the crew, and outbound captains also lifted a dram, perhaps eager to leave behind the entanglements of shore.

But David and I will go without any libation this trip. Dram Tree Park is in the throes of a major renovation—and a reclamation, since it turns out to be a hazardous waste site once occupied by the Wilmington Manufactured Gas Plant. Now it's being rehabilitated by Progress Energy in partnership with the City of Wilmington to include a kayak launch and an upgraded boat ramp with floating dock, a sure sign that the city and private enterprise are recognizing the value of the river, and of getting people out onto the river.

But for now the ramp is closed, so David and I, riding *Sea Whip*, pass under the Cape Fear Memorial Bridge and gaze up at its rusted undergirders and the flash of traffic through the gratings that make up the roadbed at its apogee.

Like all the other bridges on the river, the Cape Fear Memorial Bridge has its own ill-starred past. It's an unusual drawbridge, a so-called vertical lift bridge, which means the thirty-three-meter-long center span rises all of a piece, remaining level, to open the channel below to shipping. It's six-tenths of a mile long and opened to traffic on October 1, 1969.

I'd long heard an urban legend of how a Cadillac had driven past the roadblock while the center span was rising and went straight off the bridge and into the river. Supposedly this happened shortly after it opened. I finally tracked down the facts of the tale with the help of Ben Steelman, a reporter for the *Wilmington Star News*. It turns out that the story was basically true, though dates and details were off: On Halloween morning 1977, a 1975 Cadillac driven by Gennis Smith had nearly made it across the center span but then somehow got caught partly on and partly off the span as it was rising. The span was lifting the back of his vehicle. As he recalled for the newspaper ten years after the fact, "When it got pulled about six feet, I jumped."

Good thing he did. At some point, the rising span let go of the car, and it fell back to the lower level; when the span came back down, it crushed the Cadillac and sent it hurtling into the river. A woman in a Chevy Vega following the Cadillac braked hard enough to stay on the center span and rode it all the way to the top and back down again, screaming all the while. She drove off without giving her name to reporters, but a friend of mine at the university revealed her identity. She was a professor new to the area who didn't understand how the bridge worked. She assumed it would tilt like a traditional drawbridge and slide her back down, crashing into other cars. So her screaming was entirely reasonable—and something of a metaphor. Here she was, transplanted into a new community, and she panicked because she didn't know how things worked.

In November 2008, a flatbed truck heading eastbound on the bridge changed lanes abruptly and collided with a tractor trailer. The impact catapulted the flatbed across the guardrail into the oncoming lane, where it smashed into an SUV, killing a twenty-nine-year-old woman and seriously injuring a four-year-old boy.

The following month, a small experimental aircraft flew *under* the bridge, causing a minor stir.

These days more than 46,000 vehicles a day cross the bridge, which is showing its age. In 2009 it was rated by the American Automobile Association as one of the ten worst in the state. Most recently, the bridge has tended to get stuck open due to a malfunction of the computer that controls the lifting apparatus. Still, it is the signature of the city, the picturesque gateway to the Wilmington waterfront, and passing under it, we can generously ignore its failings.

~~~~~~

I return to Dram Tree Park on a summer morning, after the site has been scrubbed of hazardous waste and a new launch ramp installed, and I'm impressed. From a clean, newly surfaced parking lot with lined spaces for vehicles and trailers, you can launch a small boat from either of two lanes bordered by finger piers. And best of all: North of the second lane, off the dock, floats a state-of-the-art kayak launch similar to the one already installed at the boat ramp on the Brunswick River. You place the kayak on a set of rollers and then, using handrails that line the length of the roller platform, ease into your seat. You then simply use the rails to push your kayak down the rollers to a gentle splash, and you're off.

Across Water Street from the spanking-new boat ramp—and just a few doors down from the humble one-story bungalow that houses Cape Fear River Watch—stands an old white clapboard house with a new sign: "Ted's Fun on the River." "Ted" turns out to be Kelly Jewell, a tall, friendly-faced man of retirement age but with a young disposition. There is no "Ted." "When I was a kid, my nickname was Ted," he says, which explains nothing. "My father was also called Ted. My wife has always called me Ted. But in our family there's no Theodore."

The whimsical name fits the general whimsy of the place—part coffee shop, part general store, part music venue, part gallery, and part outfitter. Next to the side deck, which you climb onto to reach the main entrance, sits a small fleet of rental canoes and kayaks. Black pirate flags mounted on the railings snap in the breeze.

Kelly used to live in this house, a thousand square feet big, literally in the shadow the Cape Fear Memorial Bridge, which looms high above. He had lived other places downtown and for awhile moved out of the city altogether to a farm. But when Dram Tree Park was finished, it was time to move back. He and his wife, Julia, dreamed of opening a music venue and enjoying the river. They are two-thirds of the Port City Trio, a jazz combo that plays locally, and most Friday nights they can be found in the music alcove at Ted's, filling the living room with lively jazz standards.

The walls are covered with old movie posters, photographs, and original art. Someone donated a checkerboard, the draughts made of soda bottle caps. A piano stands against a wall, and there's a guitar handy for anyone who cares to play awhile. The whole place is like a bohemian front porch that just happens to be indoors.

The Riverwalk is eventually supposed to run all the way to Ted's front door, but money has stalled and it still has a ways to go. But when it does, Ted's will be the last stop for foot traffic. On the river, if you build it, sooner or later they will come.

For Kelly, the river is the inspiration, the reason to be where he is, and once the run-down boat ramp was cleaned up and rebuilt, he saw his chance to bring his dream to life. He's always been something of a river rat; he used to play on the Cape Fear in an eight-foot rowboat. He won't rent his boats when the river's back is up, but it doesn't stop *him.* "I've been out there on days when it looked like Niagara Falls," he says, and grins.

~~~~~~~~~

But all that is in the future as David and I cruise past Dram Tree Park, still fenced off with big construction equipment corralled inside, our johnboat slapping the river like it's concrete slabs, not water. From the Cape Fear Memorial Bridge at Wilmington, David and I have almost fifteen more miles to go, all of it a rough, pounding ride into the teeth of a freshening wind.

So we push on, me at the tiller. David drove a good part of the way and finally needs some relief—his hand has gone numb on the throttle. We pass the port of Wilmington, and it's busy. A bulk carrier is being emptied by a great claw crane.

The port used to be located right at the foot of Market Street downtown, but after World War II the state bought the North Carolina Shipbuilding Company and created a modern port with a million square feet of indoor storage space. One of the old sheds is still standing, a hangarlike structure where keels were laid for the old Liberty Ships, built fast and cheaply by riveting prefab components together.

In recent years, the port has been upgraded with four mammoth post-Panamax container cranes. In 2010 alone, it handled almost 450 ships with a combined cargo capacity of 3.5 million tons: grain, chemicals, wood products, machine parts, scrap metal, cement, foodstuffs, and general merchandise of all kinds. Whenever a ship is in port, you can see a constant parade of tractor trailers hauling the containers out Shipyard Boulevard toward Carolina Beach Road, from there crossing the river toward one of the freeways out of town.

When the U.S. Coast Guard barque *Eagle* visited Wilmington recently, it tied up at the port. The great ship, its 295-foot hull gleaming white, its three masts soaring almost 150 feet into the air, was dwarfed by the giant orange and blue cargo cranes of the port. The powerful ship looked almost quaint, a historical relic. Gorgeous, an emblem of the romance of a bygone era, obsolete in a practical sense for moving cargo, but very effective as a way of training minds, bodies, and characters toward rigorous discipline, teamwork, and sound judgment when it counts.

History, yes, an anachronism. But alive.

~~~~~~~~~

Running the river has also been an excursion into my own past history on the river. The old proverb has it that you never step into the same river twice, yet for me all the rivers of memory are the same. Time gives the river an

The old-fashioned helm station of the Coast Guard barque *Eagle* presents an anachronistic contrast to the towering post-Panamax cranes of the port of Wilmington (author photo)

extra dimension, the way its depth gives it power and the atmosphere above it creates weather and room for birds.

So passing the port brings to mind another river trip.

It's a breezy warm evening a few years back, an hour before true sundown. I cross the Cape Fear Memorial Bridge and locate the McAllister Towing dock on Eagles Island, just south of Battleship Park. I clamber across two moored tugs to reach the outboard boat, the 103-foot-long *Barbara McAllister*, a black hull with a barn-red superstructure trimmed in white. Tonight it'll work in tandem with another tug, the *Clearwater*, to dock the *Hanjin Los Angeles*, a 950-foot-long container ship of about 52,000 tons, and I'll be along for the ride.

Captain James K. Galloway steps aboard, pours a cup of strong coffee in the forward galley, then climbs up to the wheelhouse. He is working the powerful vessel that night, as usual, with just an engineer and a deckhand. A tugboat is just a pair of giant diesel engines bolted onto enough hull to make them float, with hundreds of times more horsepower than a comparable-sized boat.

Last to board are the docking pilot, Jerry Champion, and a young apprentice pilot. Champion has worked the river for more than thirty years, the previous eighteen of those docking mammoth ships.

"The biggest problem is getting the ship stopped and maintaining control," Champion tells me once we're under way. "All the rest is a matter of push and pull."

There is nothing in the way he's dressed to indicate his nautical profession—he's wearing slacks, a casual shirt, and street shoes. He's a quiet, plain-spoken man with neat black hair and a steady manner, exactly the kind of guy you'd trust to guide a big ship into port with a hard wind blowing, a current rushing downriver against a tide pushing from another direction. Everything is moving—the air, the water, the ship, the tugboats—often in several directions at once.

He says, "It's kind of like driving on ice and you have to make your car go sideways into a parking space." That is, if your car is almost a thousand feet long.

The *Hanjin Los Angeles* hoves into view coming around the last bend downriver of the port: An immense black hull, its deck is piled four high and thirteen across with containers the size of semitrailers. In fact, each will become a semitrailer once it is lifted off the ship by a giant crane and secured atop a chassis.

The *Barbara McAllister* closes the distance, swings across the current, and slides up next to the ship, dropping back along the great black hull until we're even with the boarding ladder and pacing the ship at a steady speed. Now comes the most dangerous part of a pilot's day: He'll have to climb up the rope Jacob's ladder ten feet or so to reach the bottom of the boarding stairs that run up the outside of the hull to a hatchway in the side of the vessel. Not long ago, a pilot at Georgetown, South Carolina, not very far down the coast from us, fell into the gap between the pilot boat and the ship and was never recovered.

Champion steps up onto the lurching rail of the tugboat. Then, timing the pitch and roll of the boat, he steps across the open gap between boat and ship and onto the ladder. He climbs up the side of the moving hull until he can reach the boarding stairs, then swings over and continues his ascent with steel, not rope, underfoot.

My turn comes next. I study the moving black hull, close enough to reach out and touch. Check the gap of black river between the ship and the tug. I take a breath, then step up onto the tugboat's rail, reach across, and grab the Jacob's ladder. Quickly I step across the open space onto the ladder. For

Champion, the step across the chasm was a piece of routine bravery. But I have to summon my nerve, and when I make that big step, my heart is in my throat. The ship's steel side radiates heat, and below me the black sliver of water between the two moving vessels boils with their passage—not a place anyone could survive.

As I climb, clutching the rope tight, I can feel the hot steel against my body.

I swing onto the boarding stairs as I watched Champion do, then keep climbing toward the open hatchway several stories above. Once on deck, we're ushered into an elevator for the four-story ride to the bridge.

On the bridge, the captain relinquishes command of the ship to Champion. Think about that for a moment: A guy is sipping coffee one moment and joshing with his crew, and then he climbs up a rope ladder on the outside of a ship plowing ahead through the dusky river and assumes command of a vessel he has never laid eyes on before that moment—and all with complete aplomb, the way you or I might sign for a FedEx package.

And just like that, the captain hands over command.

The bridge is wide enough for a major-league pitcher to warm up on. It's manned by the captain, four khaki-uniformed officers, and a helmsman in bright orange *Hanjin* coveralls who steers the ship with a wheel the size of a dinner plate. Since the bridge is located aft, from a bank of outward-slanted windows, we can see the gargantuan spread of the whole deck, piled high with containers.

From that perspective, the river ahead looks too narrow, the ship too wide to make it around the bend, so that before long we'll be stuck like a cork in the neck of a bottle. You have to remind yourself not to panic, that it's all an optical illusion. But you understand why the captain needs a local pilot. Turns that seem wide and lazy in a small boat suddenly become tight and constricted in a vessel this gargantuan—68 feet longer than the *Titanic*. The turning basin at the port is only 1,200 feet wide, which means that this ship, turned sideways, could block the whole river channel.

The transit upriver takes about two and a half hours, but it seems to go by in a flash.

Off the starboard bow, the towering orange top-lift cranes of the port come up fast, their peaks almost at eye level. In a voice without inflection, Champion issues an order to the captain, who repeats it to his crew, and so it goes. He slows the ship, stops it, reverses engines, engages bow thrusters and rudder, and orchestrates by handheld radio the maneuvers of the *Barbara McAllister* and the *Clearwater*, which nudge in against the port side bow and stern.

The *Hanjin Los Angeles* responds to the push of the tugs by heeling slightly to starboard, then sliding heavily sideways in a roil of bottom mud stirred by the ship's reversed engines. The ship kisses the hold-off bumpers of the wharf. The deckhands in orange coveralls swarm to their work, passing ashore mooring lines as thick as their arms. Bow and stern are snugged hard to the oversized steel mooring bollards on the wharf.

But something's wrong.

All at once, the *Clearwater*, pushing at the stern, shuts down with engine trouble. The stern of the *Hanjin Los Angeles*, caught by the river's rushing current, slides away from the wharf. The mooring lines stretch taut, ready to snap. The dockhands and deckhands scatter in a hurry—if a line were to part, it could whipsaw and cut a man in half.

Champion speaks calmly into his walkie-talkie, ordering the *Barbara McAllister* around to the stern. From the port wingdeck, I watch the green and red decks of the tugboats: the *Clearwater* slack, the *Barbara McAllister* nosing in hard against the ship's hull, slowly pushing it back into the wharf. In five minutes, the *Hanjin Los Angeles* is safely docked.

For just that couple of endless minutes, 52,000 tons of floating steel swung out into the stream, no longer under control, till another tug came barging to the rescue. It was no different, in its way, than what happened to our canoe, the Green Monster, gripped by an unyielding current and the physics of gravity and momentum: The river had it. But when docking a gargantuan vessel like that, you can't just let the current take you, as we tried to do. The current would have broached the ship onto the Cape Fear Memorial Bridge, and the whole span would have come crashing down on the ship in a maze of twisted girders, crushed asphalt, and falling automobiles.

Here, when the river has you, it's trouble. I ride back to McAllister's on the tug, and everybody is relaxed now, the hard work finished for the night.

I won't ever look at the river in quite the same way again. Now it's also an industrial phenomenon, like a railroad or a great factory. I'm ambivalent about that fact, and over the years since, my ambivalence has only deepened. So much of what has been done to the river—and probably most of what will be done to it in the future—has been undertaken to make the channel more navigable for big ships. From the earliest attempts of the Cape Fear Navigation Company to push steamboats beyond Fayetteville, to the dredging projects of the late nineteenth and twentieth centuries, to the dams that have blocked the sturgeon and shad from their spawning grounds, shipping has changed the river.

It's thrilling to watch the big ships steam downriver and stand out to sea, more thrilling to actually stand on the bridge of one of the great monsters and watch the river unfolding before you like a museum diorama, vivid and almost miniaturized. And shipping means jobs and a jolt for the local economy.

But in the lower river, much of the wildness is gone.

~~~~~~~~

Riding our johnboat *Sea Whip*, David and I bash our way past the port and downriver. With the tide ebbing and the wind now blowing at a steady fifteen knots upriver, we're experiencing a wind-tunnel effect frequent on the river caused by the temperature differential between the air and the cooler water. And exaggerated by the terms of the old mariner's maxim, "Wind against tide makes for a rough ride." The chop turns the ride in the flat-bottomed aluminum *Sea Whip* into a trial, as if we're bouncing across slabs of concrete—*slam slam slam slam*.

Ahead of us a container ship is standing out to sea, just passing the bend at Southport before making the turn toward the fairway between Oak and Bald Head Islands.

The lower river became a shipbuilding center for World Wars I and II. In World War I, Carolina Shipbuilding turned out ten steel-hulled ships—too late for service in the war, but plenty early enough to be used in the next one, in which four were torpedoed, bombed, or sunk by mines. Liberty Shipbuilding turned out concrete ships, and two smaller yards built wooden hulls. Shipbuilding was a labor-intensive operation, and all the yards together employed about 4,000 workers.

In World War II, the North Carolina Shipbuilding Company established itself three miles south of the city and set about constructing 243 cargo ships for the war effort, including 126 Liberty Ships.

The Liberty Ships, sometimes called "ugly ducklings," were constructed in sections, then riveted together. Workers could build a ship from keel to launch in just twenty-five days. The 440-foot-long Liberty Ships, cheap and fast to build, turned out to be the workhorses of the war effort. They were designed to last only a few years, but many were still afloat and working half a century after the war. Twenty-three of those built at Wilmington were sunk by the enemy.

The first Liberty Ship, the *Zebulon B. Vance*, named for the heroic Civil War governor, slid down the ways on December 6, 1941, beginning a tradition of naming ships for prominent North Carolina figures.

When it was in full production in 1943, the yard employed 25,000 workers, nearly a third of them African American and 1,600 of them women—80 percent of all the manufacturing jobs in New Hanover County. Its payroll topped

Launching a freighter in World War I–era Wilmington
(courtesy of the Historical Society of the Lower Cape Fear)

$50 million. Along with the usual amenities, such as a cafeteria, the shipyard had its own police and fire departments, its own bus depot, and its own hospital with seven doctors and fourteen nurses. By comparison, the entire population of Wilmington at the outset of the Civil War amounted to only about 15,000.

The above are just numbers, but imagine the sheer energy of those workers, the way they transformed the city. Just as during the Civil War, Wilmington suddenly got a lot more disreputable—full of gamblers, prostitutes, grifters, and opportunists of all stripes—and a lot more fun.

These were not staid retirees, but young men and women in the prime of their working lives, earning salaries that just a few years before would have been unheard of. The city was also flooded with soldiers and sailors. We have become accustomed to speaking of the Greatest Generation as if they were all stoic patriots, but they also loved a good time. A few years ago, I attended a World War II veterans reunion at which the youngster in the room was seventy-four and the senior man ninety-two. They devoured thick rare steaks, washed them down with tumblers of bourbon and scotch, smoked unfiltered Lucky Strikes, and danced to Big Band music till long after midnight. The Greatest Generation knew how to have a good time.

The shipyard workers were actually carrying on a long shipbuilding tradition on the Cape Fear. Virtually from the time of its discovery, all kinds of ships were built on the banks of the Cape Fear: schooners, barques, sloops, and brigantines, along with smaller, nimble shoal-draft boats, including sharpies, shallops, and pinks. The first were simply built by individuals on their property, but later scores of shipbuilding operations were sited from Wilmington down to Bald Head: Wimble, Beery, Corbett, Wells, Hunter, and Telfair, to name just a few.

After World War II, the North Carolina State Ports Authority acquired the North Carolina Shipbuilding Company property in stages and located the new port of Wilmington at the site, at the terminus of Shipyard Boulevard.

~~~~~~~~~~

At last David Webster and I spy the three Loran towers that signal the entrance to Snow's Cut, the man-made canal connecting the Intracoastal Waterway and the Cape Fear River. We veer left away from Sunny Point Military Ocean Terminal, the largest ammunition port in the country. By train or truck, ammunition, bombs, shells, supplies, tanks, Humvees, trucks, and troops arrive at Sunny Point and are loaded aboard ships bound for service around the globe. It's the army's main deepwater port on the Atlantic Seaboard. Sunny Point once was the location of Howe's Point Plantation, the one sacked by Cornwallis in retaliation for the defeat at Moore's Creek.

The 82nd Airborne Division, stationed upriver at Fort Bragg, near Fayetteville (remember the Sound of Freedom?) relies on Sunny Point as its point of embarkation, should it be mobilized. Long before the first Gulf War was officially launched, we could watch the convoys of troops and the flatcar trains full of Abrams tanks and Bradley Fighting Vehicles snaking toward Sunny Point and know that something big was up.

Today as we pass, the terminal is guarded by a roving patrol boat that scoots out into the channel like a guard dog, checking us out and making sure we keep out of the restricted area.

Soon the lower Cape Fear, from Bald Head Island to the Isabel Holmes drawbridge, will be lined with fifty cameras tracking commercial ships and pleasure boats, a creepy $2 million surrender to Homeland Security. It won't be the same cruising the river knowing that you are under surveillance, every action monitored by some anonymous agent staring at a console. Out in nature, one should be able to be alone, or as alone as is possible among the other boaters.

From this point on, the river will be busy with the traffic of ships and other commercial vessels, fishing boats, recreational powerboats, and even some sailboats, inbound from the south, outbound for the northern summer sailing grounds of Maine and the Chesapeake Bay.

We follow the daymarks in a left curve into the cut past Carolina Beach State Park (also closed for renovations, including the boat ramp) and pass all the way through the cut, under the single bridge that connects Carolina Beach, Kure Beach, and Fort Fisher to the mainland. At last we take out at the boat ramp situated at the southeast corner of the cut, saltwater from the Intracoastal Waterway mingling with the tannin-colored freshwater of the river. It's been another nine-hour day, more than 125 miles, plus backtracking.

On our paddling trip, Ethan spoke of this running of the river as a "good survey" of it, and that's right. We could easily have lingered for days along any short stretch, camped beside any rapids and run them over and over, just as we paused at Lanier Falls. You could easily spend a leisurely week on the stretch between Buckhorn Dam and Raven Rock and a whole day at the rapids above Old Bluff Church, which we never did spot, despite four sets of eyes, three of them using very expensive binoculars.

You could poke into every little creek mouth, though not with the old Monster or even a kayak at low water. Only a few feet back from the bank, the creek is enveloped in deep shade, almost irresistible on a sunny day. Almost an invitation to go back in time to that childhood moment when animals could talk and magical things happened in the shadow-dappled woods.

Now as we step onto dry land, my eyes are full of the river and my memory is full of birdcalls, conversation, the damp concrete smell of the great locks, the fragile clutch of turtle eggs on a sandbar, herons and hawks, the face-burning wind in the lower river, the hard chop, the great ships churning out to sea, and the towering silence of drifting backward, the only boat for miles in any direction, the river carrying us inexorably exactly where we want to go only because it happens to be going there.

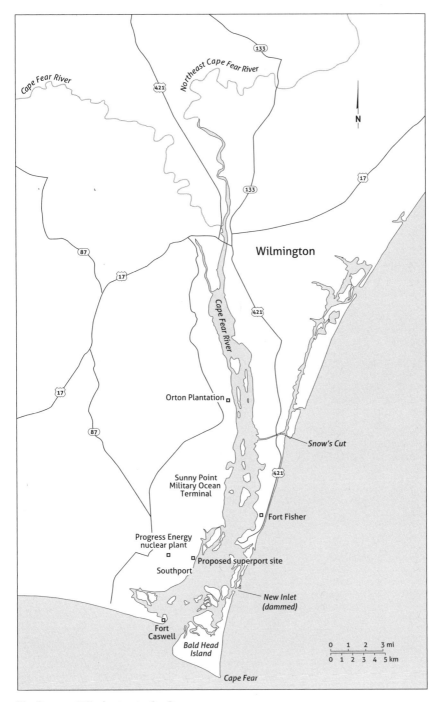

The Estuary: Wilmington to the Ocean

I've taken the journey downriver in stages, and the later stages include layovers, chances to explore the landscape and history surrounding the river and to reflect on what it's all adding up to. For me, the river presents a kind of palimpsest: All the events of history are overlaid onto the present. The colorful ship's captains and explorers and engineers and Indians and planters, the bold escaping slaves and hardscrabble farmers, the shad fishermen and steamboat pilots, the desperate victims of the coup of 1898, and the actors on James Sprunt's riverside lawn—all are still alive on the river, their faces as vivid and their voices as clear as if they were paddling along beside me.

It's a pleasure to fall into history that way, beyond the dead dry dates and names in textbooks, so that the people and their voices and deeds stay alive.

My own experience on the river feels that way, too: This one trip—beginning with a brace of canoes and continued in a johnboat and soon to finish in a larger V-hulled vessel—contains all the trips I've made over the years on the Cape Fear and its tributaries. So for me this trip is a journey of decades, start to finish.

Since arriving at Wilmington by johnboat, I've waited out a week of rainy days, sometimes starting clear but developing into violent drenching thunderstorms that have dumped more than five inches of rain on the lower basin. Even yesterday the south wind was so ferocious it drove me and my little Boston Whaler runabout back into harbor after only an hour of hard pounding on two-foot breaking swells inside the Intracoastal Waterway.

So here I am on a bright morning in early June at a quarter to nine at Creekside Marina on Bradley Creek, waiting for Frank Chapman, man of many talents and one of my favorite people to go exploring with. Frank did his graduate work on birds and is a consummate boat handler, diver, fisherman, and all-around waterman. Once on a collecting tour to Central America, he wound up in the middle of a revolution and had to talk his way onto a tramp steamer to escape home. We'll take Frank's boat, which is built for a pounding, south on the Intracoastal Waterway and back through Snow's Cut, then thread our way through the southbound channel back into the main river channel, reconnecting with our river journey.

We'll backtrack somewhat—the mile or so through Snow's Cut—but that's okay. We have about five miles to the cut. Once we're through, it's about fifteen more miles downriver to where river meets sea. "Snow's Cut" was the unofficial local name for this canal for at least a dozen years before it was officially so named. Major William A. Snow was Wilmington district engineer for the U.S. Army Corps of Engineers from 1926 to 1930. He was handsome, young—just thirty-two when he was promoted—and had a demonstrated talent for accomplishing big projects on time and under budget.

One of his secrets was simple: *People liked him.*

It's amazing how often we overlook the power of simple charm in accomplishing great things. Major Snow could get a roomful of people to agree on a course of action, then motivate others to carry it through. It was his job to extend the Intracoastal Waterway south from Beaufort to the Cape Fear River. Dredging the coastal portion was fairly routine, except that the dredgers ran into more stumps and roots than they had bargained for.

But getting across the solid ground of the lower peninsula at Seagate presented a special challenge. The tidal surge on the river was not in synch with the tidal flow coming directly into the Intracoastal Waterway through the various inlets, so water levels could vary dramatically and unpredictably. Many feared that connecting the river with the sea via a canal might create violent currents that would make such a cut dangerous to navigate, creating a kind of tidal vortex. A tidal lock might be required to ease the transition, and that would be expensive, on the order of half a million dollars.

Major Snow pushed on through anyway.

His machines moved 1.6 million cubic yards of mud, sand, tree stumps, and rock, and water soon flowed between Seagate and the Cape Fear River. Once the cut was finished, it turned out that it would be navigable without a tidal lock. The vortex theory was a myth. Any experienced boater will tell you, though, that at certain tides, a very strong flow will carry you through Snow's Cut. I've sailed through the cut engineless and actually found my boat heeling in a brisk wind, pointing east but sailing backward.

Major Snow finished his portion of the Intracoastal Waterway more than a million and half dollars under budget. The Wilmington Chamber of Commerce passed a resolution honoring him for his frugal efficiency and naming the cut after him.

So now, because of Snow's Cut, the Intracoastal Waterway is something of a tributary of the Cape Fear. The tidal flush flows back and forth, changing salinity in the river by some small fraction.

~~~~~~~~~~~~~

At Creekside Marina on the Intracoastal Waterway side of the Cut, the tide is now falling. I can see the oyster reefs appearing above the water, turning Bradley Creek, like so many tidal creeks in the area, into a slalom run.

Frank arrives, the boat is lowered into the water by a forklift, and we step aboard and are on our way at nine o'clock sharp. In about two hours, we will reach the point beyond Bald Head Island where the brown plume of the river, heavy with its cargo of muddy silt, at last gives way to the gray-blue of the open ocean. The tall sea buoy, rocking on the waves, will mark the end of the river and the beginning of the sea. More than 200 miles of river will lie behind us.

"We may have a rough ride today," Frank says, lifting his head to study the sky and feel the breeze on his cheeks.

Frank is a compact, muscular guy, with silver hair, friendly blue eyes, and a ready smile. He rarely gets flustered. He's the sort of guy you want on your side in a tight spot—resourceful and knows his way around boats, trucks, and airplanes. He can always find fish, and he seems to know every twist and turn on the river.

Our boat is a twenty-two-foot Carolina Skiff, appropriately named but, alas, made in Waycross, Georgia. It has a Suzuki 150 horsepower engine, enough power to make us fly like a rocketship when we want and to breast the seas in the estuary, if we get the blow we are expecting. The boat is immaculately white with a platform bow and a center-cockpit steering station under a bimini. It can do forty knots easy. But most of the time we are not blasting along. We head down to the cut leaving a straight foamy wake, slow considerably to enter the narrow passage, pass under the bridge that leads to Carolina Beach and Fort Fisher, and come to the forking channel at the end of the cut. We veer left, following a line of daymarks, and pretty soon we're back in the shipping channel, headed downriver.

Frank is grinning behind his sunglasses, enjoying the gorgeous day and the fast ride. "Not as rough out here as I thought," he says. "We couldn't have picked a better day."

Once through Snow's Cut and back on the river, we're in plantation country—have been, in fact, from Fayetteville on down. The Cape Fear basin didn't support large cotton plantations of the type found in the Mississippi Delta, though some cotton was raised on more inland plantations. Three kinds of

plantations found fertile ground along the river. The first was the rice plantation, with its telltale straight-line canals.

The second was a kind of generalized operation, with acres of soybeans,
peanuts, corn, cotton, indigo, and other crops, along with cattle, sheep, and
hogs. An assortment of artisan shops supported the enterprise: blacksmith,
brickmason, carpenter, cooper, cobbler, harness maker, wainwright, and so on.

The third was the turpentine plantation.

Before long, Orton Plantation comes up on our right, the great columned
house fronted by expansive gardens on the river, skirted with marshes full
of waving pea-green grass. Orton was the quintessential rice plantation. The
story of Orton is in many ways the founding myth of the lower Cape Fear. It
tracks the first permanent settlement on the lower river and the establishment of the plantation culture that would come to dominate the social and
political life of the region for hundreds of years. Some would claim it still
holds sway.

After various explorers from Verrazano onward had noted Cape Fear
(or Cape Fair) on their charts, a succession of expeditions ventured up the
river to scout it and decide whether it was suitable for colonizing. Captain
William Hilton sailed his ship *Adventurer* into the Cape Fear sometime in 1661
on behalf of a company in Barbados headed by John Vassall. The company was
intent on founding a settlement somewhere on the coast of "Virginia," which
in those days included the Carolinas. He brought back a glowing report.

Shortly thereafter, some enterprising New Englanders, exploring avenues
of trade with the Indians, showed up. But they did not stay. They turned loose
some cattle and left behind the note that Hilton found—and found so objec-
tionable—claiming that the Cape Fear was rotten country for settlement.

In 1663, Hilton returned on the *Adventurer*, anchored the ship in "The Cape
Fair Roads," and probed upriver seventy-five miles, presumably in smaller
auxiliary craft. His party sailed up the Cape Fear River, which they named the
Hilton; they considered the Northeast Cape Fear to be the main river.

Meantime, King Charles II was restored to the throne of England, and in
gratitude to his eight backers, he named them the Lords Proprietors of a huge
swath of land stretching from Virginia south through the Carolinas, which
was called variously the Province of Carolina, Carolana, or New Carolina.
Naturally, they in turn renamed the river the "Charles." There were lots of
preexisting claims and counterclaims. Somehow the Proprietors got together
with the Barbados company and the New Englanders and, on May 24, 1664,
jointly founded a settlement called Charles Town (what else?) at Town Creek,

about twenty miles upriver from the ocean. The population was large for such an enterprise: 600 colonists.

Colonel John Yeamans (sometimes written as Yeomans) was knighted by the king and named royal governor. He arrived at Charles Town in November of the following year to find out that the settlement was already in trouble. The colonists were at war with the local Indians. The Massachusetts men, it was claimed, had taken captive some Indian children and adults and sold them into slavery, igniting reprisal. The Indians killed all the settlers' cattle.

And Yeamans's arrival was fairly dramatic, as arrivals go.

His little fleet of a "Friggatt," a "Sloope," and a "Fly boate of about 150 tons" was scattered by fearsome storms. The frigate was dismasted, but somehow all three vessels rendezvoused off Cape Fear and anchored near present-day Southport. But a fresh gale blew them off their anchors, back out to sea onto the Frying Pan Shoals.

Once again the ships managed to claw their way into the estuary, but the "fly boate" had run out of luck: "But this proved but a short difference in their Fate," writes one of the colonists, Robert Sandford, "for returning with a favorable winde to a second viewe of the entrance into Charles River but destitute of all pilates save their own eyes (which the flattering gale that conducted them did alsoe delude by covering the rough visage of their objected dangers with a thicke vaile of smothe waters) they stranded their vessel on the mioddle ground of the harbours mouth where . . . the tide of flood beate her to peeces."

All aboard were rescued, but all the provisions and "Magazines of Armes powder and other Military furniture" were deep-sixed. Not a very auspicious entrance.

The colonists, it also turned out, were caught up in a permanent quarrel among themselves, especially over the issue of how they should be governed and who should select their leader.

Yeamans left for Barbados in the frigate to undertake repairs. He sent the sloop north to Virginia to bring back provisions to replace what was lost. But, Sandford reports, "the sloope in her comeing home from Virginia loaded with victuals being ready by reason of her extreme rottenness in her timbers to Sinke was driven on shoare by a storme in the night on Cape looke out."

The misadventure wasn't over.

Plan B was to hire a vessel under the command of Captain Stanyon, currently at anchor off the settlement. This they did. Sandford's enigmatic report tells us what came of that effort: "Captain Stanyon in returning from Barbados weakly maned and without any second to himself driven to and agen on the seas for many weekes by contrary winds and conquered with care, vexation and watching lost his reason, and after many wild extravagances leapt overboard in a frenzye, leaveing his small Company and vessel to the much more quiet and constant though but little knowing and prudent conduct of a child, who yet assisted a miraculous providence after many wanderings brought her safe to Charles River in Clarendon her desired port and haven."

The substance of the account is extraordinary, never mind the tortured syntax and whimsical spelling: The captain goes insane and after "many extravagances," whatever bizarre behavior that conjures, jumps overboard, leaving the ship's fate in the hands of a child—a boy? a young man? a precocious girl?

We will nevere Knowe.

All we can be sure of is how damnably hard it was to gain a toehold on the Cape Fear from the sea.

The colonists appealed to the Lords Proprietors for aid, but they were an ocean away, preoccupied with continental wars, and indifferent to the needs of the colony they controlled. Disheartened, the colonists packed it in. Yeamans led another party south to found a new colony, called (what else?) Charleston. This time the settlement stuck.

But the colonizers weren't done with the Cape Fear. Next time they wouldn't brave the sea but come upcountry by land from South Carolina.

They came from a section above Charleston called Goose Creek. The whole affair started with a massacre far removed from the Cape Fear.

In 1711, the Tuscarora Indians, Iroquoians allied with the Five Nations in New York, rose up against the colonists in the region between the Neuse and Pamlico Rivers. As Sprunt relates the affair through the words of Christopher Gale, an eyewitness to the uprising who testified before the South Carolina General Assembly, "One hundred and thirty persons were butchered in two hours under the most appalling circumstances. Women were laid upon the house floors and great stakes driven through their bodies; other atrocities were committed too frightful to think of, and more than eighty unbaptized infants were dashed to pieces against trees." One witness claimed that unborn babies were cut from their mothers' wombs and hung from the branches of trees.

There had been occasional conflicts before between colonists and other, less powerful tribes, such as the Coree and Nynee, who were overrun by the colonists, and the Bear River and Machapunga, who continued a campaign of harassment against the settlers and habitually retreated into the sanctuary of the wilderness. But there had been nothing on this scale, counting the number of dead or the degree of "fiendish cruelty" practiced in their killing. Sprunt writes, "The colony on the Neuse and Pamlico was blighted for years and well-nigh destroyed."

It's impossible to know at this late date just how accurate Gale's account of the massacre was. Certainly, ramping up stories of atrocity would be the surest way to enlist the help of the South Carolinians.

However exaggerated their violent actions, the Tuscarora appear to have had a genuine grievance: The settlers had adopted the practice of kidnapping and enslaving Tuscarora children, as well as treating the adults with disdain, subjecting them to all sorts of indignities. They had had enough. Their complaints got them nowhere, so they determined to take a hard stand against the settlers and reclaim their lands and their rights. But they did not reckon on the settlers in Neuse-Pamlico having enthusiastic allies who would welcome a chance to fight Indians.

Almost immediately, a punitive expedition was launched from South Carolina, with a war chest of £4,000 sterling, led by Colonel John Barnwell. His force numbered just 33 mounted whites and about 500 allied Indians, who themselves were promised slaves in return for their help. They burned some Tuscarora towns but ultimately were unsuccessful at putting down the uprising, as it was called.

A second, larger army under Colonel James Moore, namesake son of the governor, and including his younger brother, Captain Maurice Moore, was dispatched. Moore's army of more than 1,000 whites and Indians laid siege to the Tuscarora stronghold, a log and earth fort known as Neoherooka on Contentna Creek. It took them about three weeks to take the fort, and in the end they slaughtered some 300 Tuscarora and captured 100 or so more. The Tuscarora nation would never rise again in North Carolina.

Maurice Moore loved the Neuse-Pamlico country so much that he stayed there. When Indian trouble beckoned him back to South Carolina, he marched home through the Cape Fear region. He crossed the river at Sugar Loaf, now part of Carolina Beach State Park, and was charmed by the lands on the western side of the river. He made up his mind to return and settle there.

Return he did, after sorting out legal matters with the Lords Proprietors, a dozen years later in 1725, with yet another brother, "King" Roger Moore, founder of Orton Plantation. Roger Moore brought with him hundreds of slaves, so slavery on the Cape Fear arrived with its first permanent white settlers. Maurice Moore laid out a plan for a town to be called Brunswick on

Town Creek, where a bar across the river prevented easy access farther upstream. So prosperous was Brunswick Town that in a single year, forty-two vessels sailed outbound with cargoes from the river plantations.

Sprunt references the customshouse records from 1773 to 1776, during which time more than 300 vessels called at Brunswick Town, including the brigs *Wilmington* and *Orton* and the schooner *Rake's Delight*, bearing outbound cargoes of "lumber, tar, indigo, rice, corn, wheat, and tobacco." Inbound cargoes included "20 negroes, 50 hogsheads of rum, 1,000 bags of salt, etc." The full-rigged ship *Ulysses* delivered "furniture, leather, saddles, earthenware, shoes, linen, hats, gunpowder, silks, glass, iron, lead, and 'shott,' also port wine, rugs, toys, and household articles."

Everything to make a civilization—including more slaves.

A visitor to Brunswick Town in 1734 described his visit to Orton: "Mr. Roger Moore hearing we were come, was so kind as to send fresh horses for us to come up to his house, which we did, and were kindly received by him; he being the chief gentleman in all Cape Fear. His house is built of brick and exceedingly pleasantly situated about two miles from the town, and about half a mile from the river; though there is a creek comes close up to the door, between two beautiful meadows, about three miles length."

He does not mention that the brick walls were three and a half feet thick, with loopholes through which to fire muskets, so that the house could serve as a fort as well as a residence.

They proceeded upriver from there, past the Black River, to another of Roger Moore's plantations, called Blue Banks, "where he is a-going to build another very large brick house." Just above Roan Island, "this bluff is at least a hundred feet high, and has a beautiful prospect over a fine large meadow, on the opposite side of the river." That prospect, in present-day Pender County, is wetlands, so that the ecosystems on either side of the river are drastically different: the one very much a Piedmont habitat, the other lowland swamp.

King Roger Moore is usually credited with—or blamed for—wiping out the Cape Fear Indians in 1725, the same year he built the original manor house at Orton. It is said he and his cohort attacked the Indian town at Sugar Loaf. He was reportedly out to punish the tribe for raiding Orton Plantation and burning his original house.

In any case, as early as 1715, of the 1,000 or so Cape Fear Indians thought to reside in the lower reaches when the first Europeans arrived, just 206 remained: 76 men, the rest women and children, distributed among five villages. By 1800, they had disappeared altogether, their origin, culture, and fate all part of a mystery that haunts the Cape Fear still. All they left behind are a few

The Orton house, a paragon of antebellum architecture (author photo)

stories and some mounds containing potsherds, oyster shells, and the remains of baskets.

Orton prospered, as did dozens of other plantations along the river such as Lilliput, Clarendon, The Forks, Gander Hall, and Spring Garden—later Grovely. Orton survived a raid by troops under Lord Charles Cornwallis during the American Revolution. Orton passed to new owner Dr. Frederick Hill, who added the four signature columns at the front and raised a second story in 1840.

During the Civil War, the Federals occupied the grounds and used the house as a hospital. James Sprunt acquired it in 1910 as a gift for his wife Luola. In 1915 he erected a Greek Revival chapel for her on the grounds. She died of scarlet fever scarcely a year later, and he named the chapel in her honor. It is still known as the Luola Chapel at Orton. Sprunt also enlarged the house with two spacious wings, so that through an evolution of owners, a survival of Indian wars, the Revolution, and the Civil War, Orton finally became the paragon of classical southern architecture.

In fact it was this distinctive facade, at once elegant and definitive of an era and a way of life, that captured the eye of a location scout for filmmaker Dino De Laurentiis. He and his associate, Frank Capra Jr., chose the house for the location of *Firestarter*, and shooting the movie on the river inspired De Laurentiis to build a film studio in Wilmington—now EUE/Screen Gems.

Orton was chiefly a rice plantation, and long after the rice culture died out

The classic interior of the Luola Chapel at Orton, built by James Sprunt
for his wife, who died a year after it was built (author photo)

in the Carolinas, Orton remained in the Sprunt family. In 2011, a descendant
of Roger Moore, Louis Moore Bacon, purchased the house and 8,000 acres of
the original holding and closed it to public view. His stated plan is to restore
the property to what it was like in its heyday—complete with restoring the
rice canals and replanting the longleaf pine forest.

Grovely, owned by Dr. John D. Bellamy from antebellum days through
Reconstruction, exemplified the second type, or generalized plantation. It
spread over 10,000 acres. Bellamy acquired it after coming up from South
Carolina with 500 slaves he had inherited upon the death of his father, a
neighbor of Francis Marion—the Swamp Fox of Revolutionary War fame—
on Winyah Bay.

At Grovely in its heyday, 2,400 acres were under cultivation by 50 mule
teams; the corrals and meadows held 1,500 head of cattle and sheep, and each
year 1,500 hogs were slaughtered. Additionally, Bellamy's 1,000 slaves (he had
acquired an additional 500) included skilled blacksmiths, coopers, wood-
workers, butchers, livestock handlers, and other specialists. The slaves lived in
cabins on "the line." Field hands were allotted four shirts, four pairs of pants,
and one or two pairs of shoes per year. Every few years, each slave received a
new blanket and hat.

Of course, the clothes were not typically store-bought but made by other

The graves of "King" Roger Moore and his family at Orton (author photo)

slaves right there on the plantation from fabric spun by slaves from cotton planted and harvested by slaves. So it's hard to credit any generosity or even fairness to this grudging allotment. The slaves were prisoners, after all. They received no pay for their work. Even their earnings from hiring out to other plantations were paid to their owners. Only the occasional meager pay earned during off-hours, if the owner allowed it, went into their own pockets.

Each week, flatboats and wagons carried the bounty of Grovely into Wilmington, where Bellamy kept his large household: his wife, Elizabeth; the younger of their nine children, including William, Ellen, Belle, John Jr., George, and Chesley; and as many as nine household slaves to cook, clean, and tend the children. Son Marsden was already grown. Bellamy also kept a store and invested in railroads, among many varied business interests.

Some of the bounty fed the house and its numerous guests. Some of it became inventory in Bellamy's store. The rest was shipped downriver or hauled out by railroad.

Bellamy also owned the third kind of plantation, a turpentine operation called Grist, near present-day Chadbourne.

The economy of the lower Cape Fear had been based on naval stores all through colonial times. "Naval stores" is just an exotic way of referring to rosin, pitch, and turpentine. They are, in varying states of distillation and refining, products of the longleaf pine indigenous to the area. By the outbreak of the Civil War, about 4,000 hands, mostly slaves, were engaged in harvesting about $5 million worth of naval stores in North Carolina, and just about all of that came from the lower Cape Fear basin.

The longleaf pine (*Pinus palustris* Mill.) is the signature tree of the coastal river plain, and a remarkable piece of natural engineering it is. Like most things along the Cape Fear, it has gone by many names: swamp pine, pitch pine, yellow pine, longstraw pine, or heart pine, for the quality of its wood. It germinates quickly, within a week of hitting the ground, as a clump of grassy needles, and it may take three to seven years to become a sapling. It grows slowly. It can take up to 150 years to achieve its full size, then live another 150 years fully mature with a taproot reaching down twelve feet. To survive, it requires frequent fires to destroy the competing slash pine and other species that grow up fast around its base—and to clear the dense litter so that its seeds can fall directly onto soil.

As you would expect, the rough, scaly, red-brown bark of the longleaf pine is thick and highly resistant to fire. It produces a cone as large as ten inches long but regenerates only about once every four or five years.

In early colonial days, tar was extracted from split deadfall pine logs, so-called lightwood, by heating the logs in an earthen kiln, a pyramid of wood covered by earth and clay with a smoke hole in the top. The logs heated and the tar dripped into a sink at the bottom of the kiln, then ran out in a gutter to be collected by dippers and poured into barrels. A typical kiln, twenty or more feet in diameter, could burn for a week and produce more than 100 barrels of tar.

Tar could then be concentrated into pitch by being fired in a hole or boiled in a pitch kettle.

Later, a method was devised for harvesting gum from live trees. The basic raw product of the longleaf pine was pine gum, drawn from a living tree in a manner analogous to the way sugar tappers in New England harvest the sap from maple trees every spring (when it is warm enough to run) and refine it into syrup. Except that in the case of the longleaf pine, it was not sap but gum that was drawn out of the tree.

The gum was distilled into turpentine and rosin. Turpentine had wide and varied usage as an ingredient in certain patent medicines, ointments, laxatives, waterproofing, lamp oil, solvents, paint and paint thinner, varnish, adhesives, even shoe polish, and it was indispensable in fashioning water purification systems.

Rosin, collected as a by-product of distillation, was used in paper products,

A turpentine wharf in Wilmington's heyday as an exporter of naval stores (courtesy of the Historical Society of the Lower Cape Fear)

axle grease, enamels, roofing materials, ink, soap, and of course, waxing fiddle bows.

To collect gum, workers cut a "box" into the tree in winter, when it was dormant. The cut was made about eighteen inches up from the base of the tree with a special long-headed boxing axe. Then as the sap flowed in spring, they "hacked" the tree diagonally down toward the center of the box, causing the gum to run from the cuts and collect in the box.

The cut on a properly boxed tree resembled an inverted military chevron, pointing downward. Each season, the slashes were cut higher. When they were above a man's head, the streaking was continued with a long-bladed hack called a puller. Carefully managed by an experienced crew, a tree could continue to yield gum for two generations—some claim as long as half a century.

The gum was collected in barrels and consolidated, and then it could be distilled over hot fires into spirits of turpentine.

The unluckiest slaves (presuming there were any "lucky" ones)—ironically among the most skilled and valued at up to $3,000 apiece—were assigned to remote camps in the pine forests, where they boxed longleaf pine trees. They worked from November through March, boxing 80 to 500 trees apiece per week, and in the off-season they built barrels and tools, surveyed new stands of pine, and protected the cut trees from fire and other damage.

It was hazardous work.

The fumes were noxious and toxic in a whole host of ways. If the slaves were not provided with enough clean drinking water—in a region where summer temperatures routinely hovered in the high nineties with almost 100 percent humidity—the workers would drink from rainwater collected in the boxes. That water was, of course, contaminated by the toxic gum.

Many camps were equipped with a copper still with which to refine turpentine and its by-product, rosin, and breathing the fumes of the distilling process caused all sorts of pulmonary problems.

Slaves who worked in the naval stores operations suffered from asthma, dizziness, "griping" of the bowels, "dead" limbs, mental impairment, skin rashes, and even blindness from the fumes, in addition to more prosaic dangers such as snakebite, heatstroke, malaria, drowning in bogs, tick fever, and being burned in the makeshift kilns. The men lived in crude shacks or lean-tos without women or families for months or years at a time. The nature of the activity required that it be performed far from settlements, where the pine forests rose thickest.

Naval stores played a huge part in both commerce and war. Tar was essential to the British—and later the American—navy. In the days of sailing ships, all the standing rigging, the ropes and cables that held up spars and masts, had to be tarred to avoid rotting in the weather.

Two barrels of raw tar could be refined into one barrel of pitch, a higher-grade product with a greater viscosity. So pitch was used to seal the seams of wooden planking and for just about any other application where waterproofing was desired. A wooden navy needed a lot of tar and pitch. The industry got jump-started in the Carolinas and Virginia during the early 1700s, when an assortment of European wars, alliances, and monopolies drove up the price and reduced the availability of tar on the world market. Great Britain owed its prestige and security to its dominant navy, and so through a system of incentives it encouraged Americans to produce tar. England had no pine forests to tap.

Altogether, at the time of the Civil War, about fifty plantations could be found along the Cape Fear, providing a way of life that was prosperous, even profligate, for the white owners and their families, and an existence that varied between drudgery and hell on earth for the black slaves who actually performed the work and made the wealth on which the entire coastal economy depended.

It's often argued by partisans of the Lost Cause that the Civil War was not about slavery but tariffs, or that Lincoln could have bought off the Confederacy and stamped out the rebellion by fairly compensating the southern slave-owners for their confiscated slaves, thus effectively ending slavery.

And in fact, late in the war, when it was clear that Lee could no longer sustain his army in the field and the Confederacy was doomed, a commission brought that very proposal to Lincoln: call a cease-fire and negotiate compensation for the slave-owners, and slavery would be ended. But by then Lincoln had no need to negotiate. The war would end in a matter of months—that much was certain—and he was in no mood to compensate the class that had fomented the war. For him it had become a moral question, and an armistice would not do. He craved the vindication of absolute victory.

In any case, the argument misses the point. The slave economy of the South—including the plantations along the Cape Fear—was fundamentally at odds with the wage-earner economy of the North. It was as if the two sections inhabited different moral and economic universes. One or the other would finally have to give.

Since the North had all the factories to make cannon and rifles, could field an army of almost unlimited size due to the steady influx of Irish and German immigrants (not to mention freed black slaves), and enjoyed equally unlimited commerce with the outside world, protected by a forceful navy, any sane person could have predicted the outcome. Many did.

As the Flat River Guards marched out of Durham County to the war, they stopped at Walnut Hall, home of William Preston Mangum, a young enlistee, so he could bid farewell to his family. His father, a former U.S. senator now crippled by a stroke, admonished him and his comrades, "Boys, God bless you every one, but you can't succeed. Their resources are too great for you." He had lived in Washington and knew the might of the United States Army.

Young Willie Mangum survived for another month, until mortally wounded at the First Battle of Manassas. A pocket Bible stopped the bullet, so he lingered for two weeks until succumbing to infection. Soon after old Senator Mangum learned of his son's death, he himself fell down dead. Senator Mangum's was a warning sounded many times along the Cape Fear by those who were not part of the plantation class.

True, you could buy all the slaves out of their bondage, but the value of a slave abided not simply in his or her worth as an item of property for sale on the open market, valued from a few hundred to several thousand dollars. The slave was a *net generator of wealth* for the owner. In the course of a lifetime of labor, he or she would create value many times greater than mere purchase value, with minimal upkeep. Remember, the slaves not only made wealth for the master, but they also had to grow, harvest, slaughter, and prepare their own food; build, repair, and clean their own quarters; make their own tools and clothes; care for their own children; and so on.

The 4 million slaves—all but about 10,000 in the states of the Confederacy—collectively constituted the greatest single economic asset in the United States, larger by far than land or railroads or manufacturing: more than $1 billion—today that would be more than $26 billion.

Slaves were traded like livestock and were denied their essential human dignity, but their skills and practical training often surpassed those of their "masters." They were carpenters, blacksmiths, wainwrights, wheelwrights, coopers, cobblers, plasterers, saddle makers, seamstresses, and brickmasons. They were also managers, lockmasters on the rice plantations, river pilots, trail guides, experts at boxing longleaf pine trees, distillers, drivers, couriers, bodyguards, preachers, nurses, cooks, child care specialists, hunters, and fishermen, and they were accustomed to hard labor in all seasons.

Thus, families like the Bellamys could enjoy a life of almost obscene luxury without actually working. Bellamy inherited half a thousand slaves and a good deal of wealth from his father and so was born with the silver spoon planted firmly in his mouth.

On the eve of the Civil War, Dr. Bellamy built the grandest home in Wilmington on Market Street, only a few blocks up from the river and the open-air slave market: a Greek Revival style mansion of twenty-two rooms in four stories, capped by a belvedere or lookout room at the very top. The house featured indoor plumbing and two capacious formal parlors hung with oil paintings done by his daughter Belle, and it was ornately decorated with hand-carved moldings and Persian carpets. White marble fireplace mantels dominated the rooms. Outside, fourteen massive Corinthian pillars lined three sides of the white house. Only the rear, opening onto the four-room slave quarters and the carriage house, lacked them.

The slave quarters, by contrast, were two-story board-and-batten cabins, four small rooms adjoining the stables, with an outhouse attached. The carpentry was rudimentary—plain and practical. No time or money was wasted on amenities. The slave quarters were cold in winter and sweltering in summer. And from the doorway of the slave cabin, the view opened onto the grand porch at the back of the house, the high windows, and the towering facade of the mansion, which during certain hours of the summer months would literally block out the sun.

Bellamy was fond of boasting that he had paid for the entire cost of the house with one year's profits from Grist, his turpentine operation. That cost included the $4,500 price of the lot (more than $120,000 in today's currency) and the services of skilled masons and carpenters, slaves, whom he hired from Nicholas Nixon, who owned a peanut plantation up at Porter's Neck but kept a large crew of enslaved artisans in the city.

One of them, William B. Gould, was a twenty-four-year-old master brick-mason and plasterer. He signed his name in the plaster of the front parlor in an elaborate cursive hand. He was a mysterious character in certain ways: He had learned to read and write—not just English but also French and a smat-tering of Spanish—during a time when it was very much against the law to educate a slave. Practically speaking, there were lots of advantages to having a slave who could read a blueprint, keep accounts, or read sailing directions, so the law may have been more honored in the breach.

Gould bided his time. On the night of September 21, 1862, he and seven other slave companions stole aboard a small boat at the foot of Orange Street and rowed more than twenty miles down the Cape Fear River, aided by a steady sheltering rain. Fourteen other escaping slaves manned two additional boats.

The current swept them downriver past the moored blockade-runners; past the magisterial sprawl of Orton Plantation and Town Creek, where Bel-lamy's plantation Grovely lay; past the guns of Fort Anderson and Fort John-ston; and past the sweeping bend at Smithville, Fort Fisher looming to the left on Confederate point and Fort Caswell, an old masonry fortress, on the right. The boat had a sail, but the men were afraid to raise it and be spotted by patrols or sentries.

It took them all night to make the passage.

At last, long past sunrise, out beyond Smith's Island (now Bald Head Island), the open sea beckoned. They hoisted the sail and scudded along in the fresh morning breeze. Before long they were spied by the USS *Cambridge*, one of the blockading Union squadron, and the event was recorded in its log: "Saw a sail S.W.S. and signaled same to other vessels. Stood for strange sail and at 10:30 picked up a boat with 8 contrabands from Wilmington, NC."

Almost at the very hour that seamen were taking Gould and his compan-ions aboard the *Cambridge*, President Abraham Lincoln was summoning his cabinet to brief them on a restatement of the Union war aims, which he called the Emancipation Proclamation.

Gould was not finished with his adventure. He enlisted in the Union navy and for the duration of the war chased down blockade-runners, to sink them or run them aground. Gould and his companions were just the vanguard of an army—literally—of slaves from the Cape Fear basin who ran away to freedom and enlisted in the fight to bring it home to the families and friends they left behind. Gould was one of the few to leave behind a memoir of his adventure from bondage to freedom.

But it wasn't just the slaveholding families who prospered by the slave economy on the Cape Fear. The goods shipped out of the waterfront at Wilmington were, in the main, the fruits of slave labor. They provided employment for storekeepers, stevedores, sailors, port inspectors, teamsters, tradesmen, guards, pilots, managers, accountants, lawyers, railroad crews, and so on.

So even if you never owned a slave in your life—and most white people of the era did not—if you lived in the Cape Fear basin before the Civil War, your life was bound up in a slave economy that essentially built the city and drove commerce.

If you were white, your attitudes were formed in the culture of white supremacy: Whites were in charge because, racially, they were superior and deserved to be. God had ordained it so—if you had any doubt, just consult any Protestant preacher. (Catholics were more ambivalent, though they, too, prospered, and of course Quakers were mostly downright heretical on the subject.)

If you were black, you were a permanent suspect, even if you had been born free or legally freed through manumission. At any moment, you might have that freedom revoked under the flimsiest of pretenses, and under the law you were still a second-class citizen in terms of your rights to due process, your public privileges, and your standing among whites. You could not own a firearm, testify in court, or sit on a jury.

If you were not born free, you were, under the law, just three-fifths of a human being. You could be subjected routinely to arbitrary and sadistic violence for the most trivial offense: beating, confinement, whipping, branding, even dismemberment. You could legally be killed without consequence. Your children, husband, wife, or other family could be taken from you and sold to another part of the country without any warning, and you would be powerless to prevent it.

It's not hard to see how such a corrosive public ethic could infest a population as virulently as yellow fever, corrupting it beyond any remedy short of bloody war. Something fundamental was being fought over: the soul of a nation. This was the legacy that would come back to haunt Wilmington and the river country again and again.

The river played its role in creating a plantation culture that was, finally, a doomed house of cards.

Frank Chapman steers us past the green swaths of plantations on the western shore, now peopled only by the ghosts of the slaves and their masters, speeding us downriver in his Carolina Skiff. Behind us we raise a rooster-tail wake, and ahead of us the river opens wide and sun-dazzled, flecked with tiny boats in the distance. For the time being, I leave us frozen in place, the river basin spreading out in a luminous panorama from water to sky, so I can let my imagination wander afield on that western shore before finding the sea.

11

I want to visit one of the plantations from the river, navigating the watery avenues that served as thoroughfares of trade back in their heyday. So on an overcast day in early July, with thunder rattling fitfully to the north but no rain in the offing, we put out from Wilmington Marine Center just south of the port and chug across the windy river, splashed by swells, toward Mallory Creek on the west bank, the gateway to the old Clarendon Plantation.

We're embarked on one of the side excursions I promised myself while running the whole river to the sea, a chance to explore another piece of it with a reliable guide.

My pilot and companion is Kemp Burdette, the thirty-six-year-old Cape Fear river keeper. He's been on the job a little less than a year. Formerly he served as executive director of Cape Fear River Watch, the nonprofit organization that acts as steward of the river, supporting the work of the river keeper. He hoped that the change of jobs would allow him to be outdoors on the river every day, but in reality he still spends a lot of days at the computer, researching and emailing, or on the phone, scaring up support, advocating, and persuading people to pitch in—in his quiet, determined way, urging people to care.

Kemp is the river's official champion. People call him with tips: Something doesn't look right. Somebody's doing something he shouldn't. There's a fish kill, or an algal bloom, or somebody dumping trash. He's part investigator, part advocate, part educator, and all riverman.

He is tall, deeply tanned, fit, and youthful-looking, with short-cropped dark hair graying slightly at the temples. He grew up on the water in a whole variety of ways. He lived in Wilmington and played on the river, fishing, boating, just messing around. His parents bought a place up near Moore's Creek on the Black River, as lovely a stretch of riverine real estate as you can find in this part of the world, so the Black River was also his playground.

There are, officially, 190 water keepers around the world. He tells me, "I was just at a conference where I met the river keeper of the Upper Tigris, in the Kurdish section of Iraq.

Kemp Burdette,
Cape Fear river keeper
(author photo)

And his range of problems makes my range of problems look kind of tame sometimes, you know?"

You can't just decide to be a river keeper. You have to be sponsored by a grassroots nonprofit organization that pays you a full-time salary and provides the resources for you to do your job. This is to make sure that the river keeper is actually representing the local people who live on a river, and to make sure he or she can dedicate full attention to the task. It's not a part-time job.

Among other things, it requires that the river keeper know the river intimately, and that means getting out on it in all weathers, in all seasons. Usually we would be aboard the twenty-six-foot donated patrol boat, but it has been hauled for maintenance.

Kemp's father, Wilkes, built the boat we're on—or rather, he took an old long-line fishing dinghy and added a cabin and decks, creating a sturdy, weatherproof craft that resembles a miniature tugboat and takes the slapping waves with aplomb and keels deep into the lively current. Wilkes Burdette has built many boats over the years. His idea of adventure in the old days, Kemp tells me, was to buy an old lifeboat at salvage across the river and then turn it into a cabin cruiser. He and Kemp's mother would cruise the Intracoastal Waterway, waiting tables or working as short-order cooks along the way to pay their passage. Kemp says, "I guess it was their version of the VW microbus."

Kemp himself never got far from the river. During college at UNC Wilmington, he lived on an old houseboat on the west bank of the Cape Fear, rent-free in exchange for being the de facto night watchman for the boatyard there. The boat he was living on had been sunk and salvaged, an early exercise in repurposing.

Seated in the cozy wheelhouse, Kemp gives me a play-by-play of what we're seeing on the river. He speaks with a slight drawl, in a deliberate and thoughtful manner that carries an air of quiet authority. He points out two cargo ships docked just upriver at the port, spots a white ibis, an osprey, and a mob of pelicans working the shallow bay on the west side, near the rice canals. He observes, "The pelicans are putting on a show for us."

We can see fish jumping in small hordes, so it's no wonder the pelicans are having a field day. They spiral around above the water, waiting for a fish to show, then they dive vertically, slamming hard into the water. It always seems as if the pelican will be dashed into unconsciousness. But then it splashes free of the water, fish wriggling in its beak-pouch, and flaps into the sky, grabbing air with its huge laboring wings.

The whole enterprise seems insane, suicidal, yet it works beautifully. I never tire of watching a crazy pelican dive for fish.

The brown pelican was practically extinguished from the river by the 1970s; the culprit was the pesticide DDT: **d**ichloro**d**iphenyl**t**richloroethane. A Swiss chemist named Paul Hermann Müller won the Nobel Prize for discovering DDT. It was used widely during World War II in the Pacific theatre, and after the war was touted as a miracle pesticide: the surefire way to wipe out mosquitoes, which are vectors of malaria, dengue fever, and other horrible tropical fevers. DDT was tasteless, odorless, and seemingly harmless to humans. So benign was it considered to be that, at press conferences, scientists advocating its use — to demonstrate that the public had nothing to fear — would actually spoon it into their own mouths.

As usual, what we knew for sure turned out to be dead wrong.

It turns out DDT accumulates in the bodies of the predators who eat the mosquitoes that DDT was designed to eradicate, such as fish and birds — a process called "biological magnification." And of course, if we eat the fish or birds, it accumulates in us. It takes as much as fifteen years to break down. Humans who eat fish laced with DDT can experience reproductive failure and are more prone to liver cancer, among other maladies.

In the wild, DDT fatally weakened the shells of birds who ate DDT-sprayed insects, and all of a sudden birds like the bald eagle and brown pelican were staring down the barrel of extinction. DDT was banned in 1972, but by then there was just one lonely colony of brown pelicans left in North Carolina, about 100 nesting pairs on Ocracoke Island, not even part of the mainland.

But along came a university professor named James F. Parnell, who, in concert with a colleague named Robert Soots, discovered that birds were colonizing dredge-spoil islands in the river. This was back in the 1960s, when there was not yet such a thing as environmentalism, and isolated spoil islands turned out to be one of the few natural refuges for birds like the pelican, which builds its grassy nests on the ground. Parnell, Soots, and their students set out to protect and nurture the colonies, patiently enlisting various state and federal agencies and nonprofit groups to ensure their survival.

It was relentless, unglamorous, and at times frustrating work.

But it paid off. Nowadays, the pelicans number more than 4,000 breeding pairs.

Along with cattle egrets, great egrets, gull-billed terns, night herons, white ibis, American oystercatchers, and other waterbirds, they nest on an archipelago of seven man-made spoil islands in the lower Cape Fear, under the stewardship of the North Carolina Wildlife Resources Commission and the Audubon Society, in close cooperation with the U.S. Army Corps of Engineers and other state and federal agencies. Parnell's honorable legacy is a network of waterbird conservation lands across the state known as the Dr. James F. Parnell Colonial Waterbird Sanctuary System.

I love that story of the salvation of the brown pelican, because it reminds me that environmentalism can be an active, practical ethic of solving problems for the good of everybody. In this story, nobody loses. Which makes perfect sense to me. We live here—so why not take care of this river place the way we take care of our house and yard? For tens of thousands of our fellow creatures, it is their home and yard.

Parnell is no egghead, no rabid political radical. He's just an alert man of science who loves birds, loves being outdoors for any good reason, saw a place where he could make a difference, and quietly set about changing the world. And he's a nice guy, an inspiration to a generation of students. My paddling companion, David Webster, counts Parnell as a mentor and friend. They worked together for decades. David says, "Jim Parnell is a true southern gentleman. He does not curse or drink. He is always gracious and kind. He will do anything for anybody."

The pelican, unfortunately, wasn't the only bird in trouble. The Carolina parakeet had already been hunted to extinction. Other river birds were getting wiped out for different reasons.

The great egret, a magnificent white shorebird that stands more than three feet high, was hunted almost to oblivion in the nineteenth century to supply women's hatmakers with its fine gossamer plumes. By the early 1900s, just one nesting colony remained in the entire state, on Orton plantation, in a refuge guarded by one of North Carolina's few professional game wardens.

Being a game warden wasn't about hanging out in the woods and checking hunting licenses. In those days it could be a dicey occupation. The very first game warden hired by the Audubon Society, then just a loose-knit group of wildlife advocates, patrolled Florida's Pelican Island National Wildlife Refuge. His name was Guy Bradley, and we remember him so vividly because in 1905, after just three years on the job, he was murdered by poachers.

Audubon was a prime mover in protesting the mass slaughter of waterbirds for their plumage. In 1901, the society managed to persuade Congress to outlaw the practice. By 1915, it had achieved a law placing all migratory birds under federal protection.

The image of the great egret in flight, known in those days as the American egret, which started all the fuss and gave Audubon its mission, is still emblazoned on the seal of the Audubon Society.

Now Audubon is tackling a new crisis on the lower Cape Fear: The white ibis are deserting their favorite nesting ground, Battery Island, in ever-increasing numbers, and nobody knows exactly why. I take the question to Andy wood, education director for Audubon North Carolina. Andy is tall and sandy-haired with a graying beard. He has an open, easygoing manner that belies a passion for, as he puts it, "anything with feathers."

Is there any truth to the rumor that the storied ibis are leaving Battery Island? He ponders for a moment. "There is, but it's a complicated truth," he says. He has a patient, clear way of explaining the wild natural world to people like me. He's a born teacher. "For the past few years when the ibis showed up in the spring, there has been a pair of great horned owls nesting on the island. And when the scout ibis visit the island, it could be they say, damn! They're a predator! Maybe we don't want to hang out here."

There may be more to it. The white mulberry, *Morus alba*, a northern Chinese native, has taken root on the island in a big way. In Asia, the white mulberry is a perfect habitat for silkworms. On Battery Island, it's an ecological wrecking ball. Andy tells me, "The white mulberry overtops the other trees, yaupon holly and red cedar, shades them out, basically tries to take over the whole habitat." Some ibis try to nest in mulberry trees, but they're not an ideal homesite. "The white mulberry has long, spindly, very springy branches, and when birds settle on them it's like a trampoline."

So the ibis are moving upstream to another dredge-spoil island. There, the yaupons and red cedar are not well established, so the birds nest on the ground in the grasses, among pelicans and wading birds such as blue herons and egrets. This is a problem because the low-lying island and the ground nests can get overwashed in big storms and flooded out, the nests destroyed.

There's one other possible culprit: saltwater intrusion. The nestlings cannot digest salt, so the parent ibis have to fly to a freshwater food source—marshes, swamps, ponds—and return with dragonfly larvae, crayfish, and other salt-free food. The ibis will routinely fly twenty or thirty miles a day to feed their young. As the river has been dredged ever deeper, the saltwater intrudes not just farther upriver but also farther into the boundary marshes and freshwater swamps, so that the ibis's food source has gradually retreated farther from their island.

Like most phenomena in nature, their exodus is probably the result of a complex interplay of factors—predators, changing habitat, saltwater intrusion—hard to parse, harder to solve.

In the meantime, Andy and his colleagues have received donations of yaupon holly and red cedar from the Cape Fear Garden Club and are planting them on Battery Island while doing their best to dig out the white mulberry. But the mulberry is hardy and stubborn and hangs on tenaciously. Very likely, it's not going anywhere.

In the 1600s, when the first explorers made their way cautiously up the river, the depth of the river at the ocean bar was probably not more than ten feet or so at low tide. The natural channel of the river deepened to fifteen to twenty feet until it shallowed at another bar off Town Creek—one reason Town Creek presented a natural choice for settlement. In those days, the river flowed to the sea virtually completely fresh. The incoming tidal wash carried saltwater into the bay at present-day Southport, but not much farther, and the strong current flushed the river clean of salt twice a day.

Now the saltwater carries all the way to Lock and Dam #1 on the mainstem—thirty-four miles above Wilmington harbor—and beyond Castle Hayne on the Northeast Branch.

"Any additional saltwater intrusion in the river will have an immediate effect on hardwood bottomland swamps," Andy says. Essentially, it will kill the whole habitat. This would drive away the prothonotary warbler, for instance, that we noted in such abundance on the upper river.

Saltwater intrusion has insidious effects and has profoundly changed the river—and the creatures who live there. In addition to "glamorous metafauna"—that is, the picturesque, warm-blooded large creatures—saltwater intrusion has already killed off the magnificent ramshorn snail (*Planorbella*

*Magnifica*), the other object of Andy Wood's naturalist passion. It's one of the largest snails in North America, the diameter of a quarter, shaped exactly like a ram's horn, red-brown marled with blue.

Since 1992, Andy has been primary investigator of a worldwide effort to study and devise a species survival plan for the magnificent ramshorn snail and its cousin, the Greenfield ramshorn snail—both likely now extinct in the wild in the Cape Fear basin and surviving only in Andy Wood's jealously guarded tanks. "Which is all well and good," he says with some frustration, "but what would we say if there were a thousand Bengal tigers left, but all of them were in zoos and none of them was in the wild? What good is that?"

So here on the lower river I'm thinking about ibis and saltwater intrusion and all the creatures who call this river home as river keeper Kemp Burdette ferries us across the wind-chop toward the western shore. As we approach the west bank, Kemp points out the bleached upright bones of a stand of tall but quite dead cypress trees. "Most of the cypress in this whole area, especially as we get back in there, they're all dying because of the saltwater intrusion," he says. "The cedars are a little more tolerant of saltwater. But I don't think anything can stand too much. Periodic flooding's okay, but they can't really handle this ever-increasing amount of saltwater."

The bony, gray limbs of the cypress, bare of foliage, endow the shorescape with a haunted silhouette.

He says, "It's kind of a poster-child scene for saltwater intrusion."

At the pinnacle of one cypress tree, a lumpy osprey nest is occupied by an adult bird, while two fledglings swoop back and forth in easy range of the nest. The bare branches of another hold a white ibis and a yellow-crowned night heron.

The tide is dropping: The fall will be four feet or more on a day like today. Because of dredging in the lower river to deepen the big ship channel to forty-two feet, the result of the saltwater intrusion is dramatic. For one thing, all those cypress trees used to be alive, their tops burgeoning into thick canopies.

Likewise, the cedars close to the river are dying. They are more tolerant than the cypress—both in fact can survive the occasional overwash of tidal water during a storm—but they just can't survive permanent immersion in saltwater. The bare forest is lovely in the way that a battlefield or a graveyard is lovely: stark and a little spooky.

And speaking of saltwater intrusion, there are plans for a superport at the mouth of the Cape Fear, near Southport, the so-called North Carolina International Port. The Panama Canal is being widened and deepened, and the new post-Panamax superships—the largest ships that will be able to fit through the renovated canal—will be too big to make it upriver to the current port of Wilmington. They will exceed 1,200 feet in length and require a channel 55 feet deep. That makes them a third again bigger than the *Hanjin Los Angeles* and capable of wedging themselves tightly between both banks of the channel at the turning basin for the current port. There's no way they can make it that far up the river, and the proposed international port site is just nine and a half miles from the sea buoy.

"I'm real concerned about it, that's for sure, and I've been following it," Kemp says. But he's got a strong ally, Mike Rice, who joined No Port Southport and then broke away and formed his own organization, Save the Cape. Rice is a retired engineer and attorney who does his homework. "He is one of those people who is unbelievably sharp. He can catch a detail that nine out of ten people miss. He's kind of just devoted himself to this port issue. And I almost feel sorry for the ports people, because every time they make a mistake he is on 'em. He catches *everything*. He's really smart, and he's very unassuming when you look at him. I think he cultivates that image a little bit. He'll kind of slouch into a meeting sliding his feet and he'll sit down at a table, introduce himself, things'll get going, then all of a sudden he'll just pounce on somebody."

But if the superport gets built anyway?

"It would be terrible," Kemp acknowledges.

"Not to mention the deepening of the river," I say.

"And the straightening." There's a kink in the river that would have to be ironed out. "That's something he's done a good job of pointing out. Not only are they going to have to deepen the river, but there's actually a pretty pronounced S-curve down at the mouth where ships come in—and they can't make that turn. They have these fancy simulators of a ship's bridge, and they put in all the environmental factors and try to make that turn, and nobody's ever been able to make that turn. And he's going, 'Does anybody but me see that as a bad sign?'"

The proposed channel would pass close to the east side of Battery Island. The violence to the river, to the healthy ecosystem of the lower estuary, would be incalculable. Kemp explains why. "To straighten the channel there, you'd have to basically destroy Battery Island, which is one of the most important, if not *the* most important, white ibis rookeries in the United States. There's a huge white ibis population out there."

So there goes one of the bird islands—in this case, Battery Island, home to the greatest nesting colony of white ibis in North Carolina—some of those precious, gorgeous birds that so many dedicated people have spent the last fifty years saving from extinction. In any given season, as many as 15,000 breeding pairs will nest there and raise their young—12 percent of the entire ibis population *on earth*, and just about all of the ibis in the state. If they were humans, the comparable number would be 840 million people. Never mind the thousands of egrets and herons.

Kemp continues, "Then there's the whole issue of putting a giant port squarely between a nuclear power plant and the largest ammunition depot in the world. Again, some of these things seem to be no-brainers, but nobody seems to be paying attention to them."

The North Carolina Ports Authority has already purchased 594 acres, of which 113 acres are salt marsh, inland wetlands, or ponds. The site borders both the Progress nuclear power plant and the blast zone for the Sunny Point Military Ocean Terminal. The proposed port would require a wharf nearly a mile long.

And there's a physical challenge in the actual construction. "In order to get fifty-five feet for a shipping channel, you'd have to dredge out into the ocean for miles. It's not just dredging the river. . . . You'd be doing open ocean dredging, which seems to me to be futile. How do you expect that sand to stay where you put it?"

The dredged channel would have to extend seventeen miles offshore.

I say, "I guess you'd have to protect it with jetties, like Charleston."

"Right. And how many billions of dollars is that to build this jetty—when Charleston's already got one and they're right there? There are so many reasons why that seems like a bad idea. Because Norfolk, Charleston, and Savannah are already the equivalent of light years ahead of us."

To build the port would mean paving over hundreds of acres of tidal marsh, punching a major highway and railroad through some fairly sensitive wetlands, and dredging on a scale we have never undertaken on the Cape Fear. The Corps would have to scrape out thirteen more feet of bottom, increasing saltwater intrusion upriver.

For now, the project is just a pipedream—the state doesn't have either the money or the political will to make it happen. The latest estimates for what it would cost are in the range of $4 billion to $5 billion.

Kemp and I leave the subject there for now, distracted by more birds. They seem to be everywhere on the river today—rafting, flying, diving.

This season, for unaccountable reasons, the bird life on the Cape Fear has been particularly lush. "This year people have been seeing all the usual suspects," Kemp says, pointing out more white ibis. "But I've also been seeing wood storks, and Mississippi kites, and swallowtail kites. I saw swallowtail kites three different times this year, three different places on the river. Once at the mouth of the Black, and once on the Northeast Cape Fear up around Castle Hayne, and then once up at Lock and Dam #1."

I'm thinking that the last one is the same one that David and I saw, who has taken up residence.

He says, "The swallowtail kite is a really beautiful bird that typically doesn't come to this area."

With the dropping tide, we have to be alert for underwater obstacles. The ones that will punch right through the bottom of the boat are the sharp remains of pilings, a whole line. They are the artifacts of a primitive alternative to dredging, dating back to the early nineteenth century. The pilings anchored a wooden jetty that angled downriver and helped to push the flow of the current into the middle channel, accelerating it and scouring the bottom in the process.

Far upriver, David and I canoed over the ruins of their rockier cousins, but the principle is the same: to canalize the river into a usable, reliable channel that will take a long time to silt up. Using the river's own power to create a navigable channel.

On a low island at the entrance to Mallory Creek, nearly obscured by hardy stands of bright green and yellow giant cutgrass, Kemp points out a pile of ballast stones—deposited during the nineteenth century. Small sailing ships would off-load their ballast before navigating the shallower waters of the creek to pick up rice and other goods at strategically placed wood-planked staging areas. They could retrieve the ballast stones on their way out of the creek or, if fully ballasted by cargo, leave them for another vessel.

As a double major in geology and history, Kemp conducted an honors project on the stones. He would examine each specimen, determine its makeup, then correlate that kind of stone with a shipping route. "So I went out to Campbell Island, which used to be the big dumping area, and I collected ballast stones. And then I made midsections out of the stones and used them like fingerprints, traced them back to their origins, used them as a way of guesstimating shipping routes."

He hadn't yet discovered this little island of ballast stones at the entrance to the creek, which probably served smaller vessels, sailing lighters trading directly with the plantation. But he made some useful discoveries.

"Everybody just assumed that any flint that you had and any chert that you had was coming from the Cliffs of Dover area. You'd have these white cliffs and embedded in the chalk you'd find theses nodules of chert—the same thing as flint, just a different color. But if you look at the fossils, the fossils are vastly different, and they show they're actually a Caribbean chert and flint. I was able to contradict this Harvard geologist, which was kind of fun."

And again I'm thinking, save us all from those things we know for sure.

We pass close enough to shore to spy the plantation house, a wood-frame structure that does not seem particularly imposing, not like the grand house at Orton with its antebellum columns and spectacular gardens. "That's not the original house," Kemp tells me. "The plantation burned a couple of times. That was actually built in the early 1900s." He points. "Beautiful live oaks up there. Old water tower here." A lot of the plantation is held by land trusts to ensure perpetual conservation easements.

From time to time, we hear loud splashes ahead of the boat and arrive in time to see just a swirl of water, the telltale eddy caused by an alligator's tail. A couple of times we bump hard over something on the bottom—a lump of mud, or a submerged 'gator. This is prime alligator season, a time when kayakers stay out of these creeks.

"Earlier in the spring we would see a couple of small ones, and then there was one big one and he's a good size. He's probably ten plus feet," Kemp says. "And some of these smaller ones were five-six feet."

I say, "Six feet still has a lot of teeth on it."

He laughs. "Yeah, it's still a dinosaur."

In these waters, too, roams the alligator gar, a bony, toothy fish. We saw some of their snouts on the upper river. "Gar will get four or five feet long, so it wouldn't surprise me if that's what's making some of these big swirls."

We're running down one of two parallel canals separated by a berm just a few feet wide. Kemp says, "I've never read anything where I really understand the system of the double canals. But I'm guessing they could flood one side with this canal and the other side with that canal."

Then the boat bumps rather hard, the stern lifting just a bit, and he quickly cants up the motor to lift it clear of whatever it was our keel just found. "That makes me think we might be pushing our luck a little bit," he says. "We might ought to head back out that way. This wouldn't be the best place to spend the night."

He smiles and adds, "I've never bumped anything there—maybe it was a 'gator."

We chug back out into the bay and poke into the mouth of the creek from another direction. Mallory Creek is a bona fide creek—it has natural curves, unlike the rice canals. We slip outside the maze of canals into the open water beyond, still prowling around at the edge of the old plantation. "When you look at this from the air, it's just straight lines, and anytime you see a line that straight in nature, you know it's man-made."

We are on the verge of miles and miles of deep canals, each fifteen or sixteen feet across, dug entirely by hand—specifically, by slaves using shovels, buckets, and other basic tools. The labor was backbreaking, the heat intolerable. It was the kind of hard work that, quite literally, could kill you. The water hid alligators and snakes. The stagnant water bred swarms of mosquitoes that carried malaria and other fevers. There was always the risk of injury and, since many slaves did not swim, of drowning.

We see what I take for wild rice waving in billowing fields in the shallows near shore and along the canals. My mistake is a common one—people often mistake the giant cutgrass for rice—but the rice has been gone for generations. "There's virtually no rice left," Kemp explains. "The story you hear sometimes is that saltwater intrusion killed the rice. And that's not actually the case. The Emancipation Proclamation killed the rice production. No white folks are going to come out here and do this for any other reason than that you'd be killed if you didn't."

And it's true enough: Rice cultivation disappeared soon after the Civil War.

We get to talking about the challenges facing the river, and several of them loom large.

"For me, and this isn't a new one, but important aspects of it are new, and that's the big factory farming problems that you get. On the Cape Fear, the swine farms have gotten a lot of attention, and justly."

Hog farms in North Carolina are big business, approaching $2 billion a year in revenue. Two million hogs are slaughtered annually, most coming from factory farms of more than 2,000 animals each, crammed into long sheds. Such operations are known in the regulation business as CAFOs: Concentrated Animal Feeding Operations. Some animal rights activists prefer the more literally descriptive term "Confined" Animal Feeding Operation. Each hog produces about two tons of waste per year, typically pumped into waste lagoons, where it simply sits, untreated—unlike human waste—until being sprayed onto fields in a kind of slurry.

Since 1997, North Carolina has placed a moratorium on new hog farms in the state. But that doesn't quite solve the problem for the river. Somehow seventy-three new farms have been built anyway and another twenty-five have expanded, adding half a million new hogs. Loopholes in the legislation allowed farms to expand or be established if certain planning was already in process at the time the law was passed.

"They're still pumping hog waste into giant lagoons and then spraying it on top of fields. Completely untreated, considerably more waste than human beings produce in the state of North Carolina," Kemp tells me. "It's just being land-applied. And you can get up in a plane and you can see this stuff being applied to fields that are already saturated, there's already standing water on the fields, and they're spraying more hog waste on top of it, as if the fields can soak up any more. Or you can see 'em spraying in the rain. They've started spraying at night now because they know the planes can't see it as well."

The hog lagoons seem to fail with a depressing regularity. And when the waste is sprayed onto saturated fields, it finds its way into the watershed.

Nitrogen, phosphorus, and ammonia are the chief culprits, leading to algal blooms and hypoxia—decreasing the oxygen level so drastically that fish can no longer survive. Suffocated, they bob to the surface in a mass fishkill. But salts, heavy metals, and a boatload of pathogens also float down the river along with the chemicals, spreading *E. coli*, and other nasty microbes.

And that's not all, reports Ayako Sato of American University in a 2003 study of CAFOs and water quality: "Living near a CAFO has very serious consequences for communities already burdened by other economic, social, and health inequalities and disparities. In terms of health, the North Carolina study found that residents living near hog CAFOs reported headaches, runny nose, sore throats, excessive coughing, diarrhea, and burning eyes more frequently than a control group."

Factory farms by their nature are disproportionately located near nonaffluent rural communities where the drinking supply often relies on well water, which can turn toxic when the groundwater is polluted by massive spills, as it has all too frequently in the past few years. This brings to bear an issue of social justice, since many of those communities' residents belong to a minority or are poor, or both. There's also the ethical issue of confining thousands of animals to live their entire lifespans mired in their own waste, with no room to move, while being pumped full of antibiotics and hormones.

The slaughtering and processing take place at megaplants like the one operated by the Smithfield Packing Company, Inc., in Tar Heel, on the river. We drove right past it on our way upriver toward Buckhorn Dam on the first day of our adventure.

Socially, ethically, environmentally, the CAFO is not a sustainable model— but it is an economic gold mine for the large corporate factory operators. Organizations such as the Union of Concerned Scientists have supported the work of various local communities and river watch programs in North Carolina who want a better, less repugnant way to create a sustainable agriculture.

Meanwhile, the river basin remains the drainage sump for the hog lagoons.

~~~~~~~~~~

Even in ordinary times, hog waste presents a monumental problem of disposal and hygiene. During what are politely referred to as "weather events," they can be time bombs waiting to explode with calamitous consequences.

Hurricane Bertha scored a direct hit on Wilmington on July 12, 1996. Luckily for the Cape Fear, it careened up the coast instead of inland, but it brought severe and sustained rainfall for several weeks afterward.

When Hurricane Fran hit just eight weeks later, on September 5, 1996, it smacked head-on into the Cape Fear estuary and slammed up the coast, took an inland turn at Topsail Island, and ravaged the Cape Fear basin all the way to Raleigh. It snapped trunks, knocked down trees, destroyed nesting habitat, killed individual animals of all kinds, and displaced thousands of others. Our canoeing party paddled past all those strainers on the upper river—many of them trees knocked down by hurricane winds.

In addition to destroying homes and businesses and flooding crops, the heavy wind and rain caused erosion and significant *nonpoint source* pollution—pollution that enters the watershed from a thousand invisible sources rather than from a single big identifiable outflow—as oil and debris washed off impervious surfaces such as parking lots directly into Cape Fear tributaries, and streambanks overflowed and eroded, dumping thousands of extra tons of sediment into the river basin.

From saturated wetlands, oxygen-starved swamp waters overflowed into the river.

Half the hog population of the state resides in swine operations in the Cape Fear basin—almost 5 million animals. Forty percent of the state's turkey population is concentrated in just two counties, Sampson and Duplin, drained, respectively, by the Black and Northeast Cape Fear Rivers.

According to "Hurricane Effects on Water Quality and Benthos in the Cape Fear Basin," a study conducted by scientists from the Center for Marine Science Research at UNC-Wilmington not long after the one-two hurricane punch, "Additionally, during the week following the hurricane, at least four hog waste lagoons ruptured, overtopped, or were inundated, releasing millions of liters of raw or partially-treated animal waste into the Northeast Cape Fear River (NECFR), a major tributary of the Cape Fear Estuary." All told, twenty-two lagoon "incidents" were linked to Hurricane Fran.

In order to avoid overtopping their rising lagoons, other hog farm operators sprayed unknown amounts of liquid wastes onto already saturated fields, creating in effect shallow waste lagoons, which also rinsed directly into the watershed.

All along the floodplain, septic systems overflowed. When power failed, municipal sewage treatment plants shut down. They had no backup generators, and when local industry stepped in to provide such generators, it turned out that the plants weren't wired to handle them. So 70 million gallons of untreated human sewage were pumped directly into the mainstem of the Cape Fear.

Another 1 million gallons were released into the Northeast Cape Fear, and 4.7 million were pumped directly into the Black River, upstream of Wilmington. A huge fishkill followed—bass, carp, sunfish, shad, eels, pickerel, hogchokers. Their bloated carcasses filled the river long after the hurricane had passed on.

The problem was hypoxia: low dissolved oxygen. The waste feeds bacteria, which suck away the oxygen needed by fish and mollusks. The oxygen-starved fish die. The shellfish, biofilters essential to cleaning the river water, also die.

Because of its strong flow and the flushing action of a salt tide, the Cape Fear is more resilient than meandering rivers that empty into sounds, which tend to back up like a stopped drain. Instead of experiencing bottom waters that go *anoxic*—that is, in which the oxygen level falls to zero—even after great stresses the river usually remains at worse *hypoxic*—that is, with low levels of oxygen mixed throughout the water column.

But Hurricane Fran was different.

It brought together a lethal combination: heavy upstream rain, carrying with it runoff and silt; the devastating shock of the hurricane on such a large portion of the watershed; and human negligence.

Hurricane Fran killed the whole water column—for weeks.

When I interviewed him in the months following the hurricane, then–river keeper Bouty Baldridge recalled sampling the river in the immediate aftermath: "We found levels of oxygen in the Northeast Cape Fear to be zero for almost three weeks after Fran."

Dr. Michael Mallin, a biologist and the lead investigator of the study, told me then, "It is important to think in terms of the whole watershed."

He's a scientist, but he's also a passionate advocate for the river. Mallin has steady blue eyes, longish blond hair, and a casual manner, and like many scientists would rather be out in the field than sitting in an office. Cumulatively, over the past twenty years, he has spent whole weeks on the river.

He told me, "You know how I get involved in it is when I'm out there and

I can actually see how the river functions, ecologically speaking. For instance, if you go up the Black River, you see these extensive streamside wetlands. And at high tide, the water goes back into these wetlands. You look at that and you understand their function in nature, their function as these natural filters for pollutants that come down the river."

Mallin's study concluded, "We contend that human activities, particularly those concerned with waste treatment, significantly magnified the deleterious effects of Hurricane Fran on water quality." The study cited in particular the hazardous folly of building hog waste lagoons on floodplains.

The good news is that, since Hurricane Fran, the state no longer allows hog houses or lagoons to be built in 100-year floodplains. The bad news: Overspraying is still permissible on fields within floodplains.

"Basically, history repeated itself when Bonnie came through," Mallin said.

When Hurricane Bonnie hurtled through in September 1998, after hog farmers and municipalities had two years to learn from their mistakes, virtually the same amount of hog effluent and human sewage spilled into the Cape Fear watershed. Even the City of Wilmington contributed to the mess: When its backup system failed, it emptied 10 million gallons of partially treated sewage right into the river.

The Northeast Cape Fear fared the worst: "The river was anoxic for three weeks. It was stressed for a period of three months," Mallin said. "There was a massive fishkill there. And the fishkill killed everything. Even eels—which usually can survive just about anything—even eels were dying."

Mallin concluded, "Okay. Hurricanes themselves are natural events. And it's fine for a natural system if you have flooding—that's not a problem. That's what floodplains are for. It's only when you add all these human-induced factors such as hog lagoons on floodplains, wastewater treatment systems that will fail when the power goes out."

And it doesn't take a catastrophic event to stress the river. In April 1999, in clear weather with no storms, a hog waste lagoon operated by Murphy Farms on Persimmon Branch, a tributary of the Northeast Cape Fear, ruptured and spilled 1.5 million gallons of waste into the watershed, where it pooled and stagnated for a week, waiting for rain to flush it downriver. A beaver dam held the hog waste back from reaching the mainstem, allowing much of it to be filtered through wetlands vegetation—a mixed blessing.

As Mallin said, "Good for the river, bad for the critters in the swamp."

Chugging along the fringe of the rice canals in Kemp's picturesque boat on a perfectly clear, breezy day, watching brown pelicans dive and osprey fledglings try their wings and listening to the racket of passing gulls, it's hard to think in terms of hog waste slurry and pollution, of anoxic events and ecological catastrophe.

But listening to Kemp spell out the dire challenges facing the river, I recall an image that was burned indelibly into my memory in the aftermath of Hurricane Fran in 1996. I was a passenger in a small airplane skimming the coast to review the damage. I saw the dark brown plume of the river mouth blossom into the shoals, carrying the wreckage of houses and docks, tangles of broken trees, and rafts of flotsam.

When we dipped lower, the flotsam turned out to be the bloated carcasses of hogs.

Now Kemp tells me that there's a new twist to this old pollution source. "Poultry CAFOs are making a push into North Carolina because they've been basically regulated out of other states."

Up on the Chesapeake Bay, for example, regulators have cracked down on mass livestock operations, so they're moving down into North Carolina, where they are not regulated.

Not regulated? At all? I ask him if I'm hearing him right.

Kemp explains: "The poultry farms are what they call 'deemed permitted,' so if you build a poultry farm, it is considered to be permitted without any permitting process at all."

Like many aspects of private enterprise, the distinction comes down to a technicality: Poultry farms produce a so-called dry litter rather than the wet litter of the hog operations. But in the real life of the river, that distinction may not make much difference.

"Dry litter" is a polite euphemism for chicken shit.

"I've been sampling at this one farm, and there's *always* a giant pile of chicken shit," Kemp says. "It's out in the open, it's not covered, it's not anything, and it's sitting right adjacent to wetlands—a creek called Limestone Creek, which drains right into the Northeast Cape Fear. And this is happening all over the place, and there's no regulation around it, making it really easy for them to get rid of their waste problem by just letting it wash away."

A watershed is a giant circulatory system. What washes into the drainage ditch sluices into the creek, which runs into the river, which sooner or later carries it to the intake pipe for our drinking water.

"What we have to do, in theory, is to show the state enough evidence that these things are polluting on a regular basis to basically make the state do their job, because right now they're just kind of saying to themselves and anybody else, well, we don't really have any evidence that they're polluting. And we're saying, it's a *giant factory* where you're cramming thousands of animals into a tiny little room and feeding them full of antibiotics, because they couldn't naturally live that way, and they're pooping *a lot*. Where do you think all that's going?"

Where it is going is onto giant standing piles, he says.

"They're saying, well, we're not really seeing any problems, and we're saying, well, that's because you're not really *looking* for problems. So we have go out there and find the problems, collect all the evidence, send it to a lab, pay all the money to do that, get evidence that will stand up in a court of law, then bring it to the state and try to get them to enforce it."

I ask, "How do you get access? The owners probably don't want you on their land."

"They don't want you on their land, but they don't always post their land with 'no trespassing,' either. Theoretically if asked to leave, you have to comply and not come back. But if you can get to a ditch that runs along a property and sample, you know, you can see a pile of manure there, you can see the slope of the land, it's clearly running into the ditch."

You might not care about a few truckloads of chicken shit rinsing into the river—won't the river just wash it away, dilute it into harmless inert amounts?

Well, multiply that load by the all the factory farms in the basin, and then realize what that so-called dry litter (now all wet and slushy and floating down the river toward the intake for the Greater Wilmington water supply) contains a hearty helping of poison—yes, poison. Arsenic. It's fed to chickens that live jammed together in their miserable thousands as a means of killing many of the microbes that would otherwise wipe them out in epidemics. Chickens who live spread out on old-fashioned farms, a few dozen to a coop, don't need arsenic.

"This farm we're looking at up around Beulaville—it takes going into wetlands, it's roaming around on a creek until you can get to a ditch that's clearly draining that manure. And you take a reading in there and you find an arsenic level that's a *thousand times* higher than the EPA's safe standard for groundwater, and you think to yourself, well, there's a reason for that!"

"A thousand times?" I say. I wonder if he's exaggerating to make a point.

"Yes—we actually found that level."

Beulaville is just north of the Holly Shelter Game Land, miles away, up on the Northeast Cape Fear. For the last two weeks or so, Holly Shelter has been on fire, ignited by a lightning strike, fueled by a long-standing drought. More than 30,000 acres burned inside a forty-mile perimeter before the blaze was contained. Teams of firefighters converged on the scene from as far away as Tennessee, plowing it back with bulldozers, using up its fuel with backfires of their own. The smoke drifted over Wilmington and settled in a gauzy haze reeking of char, and there hasn't been much of a breeze to clear it away.

Today it's not as bad; a breeze is stirring on the river, and the choking haze is finally dissipating. Holly Shelter is prime paddling grounds, a web of tributary creeks and a wild swamp full of critters of all kinds. I ask Kemp how he feels about the wildfire.

"I know that burning is part of that ecosystem, and that it needs fire. I understand that scientifically, but still part of me kind of hates to see it burn."

Holly Shelter Creek is where I first met Kemp on an early Saturday morning paddle sponsored by Cape Fear River Watch. I had hauled an ungainly plastic canoe off the rooftop of my Pathfinder, and he helped me drag it down to the put-in near the confluence with Shaken Creek. An extra person showed up for the paddle, so Kemp gave up his seat in another canoe and asked to join me in mine. I was delighted for the company, and we paddled the six or so miles to Holland's Fish Camp with an unhurried stroke, enjoying the cool morning and the pretty scenery, along with some quiet conversation. Holly Shelter is unusual among local creeks in that it has high cutbanks and a brisk current along that stretch.

Over a catfish sandwich at the fish camp we talked about the Cape Fear River, how remarkably wild it remains even after hundreds of years of humans trying to "improve" it. Now we're back on the water together, and he's teaching me how to see the history of the river hidden in its mud and current, preserved like the lenses of an archaeological dig, story overlaid on story.

"See that piece of wood on the bank?" He points to a rotten stub of plank protruding from the mud, hardly discernible among the cutgrass. "That was a piece of lumber at some point, not just an old log. They could have had a little area right there where they staged rice. You see little things in the mud like that all the time."

It's one more souvenir of our heritage, a clue of past enterprises, of the ambitions of those who settled on the Cape Fear, those who fought over it, sailed and paddled and steamed upon it. But you can only see it if you are looking, and for that you have to be on the river.

That's the most important part of Kemp's job as river keeper, to pay attention to the river, in this stretch really three rivers: the main channel of the Cape Fear, the short detour that forms the Brunswick River, and the Northeast Cape Fear. It is the Northeast Cape Fear that has been occupying much of his effort these days, ever since Titan America, the American subsidiary of the Greek company Titan Cement, S.A., announced plans to reactivate the defunct Ideal Cement Plant located in an otherwise pristine location, on land adjacent to where Island Creek joins the Northeast Cape Fear.

Already more than 200 doctors, with the support of nurses and other health care professionals, have taken a hard stand against the proposed plant.

They cite a variety of alarming predictable consequences to the health of local residents, especially children.

A grassroots organization has sprung up to block the effort: the Stop Titan Action Network. In its advocacy against the project, the network says,

> In New Hanover County, we estimate that Titan will be the largest source of benzene and polycyclic organic matter—pollutants associated with causing cancer in humans—and the second-largest source of particulate matter, nitrogen oxides, carbon monoxide, volatile organic compounds, lead, arsenic, ammonia, beryllium and selenium. Titan will also be the third-largest source of mercury in our area. New Hanover County already has some of the highest mercury emissions in the state. Our area is very susceptible to the conversion of airborne mercury from smokestacks like Titan into the highly toxic form of methylmercury that accumulates in fish and other wildlife. Numerous studies have documented the toxic effects of mercury. Developing fetuses are at particular risk.

It's pretty scary stuff, and with every meeting, every press release by any party, the rhetoric has ramped up. There are lots of issues to sort out. The first came about when the New Hanover County commissioners suddenly—that is, with almost no notice or public discussion—handed out $4.2 million in tax incentives for Titan to reopen the plant.

Clearly the whole issue touches a sore nerve with Kemp. "What I'm learning is that so much is like the Titan thing—trying to stay one step ahead of people who are keeping projects under the radar. Titan. They announce on a Thursday that they are going to have a county commissioners meeting on a Tuesday to approve a $4.2 million incentive package to a cement company. That's basically *two business days* of notice. How do you expect people to be able to change plans and show up and actually find out what this project's going to be about?"

I don't have a good answer for him. I admit that I, too, have found the whole process troubling and secretive.

Kemp goes on: "And then you get there and it's very clear that everybody involved in the decision-making process—the county commissioners, Titan—everybody has known about this thing for months, if not years. But the public has been given two days' notice to provide input on what would be the fourth-largest cement plant in the entire country. And you're thinking, why was the environmental piece of this completely left out of consideration? Why are we thinking of giving these people $4.2 million to come here and destroy our environment and get rich doing it?"

The tax incentives went away. Not because the commissioners took them back, but because a judge decided that they constituted government funds and therefore triggered a more stringent permitting process. Titan *gave* them back.

The tax incentive deal wasn't the only issue. Back when the old plant was in operation thirty years ago, Castle Hayne, the community closest to the site, was a rural farming crossroads, thinly populated. In the generation and half since the old plant closed, it's grown into a real town. These days, 8,500 kids—the ones most susceptible to the kinds of health problems related to benzene and mercury emissions—attend two local elementary schools within five miles of the site.

Moreover, the plan calls not just for reopening the plant. It also calls for a massive limestone mining operation on the site. To reach the minerals it wants to extract, which lie beneath the Castle Hayne aquifer, Titan plans to pump out between 8 million and 16 million gallons of groundwater daily—an average of 4.4 billion gallons per year—drastically lowering the water table in a community largely dependent on wells and already prone to saltwater intrusion.

Probably the last straw came in March 2011, when Titan announced it was suing two citizens who spoke out about the project at a public meeting of the county commissioners. Titan claimed they had made maliciously false and defaming statements. Titan officials were especially upset by a video posted to YouTube. Rather than tamping down the opposition, this action was widely seen as arrogant and bullying, Goliath swatting down David, a lawsuit meant to intimidate Titan opponents into silence. But the Stop Titan Action Network, and much of the public, rallied around the two litigants. A sense not just of threat but of democratic outrage infused the movement. A defense fund was started, and one of the first people to pledge money to it was one of the five county commissioners—newly elected—who had not voted for the original Titan tax break.

And of course all the inflammatory things that were said against the project were repeated in public and social media, so it feels as if Titan made a major tactical blunder, simply amplifying all the claims it says are malicious and untrue.

As Kemp and I chew over this latest development, I'm thinking of my colleague David Gessner's take on why people become environmental activists, as he makes the case in *My Green Manifesto*. He writes, persuasively, "If you aren't going to fight for your home, you aren't very likely to fight for any place. And if you don't have a connection to a particular place, and to particular animals, human and otherwise, who dwell in that place, then you don't fight. It's that simple."

~~~~~~~~~~

The people who gather at Holly Shelter School a few days after my excursion with Kemp all have that connection to place of which Gessner writes. Their children attend that spanking-new school. They fish the river. They paddle it. Their doctors have told them how bad a cement plant can be for their kids' health, how it can make them more prone to asthma and emphysema. This is their homeplace. From their kitchen taps, they draw cool well water to make sweet tea on a Sunday afternoon. They're not keen on watching a pall of toxic limestone dust settle on their cars, on the wash hung out on the line to dry, on their kids' wading pool.

They march in ragged lines up Holly Shelter Road to gather across N.C. 133 from a Stop Titan billboard, bearing signs that read "Sue Us All!" and "Bullies Make Bad Neighbors" and "People, Not Profits."

One captures the whiff of insider deal-making that characterized the original tax incentive package: "It's not just the air that stinks—it's the politics!"

The sign that best sums up the ethic of the crowd, misspelling and all, seems to be "Titan Cement Will Not Decide Our Communities Future."

The left side of the billboard reads, over a billowing pall of gray smoke, "How many jobs is a child's health worth?" The answer appears on the right panel, over the smiling faces of four children: "Not even one."

It is a surprisingly nonpartisan gathering—or maybe not so surprisingly. I overhear three middle-aged men in cargo shorts and T-shirts conversing amiably as they walk. One is an avowed liberal Democrat. One says he voted Republican in the last presidential election. The third expresses a political bent that can best be summed up as "A pox on both your houses," which I take to mean he is an Independent or perhaps a Libertarian. They actually talk about whether this is a liberal or conservative issue, and *all three agree* that it is not— politics is irrelevant. This is about the safety and quality of life of their community. This is about outsiders, a big multinational corporation, assuming it can just come in here and take what it wants, leaving behind waste and a big hole where the lowland forest next to Island Creek used to be. They don't need the jobs *that* badly.

Lots of women of all ages fill the ranks of the marchers, many hauling along toddlers or infants. And the leader of the march is a young woman, a college student. Kemp is here with his family. Some of the marchers carry American flags.

Much has been made of the fact that Titan is not just *not* a locally owned

Demonstrators gather at Holly Shelter School to protest Titan American's proposed cement plant and quarry on the Northeast Cape Fear River near Island Creek (author photo)

company—it's not even an American company. The decisions that could have such profound, even disastrous effects on the river and the surrounding population are being made in boardrooms far away from Island Creek and Holly Shelter School by people who will not have to live with the consequences.

As public protests go, it's not such a big deal. A hundred or so citizens chant their message, waving at cars as they slowly cruise by, drivers honking their horns and cheering in solidarity. But it's a moment I like, a democratic moment, a moment of people standing up for the river I have come to feel attached to, and my gut tells me the same thing my head does: Titan Cement doesn't belong on our river.

For me, it's not an abstract position. It's a picture in my head of a small, verdant, namesake island at the mouth of Island Creek, a quiet fishing hole, an unspoiled riverbank under which lurk big lunker catfish. A little shady creek that offers several quiet hours of paddling. In my mind, I plant an American flag squarely on that island. But it's a local American flag, homegrown, an emblem not of dominion but of community stewardship over a place, a river, our place.

And I just have no idea whether or not this protest will work.

So the sidetrip with river keeper Kemp Burdette to the old rice plantation canals leads to another side excursion before we proceed down to the estuary, and for this one I seek out my old canoe partner, David Webster.

One cool morning in August, David and I drive up Holly Shelter Road, paralleling the Northeast Cape Fear River, headed for Island Creek, near the site where Titan wants to locate its operation.

The Northeast Cape Fear begins about two miles south of Mount Olive and courses some 130 miles down to Point Peter, where it joins the mainstem of the Cape Fear in Wilmington harbor. In addition to the Holly Shelter Game Lands, it passes through Angola Swamp. Long Creek, Prince Georges Creek, and Morgan Creek are some of its other significant tributaries. Like the mainstem, it is prime fishing grounds, home to forty-five identified species.

David Webster has strong feelings about the Titan matter. Surprisingly, his first objection has nothing to do with science or the environment. He says, "We've got a player who first off plays dirty and who will attach riders and amendments to bills that are going through the legislature and not advertise them — so there's not opportunity for public comment. So they've already indicated their modus operandi. They will cheat, lie, steal, do whatever they need to do to get to where they want to be. Is that the kind of people we want here? Environmental concerns aside. I'm just talking about *morally*. Ethically, do we encourage that kind of behavior here in southeastern North Carolina? I'd like to think we don't."

For David, Titan is a bellwether of the kind of choices that collectively we will make regarding the future of the Cape Fear basin: "How do we want to label ourselves in southeastern North Carolina? What do we want our future to be like?"

The damage can be inflicted almost overnight but last for hundreds of years.

"From the environmental side, it's clear we're looking at a tremendous increase in particulate matter, especially things that are very noxious," David explains. "And at the top of that list — and this is why we have the doctors involved — is methylmercury. Once you get mercury in the air and it gets down in the water column, and it goes through those steps it goes through and becomes methylmercury, you're talking about tremendous developmental abnormalities in young children. And we accumulate it too, but we're big enough that it doesn't really show — *unless you're a nursing mother*. And then that baby's getting it through the milk. And that's where it's going to really affect our offspring."

He doesn't believe in any quick technological fix. The problem is chemical and biological and won't go away.

David says, in the matter-of-fact tone of a scientist who is used to making judgments based on evidence, not promises, "There are people who say, 'Oh, society will take care of this, we'll develop ways to deal with it.' Well, when you're talking about things like methylmercury that have half-lives—half-life, this is half the length of time it will take to decompose—that are hundreds of years long, it's not gonna go away. I don't care what you do to come in and put scrubbers on the smokestacks. Once you've already dumped fifty thousand tons of it, it's going to be there for a long time."

As usual, David gets to the crux of the matter. He says, "I want to see them live in the affected area. I think that's the true test of whether you think you're doing environmental damage: if you'll drink the water."

We detour down the long hardpan road to the Martin Marietta aggregate quarry, and David pulls over. He scoops up a chunk of marl and brings it back to the Jeep.

"It's calcium carbonate," he explains. "It's full of marine fossils. You can see a fossilized bivalve right there." He puts his finger on the marl and hands it over to me. Embedded in the chunk is a tiny seashell. Marl is great stuff for paving—we drove in over it. It packs hard and drains well. And when the big dump trucks roar past us, they trail a choking plume of limestone dust. Marl or marlstone forms one of the sedimentary layers in a limestone deposit such as the one found above the Castle Hayne Aquifer along the Northeast Cape Fear. In other words, it's a fairly impure brand of limestone, composed of about 35 percent clay.

But the pure limestone at the top of the sedimentary plain is what all the fuss is about: That's the stuff used for making cement.

We U-turn back onto the main road, and farther on we pass the entrance to the old Ideal Cement Plant, which shut down in 1982. Soon we come to a short, narrow bridge, the dividing line between New Hanover and Pender Counties. On the other side of the bridge, the road becomes Island Creek Road, named for the little creek that runs under the bridge and makes a twisty passage to the Northeast Cape Fear River. We drive past the bridge, turn around, and return, parking on the one patch of cleared dirt and gravel near the bridge. Here the creek is only about twenty feet across.

David wants to show me the place that will be ruined if a giant open pit mine chews up the thousands of acres between the old Ideal site and the creek.

The morning is mild and breezy, the creek shaded by the bent arms of water oaks, green ash, and pond pines. We board the canoe carefully, and for this little voyage we soon abandon our seats and settle onto the floor of the boat for stability and to be able to pass under the overhanging branches. It is so shady even on a bright sunny day at 9 A.M. that I take off my sunglasses. Island Creek is a black-water creek, rich with tannin, colored very much like the Black.

We hear the trailing *cuk-cuk-cuk-cuk-cuk* of a pileated woodpecker and before long see the actual bird, big as a crow, black and white stripes on its neck accented by the telltale red crest, zipping low across the sky ahead.

We paddle slowly along the creek, ducking the low branches of willow and red maple. On either hand, living cypress trees rise up heavy and gray and straight, their canopies lush and tangled, not yet burned to stark skeletons by saltwater intrusion, as are the ones on the lower Cape Fear River. Pond pines, alders, and sweet bay grow thick on the banks. Wax myrtle erupts everywhere in profuse green clouds. White and lavender swamp rose pokes out here and there, lively bursts of bright color amid all the greenery. The small sloughs are thick with cattail and lizard tail.

We maneuver through a passage narrowed by branches protruding into the stream from both sides and pass between two wasps' nests, each the size of a large grapefruit, suspended in the limbs. On the right bank, David points out a green ash tree that has been girdled, methodically stripped of a ring of bark low on the tree to cause it to die and topple and become building material for a lodge or dam. "Well, we know there are beavers here," he says.

"What else lives out here?" I ask.

"We've already seen pileated woodpeckers. There are also otters, yellow-bellied sliders, snapping turtles, I imagine. Minks. You won't see them. We're past mating season for birds, so the ospreys are down in South America by now. Although we are seeing some northern parulas, warblers."

For sure, the creek is full of catfish and bowfin. "Bowfin is a real ancient fish," David tells me. "Around here, it's also called blackfish." Bowfin, like sturgeon and gar, was already swimming around during the age of dinosaurs. It is not a table fish.

David continues reeling off the species of wildlife that inhabit the creek. "And there's a kind of mole, the star-nosed mole, that's pretty interesting. It has twenty-two electrical receptors in its nose and can find worms by the contractions of their muscles. Isn't that amazing?"

Pretty much. The star-nosed mole looks like something invented for a sci-fi movie, if it were twenty feet tall. Instead, it's a tiny critter with a nose that develops in the form of a bright red star with twenty-two nasal rays or tendrils, the whole star just under half an inch in diameter. The star-nosed mole holds the record among mammals for being the fastest to detect whether something is edible and eating it, a matter of microseconds: worms, insects, mollusks. Not bad for a critter that is, for all intents and purposes, blind. Fully half of its tiny brain is devoted to processing what comes in through its starry nose.

And it can do one other thing, something that until very recently was thought to be impossible for a mammal: It can smell underwater. Nowadays, it is listed on the state's endangered species roster.

That roster of endangered and threatened species is growing disturbingly large.

Far upriver, on the Deep and Rocky Rivers, which drain into the Cape Fear River, the Cape Fear shiner (*Notropis mekistocholas*) is endangered, its numbers dropping every year. The shiner is a modest critter, a two-inch-long yellow minnow with a black sidestripe. It likes clean water with a low silt load, shallow white-water runs, and deep pools, so it congregates in areas with gravel or cobble bottoms. But it's long been a victim of dam construction, which changed the flow of the river.

The river frog (*Rana hecksheri*) is another historic denizen of the Cape Fear, though none has been sighted in the basin in thirty-five years. It's currently state-listed as a Species of Special Concern and may be extinct along the river. That's a shame, since it is a big, boisterous critter, brown or olive with a mottled gray-black-and-white belly. Among North Carolina frogs, only the bullfrog is bigger. The river frog's tadpoles are huge, as tadpoles go—up to six inches long—and swim in big schools for as long as a year before morphing into frogs.

Whenever a frog disappears from a habitat, it's a cause for alarm, since frogs—like mollusks, minnows, and turtles—are indicator species, telltales of water quality. The silt loads from farm and development runoff, pesticides, and toxic urban runoff seem to be the chief culprits whenever a species such as this one goes missing in action.

Also endangered: the green floater (*Lasmigona subviridis*), a small mussel with a thin, fragile shell, which is being out-competed by the Asian clam, our old friend *Corbicula fluminea*. Ditto the three-inch-long Cape Fear spike (*Elliptio marsupiobsa*), a wedge-shaped mussel found in loose muddy or sandy substrates downstream of logjams. This one, remember, used to filter the entire volume of the river every mile. Now it, too, has made the Special Concern list. The Cape Fear three tooth (*Triodopsis soelneri*), a snail, is a North Carolina Threatened Species.

David and I continue paddling, north, curving west, now angling north again, and so on, following the long, shady channel. On both sides of the creek, we're seeing lone cypress trees and splay-limbed water oaks sprouting flags of resurrection ferns, which live on the outer surface of bark. In times of drought, the ferns curl up and appear dead, but just add water, and they open in wide, bright green plumes. All along, in the placid shallows near the banks, we admire the spatterdock. Spatterdock looks like water lily, with a floating, heart-shaped leaf anchored to the bottom. Among the floating leaves, the yellow cups of flowers poke up on bendy stalks.

David remarks, "One thing I'm not seeing is alligator habitat."

Then only a little way farther, we cross the inflow of a small shallow branch. A hundred yards or so back from us we can see a mat of grasses, some open boggy ground fronted by a pool of still, murky water. David points. "Look down that branch—that's where you're going to find alligators." An alligator will create its own pool by swishing its enormous, heavy tail. The pool will function as insurance against low water or drought.

From here on down to the Cape Fear estuary, alligators are right at home. They tend to avoid humans, given the chance. You're most likely to find the females by their nests. The alligator mating season begins in April, and the bull alligator doesn't stick around after mating. The female scratches out a nest with her back feet in a clear, marshy area near quiet water. The nesting site may be eighteen feet across. She then deposits a clutch of thirty to fifty eggs at a depth of fourteen inches or so. Next, she piles dirt and plant debris—mainly grasses, cattails, and the like—in a mound two to three feet high. Turtles do much the same, but then they leave the nest to its fate.

The mama 'gator, though, will stick around not just until the hatchlings break out of the nest but for a full year afterward, till the next mating season comes around. She and her pod of young ones will stick close to their nest.

If you come across an alligator nest, you might mistake it for a brushpile, a kind of compost heap. In fact, that's exactly what it is. The chemical reaction caused by the decay of the vegetable matter gives off heat, and the temperature of incubation will determine the sex of the offspring: From about 82 to 86 degrees, the young will become females; at a temperature greater than 90 degrees, males. The mother will actually monitor the temperature of the nest with her own belly and either add or remove material in order to heat or cool it.

How she knows whether it will be desirable in a given season to hatch males or females is not quite clear, a euphemism to say that we haven't got a clue. Scientists agree that if she did know, this method is an excellent way of controlling the sex of the offspring.

About sixty-five days after laying the eggs, the mother will help them hatch by excavating the nest carefully with her front legs and muzzle, removing the eggs with her mouth, and gently chewing them open. Depending on how close she is to water, she may carry the hatchlings there in her mouth and release them.

The hatchlings don't look very fierce. They're only six to eight inches long and will be hunted by just about every other predator in the swamp—until they themselves are big enough to be apex predators, right at the top of the food chain.

We move on. In half an hour or so the creek widens considerably, still meandering. We can feel the current slackening under our boat. Perched on a branch just higher than our heads is a large anhinga, its back to us: body black and gray, wings gray with silver-white feathers on top, with an orange bill and webbed feet. We can see its full coloration because it perches with wings semi-outstretched. The conventional explanation for this odd habit is based on the observation that the oil glands that waterproof its wing feathers are underdeveloped, compared with those of other birds, so it needs to air-dry them. The anhinga seems completely indifferent to our presence, and we ease by so close we could reach up and grab it.

David says, once we've glided by, "There's a new theory that it's really about biothermal regulation." That is, it controls its body temperature by exposing more surface to the air, in order to cool itself.

The anhinga resembles a cormorant but has a long tail, hence its nickname, the water turkey. To me its long, S-shaped neck and pointy head resemble those of a snake. "That's right," David says. "It's also known as the snake bird." The anhinga will dive completely underwater and then swim with only its head and neck protruding from the surface, looking exactly like a large water snake.

We've been paddling now for well over an hour, so the river must be getting close. We slide round a bend and encounter two fishermen in ballcaps maneuvering a bass boat into a small bay fringed by spatterdock. We trade greetings. "What are you fishing for today?" David asks.

One of them answers, "Bream," which in local usage could mean any of several freshwater table fish, including bluegill, fliers, and red-ear sunfish.

"Where you gonna take out at?" one of them asks.

"Back at the bridge where we put in."

"Well, you better get back soon, or you'll be fighting the tide the whole way."

"The tide's turning?" David asks.

"That's right."

To me, David says, "I wondered how much tidal surge we'd get up here." Then to the fisherman, he asks, "How much farther to the river?"

The fisherman shrugs. "Oh, two curves."

We thank him and paddle on our way. I smile at the directions, which are so succinct and perfect. Measuring distance by the number of curves—what a foolproof way to convey the truth. And indeed, rounding the second curve only a few minutes later, we spy the river, broad and sunlit beyond the narrow passage between two islands.

The breeze is full and constant now, pushing at us from the river. The small island on our left is round and thickly forested. The larger one, closer to the river, is oblong, just as thickly forested, a natural fortress. It's exactly the kind of place where as boys my brothers and I would have built a fort to protect the creek from pirates. We never figured on this kind of pirate, the kind who could take the actual land itself and turn it into a hole in the ground where something valuable used to be.

It's taken us an hour and forty-five minutes to paddle from the bridge to the river. Now we slowly turn, cast a backward glance at our sentinel island, and follow the channel back the way we came. In an hour the tidal current has carried us back to the bridge. We slide the bow of the canoe into a slough and one at a time step out without upsetting it, then carry it back to the road, where David's truck is parked on a narrow slice of cleared dirt near the little concrete bridge. We lift the canoe onto the roof and secure it.

Meanwhile, massive dump trucks loaded with marl and limestone barrel past us on the narrow two-lane straightaway, shivering us in their windy, choking wakes.

~~~~~~~~~~~~

Titan's presence or absence will change the nature of the river, and it may be years before the issue is settled. The project has received an air quality permit, which guarantees nothing but also illuminates the problem quite clearly: The various permits are issued separately, but the effects of pumping millions of gallons of water out of the aquifer, scraping out a monstrous open pit mine in the middle of sensitive wetlands, and emitting mercury and other toxins into the air are all connected. They all form one complex impact. The mercury may be bearable in certain amounts in the atmosphere, but as soon as it hits the water, it poses a water quality emergency.

So an air quality permit issued without the full context of the impact is fairly meaningless as a guarantor of a clean, safe environment. Soon after the permit was issued, four environmental groups, including Cape Fear River

Watch, challenged it with help from the Southern Environmental Law Center. Their lawsuit contends, "Ignoring available pollution controls, the state granted Titan's toxic recipe to pollute the air we all breathe."

The Titan controversy perfectly encapsulates the competing political and environmental forces along the river. Not political in the sense of Democrat or Republican. Political in the sense that people are fighting over the soul of a place, what it is, what it means, and ultimately who owns it. The Stop Titan Action Network is not just standing up *against* a particular company. It is standing up *for* the proposition that a community has a deep right of ownership of its natural place, this river.

It's the same logic that has kept North Carolina's beaches open to all citizens, that says you can't tear down historic buildings willy-nilly, that you can't turn a hallowed battlefield into a strip mall. Private property stops at the boundary of community ownership, and the battle is about where to draw that line.

The Stop Titan march is still a few days in the future as Kemp and I cruise back across the river, with following seas slopping over the stern and pushing us along.

Kemp muses that the seacoast is a lot sexier—the beaches and tidal creeks and Intracoastal Waterway. People swim there, buy or rent lavish beach homes, have a sentimental affection for dolphins and loggerhead turtles. When a sewage spill happens in the Intracoastal Waterway, people are outraged—they swim in that sewage.

"I wish the river got as much attention as the coast," he says. "Somehow people don't get as mad about putting something into the river that shouldn't be there. They say, oh well, it's just the river."

But he has a kicker, a final, visceral argument that gets them every time. "There's a lot of people who don't know we *drink* the water out of the Cape Fear River. You tell them that, and they go, *What?!*"

And I have to admit that I've never really thought about it. I mean, at some level I have known it as a fact for years, but I have never pondered it. Here I am writing about a river I've been *drinking* for more than twenty years. It's quite literally inside me, running in my bloodstream and inside my cells, which are made from the water I drink and are rejuvenated every eight years. The Cape Fear River has made me—and tens of thousands of others—what we are today. For a moment the thought stuns me with its utterly obvious implications.

We're not just looking at the river or riding on its current. We are taking it inside our bodies, not just once but many times a day. Every time we sip a cup of coffee or order iced tea at a restaurant. With every glass of cold water that slakes our thirst on a hot day and every ice cube we plop into our scotch and soda.

"See?" he says. "I tell them, that's what you're drinking every day—you're in Cape Fear River water. So think about keeping it nice, you know? And they look at me like I'm trying to trick 'em. *We're* not drinking Cape Fear River water—I'm not falling for that one! So I take 'em up and show 'em the pipe. Where do you think that pipe comes from? I don't know. From Lock and Dam #1, they're piping it all the way down here to the treatment plant. Then it starts to sink in."

*Sink in.* An apt choice of words. In some sense, we're all sinking into the river, and it's sinking into us.

Now the rice canals, Island Creek, and the Titan controversy are all behind us, as Frank Chapman and I speed downriver from Snow's Cut toward the sea, resuming the journey in his fast Carolina Skiff. The day turns out not to be as rough as we anticipated—the wind stays steady from the west at thirteen to fifteen knots, the seas mainly flat or just a little bumpy. We'll endure some pounding on the way back upriver, but in general it's a dream day to be tooling around the open waters of the estuary.

We fly downriver past spoil islands, derelict docks, long swaths of forested shoreline.

Frank noses the boat in near the Archer Daniels Midland dock, a freakishly long concrete and steel pier jutting out from the west side of the river and lit after sundown by a battery of powerful sodium vapor lights. He says, "The fishermen like those lamps. At night you'll see them out here fishing by the lights." They're after croaker, spot, black drum, and trout. The lights also attract schools of baitfish and also ladyfish, a favorite among fly fishermen.

Farther on is the ferry dock for the Southport–Fort Fisher ferry. Alligators lurk there. North of the ferry dock and just south of the long chemical pier stands a twenty-foot-tall lighthouse—or the brick remains of one: Price's Creek Light. Built in 1849, it was one of eight lighthouses along the lower Cape Fear used to mark the twenty-five-mile passage from Oak Island to Wilmington. The other seven are long gone. Price's Creek Light was a valuable signal station for the Confederate blockade-runners during the Civil War, and after the war it fell into disuse. All that remains is the conical brick base. The carousel and light have disappeared, and only an iron axle sticking up from the flattened top reminds us that it is headless.

And there's no mistaking the nuclear power plant. A wide canal guarded by gates and booms to keep away boats carries cooling water into the plant. About 1 percent of all the water in the Cape Fear River is pumped into Progress Energy's nuclear plant—36 million to 40 million gallons a day. Though the intake gate has screens to keep out juvenile fish and crabs,

Frank Chapman, boat driver, divemaster, adventurer (author photo)

many are sucked into the plant anyway, but 95 percent are returned alive down a specially constructed flume.

From time to time, Frank points out the resting places of various shipwrecks. He gestures off to a square concrete frame in the middle of the estuary. "That's the old quarantine dock. All the ships used to have to stop there before they went upriver," he tells me.

When it was built in 1893, the quarantine dock was a cross-shaped pier 600 feet long, reaching into the 20-foot-deep shipping channel, with a medical station, gangways, a ballast crib, and a special sequestered landing where infectious passengers could be off-loaded to hospitals ashore. All vessels were required to stop there before proceeding upriver. The state legislature appropriated $20,000 to build it, on the condition that Wilmington pony up another $5,000 for state-of-the-art equipment. But Wilmington reneged, and the station was turned over to the federal Marine Hospital Service, which stepped up with cash.

Shipborne epidemics were no idle concern. On November 12, 1918, during the height of the Spanish influenza pandemic, the government transport *City of Savannah* arrived carrying 1,900 Puerto Rican workers bound for Fayetteville, where they were to be employed building Camp Bragg. Twenty-eight of them died before the ship cleared Wilmington.

Farther on, Frank points again. "Battery Island, that's where the white ibis are." With nesting season coming to a close, today it's full of gulls and turkey vultures.

He indicates a spot inshore. "That's where an old Confederate ironclad went down. The *Raleigh*." The CSS *Raleigh* was one of two Confederate ironclads stationed in the Cape Fear River. Skippered by Captain Maffitt's old surveying partner, J. Pembroke Jones, the lumbering vessel fought exactly one battle, May 6–7, 1864, against blockading Union ships. As it returned from the sea through New Inlet, it ran aground and later broke up.

"There was another ironclad that sank at Southport." The CSS *North Carolina* was not seaworthy enough to venture beyond the river and was assigned to guard duty at Southport. The superstructure may have been clad in iron, but the hull was wooden and riddled with teredo worms. It sank at its moorings.

Today as Frank and I cruise down the estuary, it's as if the cosmic director has cued up everything just right: The weather is perfect, the seas lying down in places where normally they would be slamming us around pretty good. The sun is shining out of a bright sky painted with clouds, but it's not stiflingly hot. Down in the estuary, the Bald Head commercial ferry is carrying back to the mainland a garbage truck and a Mayflower moving van. The people ferry, a dashing catamaran, zooms by crowded with vacationers bound for their getaway rental homes on Bald Head, along with residents who came ashore to shop or work and workers who will provide the various services the island requires.

The car ferry *Duke* (like the other Southport ferries, named for a North Carolina university) is passing between Southport and Federal Point, and an orange Odfell Chemical tanker, *Bow Fagus*, is heading out to sea. Tugboats come and go; the pilot boat is running out to take off the ship's pilot. The Cape Fear Community College research vessel *Dan Moore* is heading out to the channel by Bald Head to deploy a monitoring buoy, its deck crammed with students. Later as we return through Snow's Cut, we'll encounter the UNCW research vessel *R/V Cape Fear*, at seventy feet long the flagship of the UNCW research fleet, bound upriver for maintenance. It can keep at sea for extended periods, manned by two crew and accommodating eight scientists.

Meantime, dozens of small runabouts, larger trawler yachts, a shrimp trawler, a small fleet of commercial fishing boats, and sailboats of all sizes join the traffic in the estuary.

I mentally contrast this scene with the one at Buckhorn Dam, more than 200 miles upriver: In two canoes we passed a single fisherman in a johnboat, then we had the river all to ourselves for miles until Lanier Falls. We had it mostly to ourselves after that for mile after mile as the river widened and constricted, deepened and channeled, widened again and fell with insistent gravity across ledges, through the locks and dams, to the meander of the coastal plain.

We pass old Fort Caswell to starboard, named for the first governor of

(top)
The Odfell chemical carrier *Bow Fagus* disembarks the river pilot and stands out to sea (author photo)

(bottom)
The Cape Fear Community College research vessel *Dan Moore* steams out the Southport channel to deploy a monitoring buoy (author photo)

North Carolina, Richard Caswell, hero of Moore's Creek, who died in abject poverty. No one is quite sure anymore where he is buried. The site thought to be his grave was excavated, but all that was found were scraps of wood, presumably from a coffin. Fort Caswell is a neat establishment of residences and larger communal buildings, by turns a Confederate and Federal army post, owned by the Baptist Assembly since 1948 and used for conferences. As the assembly describes the place, it is now "an instrument of peace." The fort is a compound of tidy white clapboard buildings roofed in green. The concrete battlements remain, stripped of guns. The whole place feels more like a summer camp than an outpost against invasion, and in fact it's now a place of retreat and spiritual contemplation for thousands each year.

Just offshore stands a weather station—a hefty steel piling on which is mounted a platform containing electronic sensors powered by a solar array. It has one odd feature that speaks volumes about where it is: a second, smaller platform, located just a couple of feet higher than the main platform. Through binoculars, we can see the ragged straw of an osprey nest. So the platform was deliberately built with a "decoy" platform to accommodate an osprey family and keep it out of the instrument array.

The water is boiling with small fish. Frank identifies them: "menhaden." A small, blunt-headed, bony fish about a foot long and weighing about a pound. This year, for unaccountable reasons, has been a banner year, and they have been spotted far upriver.

The menhaden, also called bunker or pogies, congregate in vast schools—as large as an acre—in shallow coastal waters. The fishery used to be busy, with factories for processing the fish into oil and fishmeal up the coast at Morehead and Beaufort and some right here in Southport. In fact, during the twentieth century the menhaden fishery was the largest of all American fisheries, in terms of both number caught and tonnage of fish.

The method of choice for catching the menhaden is the purse seine, a net circled around the school and pulled taut, like a purse string, by men in small boats. It has traditionally provided employment for African American men, who created a tradition of chanteys sung while working the heavy purse nets from the small boats. In the nineteenth century, the pulling was done by hand, and the chanteys helped to coordinate the haul and pace the men through the arduous labor.

These days the industry is mechanized: Spotters in small planes identify the schools and direct the mother ship to the site, then two small, fast, motorized boats surround the school with a 1,500-foot-long net weighing two tons. They draw it closed using a system of hydraulic blocks, augmented by old-fashioned muscle power. Closing the purse seine is still backbreaking work that calls for both strength and endurance. The fishermen haul most of the net aboard, leaving just the bunt in the water, now swarming with fish.

The mother ship lowers a large vacuum pipe, which literally sucks the fish aboard in a silver slurry of water and fish. A single catch might net 300,000 fish. The mother ship typically has room in its refrigerated holds for a million. The last menhaden factory on the North Carolina coast closed, and overfishing of the inshore waters by out-of-state boats has led to some fairly restrictive regulations.

The menhaden fishery is an efficient one. Unlike, say, the shrimp trawl, which scoops up all manner of other species, the menhaden net catches nothing but menhaden. The fish oil is used for lubricants, lipstick, cookies, soap, health food supplements, even linoleum. But there's an irony here—one that has consequences for the river. As Greenpeace points out, much of the processed fishmeal goes into livestock and chicken feed, which comes out in the animal waste, and the nutrient-rich runoff from factory farms is a prime source of pollution in river basins.

Everything's connected. A small, bony ocean fish can change the oxygen balance of the river far upstream of the estuary and affect all the other fish that swim in it.

We're off Snow's Marsh, near the intake for the nuclear plant and across the river from New Inlet, which has been closed for a century by a rock dam to stem the inflow of sand into the river channel, and another story intrudes on our cruise.

~~~~~~~~~~

Somehow the Cape Fear has managed to insert itself into just about every national issue we've faced in the last several centuries, including airline terrorism.

National Air Lines (NAL), though headquartered in Florida, used to operate out of Wilmington International Airport, in those days known simply by the name it had acquired as an army air force base in World War II: Bluethenthal Field. It was christened after World War I aviator Arthur "Bluey" Bluethenthal, a Wilmington native.

Bluethenthal played varsity center for Princeton University's football team from 1910 to 1912 and later coached at Princeton and the University of North Carolina. When war came, he enlisted (like Ernest Hemingway) in the American Ambulance Corps. Bluethenthal won the Croix de Guerre with Star for his conspicuous bravery at the horrific Battle of Verdun. By 1917, he had transferred to the French Foreign Legion for flight training and wound up a sergeant in the Escadrille 227. He lasted just three months. He was flying an artillery-spotting patrol when he was knocked out of the sky by ground fire. He was posthumously awarded a second Croix de Guerre with Palm and the Medaille Militaire.

One of NAL's most popular routes was its New York–to–Miami run, which passed right over Bluethenthal Field on its way south. On the morning of January 5, 1960, an NAL Boeing 707 prepared to take off from Idlewild Airport (now JFK), but a crack was discovered in the copilot's cockpit window. Passengers were deplaned and divided between two substitute propeller-driven aircraft, a Lockheed Electra and a DC-6B, which was designated NAL 2511.

The four-engine DC-6B, carrying twenty-nine passengers served by five crew, pushed back from the gate at 11:34 P.M. into a rainy night. Storms covered much of the Eastern Seaboard. In the mountains of western North Carolina, it was snowing. The coast was socked in by heavy fog, rain, and cloud cover. The flight was uneventful, so far as anyone knows, for almost three hours. At 2:27 A.M., the airplane passed over Wilmington at 18,000 feet, and four minutes later, the pilot reported they were over the radio beacon at Carolina Beach.

It was the last transmission ever received from the plane.

The *Wilmington Star News* reported what happened next in a retrospective story a half-century after the event: "Around 2:45 A.M., Richard Randolph, a farmer who lived about a mile outside Bolivia, heard an explosion 'like dynamite.' He and his wife saw a bright light hit the ground. 'It looked like it was going to hit the house,' Lottie Randolph later told reporters—then they saw a fire that lasted for five minutes. Others in the neighborhood later said they heard a blast, too."

Unaccountably, no one investigated further that night. It wasn't till the next morning that McArthur Randolph, the young son of the couple who had first heard the explosion and watched the plummeting fireball, went outdoors early to feed the hogs and discovered the wreckage of a plane strewn across a field. Since the family had no telephone, Mr. Randolph drove into Bolivia and called the authorities around 7:00 A.M. When police arrived on the scene, they found a debris field that covered twenty acres off Route 17 northwest of Bolivia.

The *Star News* reported: "'It was a gruesome sight,' recalled Clarence 'Lucky' Swartz, a retired State Highway Patrol officer who was on the scene.

'The plane was broken into two sections,' said Swartz, who was directing traffic at the scene. 'Several people were lying on the ground, but most of them were still strapped in their seats.'"

Some of the bodies had been hammered a foot and a half into the ground by the force of the crash. It was a scene that would become all too familiar over the ensuing years: suitcases broken open, clothing, plane parts, and at least one life raft strewn across the rural landscape. Some strange details imprinted themselves on the minds of onlookers and investigators: Most of the dead had had their shoes blown off. A number of the passengers were still wearing life jackets, as if they had expected to ditch over water.

And all but one of the wristwatches recovered were still running. The lone exception had fixed the precise time of the crash: 2:45 A.M.

There were no survivors.

A Catholic priest moved over the field administering last rites, and investigators began the macabre task of transporting the bodies to a makeshift morgue set up at the Moore Street Gymnasium in Southport. Among the dead was a World War II Medal of Honor recipient, Vice Admiral Edward O. McDonnell, who had survived combat in the Pacific but not this ill-starred flight.

Not all the bodies were found: Two were still missing.

Since it was too foggy for an aerial search, 450 marines from Camp Lejeune joined forces with 125 national guardsmen and tromped through the fields and marshes around Bolivia on a grisly treasure hunt.

Meanwhile, hunks of fuselage turned up far downriver at Kure Beach.

Three days after the crash, one of the missing bodies was found floating in Snow's Marsh, near the New Inlet Dam, more than fifteen miles from where the plane went down. And it wasn't found by accident. As soon as the doomed airliner disappeared from radar on that rainy night, the director of the Wilmington airport called up a menhaden spotter pilot by the name of Hall Watters and rousted him out of bed in Southport.

Douglas Cutting, a fishing guide and writer who lived for years in Southport, knew Hall Watters and interviewed him extensively before Watters's death. In an evocative personal essay about his relationship with the legendary flyer, fisherman, and hunter, called "Pilot," he writes, "He could fly over the open ocean, find a sunken wreck, mark it, drive a boat to it, dive its treasure, donate what he found, go back with a fishing rod, and go to bed with nothing more than grouper sandwiches in his belly and a memory. In my mind, there's not much he couldn't do."

Watters was thirty-five years old, trim and compact, a flyer who knew the coast as only a seasoned fisherman can. He located the wreckage of the four-engine plane just after daybreak, and the pattern of the wreckage didn't look right to him. "Somebody blew it up, cause it don't come apart like that," he told his brother Robert. He snapped a picture and left the recovery to those on the ground. When bodies were still missing days later, he took his Piper Cub up for another look.

As Cutting tells the story,

Only a few days later, on a clear January morning over Snow's Marsh, he saw something below him. Just a slight eddy in the current of some shallow water, some lines creasing off a sunken object. He radioed the FBI agent and told him they might want to bring a boat into the marsh.

First they recovered an oxygen bottle, then a pair of seats—aisle and window—that had blown out the side of the plane. Hall made another pass over the marsh, talking on the radio the whole time. Then he saw something that made his skin crawl—something he'd seen in the ravaged dunes after Hurricane Hazel and days after some fishing boat had capsized off Southport.

"We got a body down there," he said, giving the coordinates to a small creek mouth near the confluence of marsh and river.

"He's face up, part of his right leg missing, still has his boxer shorts on and a Windsor knot around his neck. No shirt, no tie, no pants," Hall said.

The body turned out to be that of Julian A. Frank, a Connecticut lawyer. His body, unlike the others, was badly mutilated. Blast debris—including steel wire and brass—was embedded in his tissue. Also, crusted on his right hand were particles of manganese dioxide, used in dry-cell batteries. Watters allowed investigators to use his hangar at Southport as a staging area to reconstruct the wreckage of NAL 2511 on a frame of wood and chicken wire.

The last body was recovered near the crash site, but attention remained focused on Frank, whose body clearly had been catapulted out of the plane and kept rocketing through the night far beyond where the fuselage went down.

It turned out that Frank had purchased a life insurance policy worth $900,000 from an airport vending machine just before his flight—you could do that in those innocent days—and that he was under investigation by the Manhattan district attorney for misappropriating money—a lot of it: almost $600,000.

Other clues turned suspicion on Frank: Components that could have been part of a bomb were found among the wreckage, including an alarm clock. The Civil Aeronautics Board determined that *something* had exploded aboard the plane at 2:33 A.M.: "Medical experts with extensive experience with battle field 'landmine injuries' and other injuries resulting from explosives indicate that the injuries sustained by the body found at Snow's Marsh could only have been caused by an explosive blast. . . . At approximately 0233 a dynamite charge was exploded, initiated by means of a cell battery within the passenger cabin and at a point beneath the extreme right seat of seat row No. 7."

For Cutting, the disaster illuminated the character of an extraordinary man: "He landed his plane on Bald Head's beaches and caught red drum in the shoals. And he made tens of thousands of landings on the grass strip across from my Oak Island creek house long before I was born. As I ate breakfast with this story every morning, watching ospreys circling, herons fishing, and the planes touching down, it finally made sense. He was the real thing. . . . And he didn't help solve the mystery of Flight 2511 in 1960 to be a hero. He searched because he had the capacity to find. He did it because it was the right thing to do."

Exactly who planted the bomb on NAL 2511 was never proven: Frank, in a fit of guilty desperation, or some other party, for reasons unknown? Was the bomber even aboard the doomed flight?

Watters testified in the successful lawsuit brought by the families. For them, the case was closed: Frank was the bomber.

But that was a civil action. Officially, the bombing remains another mystery, one that dropped out of the sky right into the river.

Frank slows the big powerboat as we approach Southport.

Onshore, a line of stately homes faces the estuary. Just offshore, the UNCW *R/V Sturgeon* is anchored, three scientists busy sampling the water column. The estuary is a rich environment for science, an ecotone containing multiple species of fish, birds, and wildlife in all stages of their life cycles.

And once again, we're cruising through history. Off to starboard lies the mouth of Bonnet's Creek, named for Stede Bonnet, the "Gentleman Pirate," scion of a wealthy Barbados family who reportedly carried his voluminous library to sea with him. Here he and his crew holed up in the summer of 1718 to repair their ship, the *Royal James*, formerly the *Revenge*, which was leaking badly. Bonnet had changed the name of the pirate ship after receiving a pardon and was sailing under the alias "Captain Thomas." They captured a smaller vessel and broke it apart to use in refitting their own ship, careened their own vessel in shallow water to replank the hull.

But they overstayed their welcome.

Bonnet had once sailed with Blackbeard, and in those days they had blockaded Charleston harbor, wreaking havoc on the local merchant fleet. Now it was South Carolina's turn for revenge. Royal Governor Robert Johnson ordered two British sloops of war under Colonel William Rhett to seek out Bonnet and bring him to justice. Rhett found Bonnet here, so the legend goes, and overpowered his much smaller crew.

The battle was apparently a rather haphazard affair in which the river played a decisive role. Both of Rhett's sloops ran aground on sandbars, as did all three of Bonnet's vessels. The crews fired at each other for five or six hours without much effect, until the tide came in, Rhett's ships were refloated and could maneuver, and he boarded the *Royal James*. Sheer force of numbers carried the day. Bonnet and thirty-four survivors of his original crew of seventy were taken to Charleston, tried, and hanged.

Bonnet is not the only pirate to have sailed these waters. Local lore has it that Blackbeard buried a chest full of treasure on "Money Island," south of Masonboro Inlet—the reason Sprunt's pageant included the replica of the *Queen Anne's Revenge*.

We run past Oak Island, past Fort Caswell, past the long beach at Bald Head Island, and into steep chop. It's too noisy to talk, and there's not much to say. I'm just holding on, enjoying the ride, mentally comparing this wide open, busy estuary, these boisterous seas, with the serene, narrow river at Buckhorn, the only sound the steady rush of water over the dam. Out here we are bucking waves, the hull under us airborne between crests, as the river loses its contour and blends with the sea. We follow the fairway between rocking buoys that mark the big shipping channel, and at last there's the sea buoy, the end of the river.

This is what I've come all these miles for, the finish line. Here is the Cape Fear River joining the rest of the waters of the planet.

Frank slows the engine, and we rock around for a few minutes, savoring the moment, no land between us and Bermuda, 600 miles east. After a couple of minutes, he grins and says, "See what you came to see?"

"Yeah—we can go back now." But I'm not quite finished. There are still two more pieces of the journey to complete: the short stretch of river from Mermaid Point down to Buckhorn Dam, and the Cape of Fear.

The horizon is full of nothing but sky and sea. We turn and speed back the way we came. We'll dock at Southport and enjoy lunch and cold beer to celebrate.

~~~~~~~~~~~

Life on the Cape Fear estuary at Southport inspired Robert Ruark to write his most beloved books, *The Old Man and the Boy* and *The Old Man's Boy Grows Older*, memoirs that capture the heyday of river pilots, fishermen, and other denizens of the water.

The books derived from a column of the same name he wrote for *Field and Stream* magazine. Ruark began his writing career on local newspapers in Hamlet and Sanford, then wrote his column for ten years. He wrote for all three Washington, D.C., dailies, became a syndicated columnist, and spent his adult life roaming the world, from Washington, D.C., to Europe and Africa. He was a big-game hunter and adventurer in the mold of Hemingway, with whom he is said to have felt a rivalry—jealous of Hemingway's fame and reputation as an outdoorsman, a reputation Ruark felt was undeserved. Ruark, born in Wilmington in 1915, was almost a generation younger than Hemingway.

His novel *Something of Value*, about the Mau Mau uprising, made him a millionaire and became a blockbuster movie starring Rock Hudson and Sidney Poitier. He wrote other novels, made a fortune, drank like a hussar, and retired to a castle in Spain. He never came home; he lies buried near Barcelona in a small village called Palamos.

Yet for all his manly bluster, hard-nosed reporting, and books about far-off wars and revolutions, he is remembered best for his tender reminiscences of growing up at the feet of two grandfathers who were both river pilots, learning the wisdom of the seasons along the Cape Fear River, claiming the salt marsh and low river country as his true home. He combined the two old pilots into one inspirational composite character, the Old Man: part grandfather, part seer, part mentor in all things wild—the kind of Merlin figure every boy wishes he had in his corner.

In *The Old Man and the Boy*, Ruark writes,

When I think of it now, I think of it in terms of sounds and smells rather than sights. The catbirds quarreled in the low bushes around the house, and the big, fat, sassy old mocker that lived in the magnolia mimicked the catbirds. The doves cooed sadly from a great distance, and the quail called from the brushy cover at the edge of the cultivation. They came marching boldly into the strawberry patches, not in coveys but in pairs, walking through the back yard as if they owned it.

The killdeers wheeled and dipped in clouds over the wet fields, the skies filled with the mournful *kill-dee, kill-dee*, and the meadowlarks sang in the fields, and out of the wet places came the wild, sweet song of the woodcock. The crows and the jays raised general hell with everything, including the spring, and you could hear the rain crows' hollow *tonk* from some hidden position in a tall pine, and the solid knock of the woodpeckers, and the sweet chirrup of the little bluebirds.

Here we meet Ruark not as a blustering, macho man-of-the-world but as a boy captivated by birdsong, who somehow knows already deep in his heart that this place of ragged boyhood is the best, truest place he will ever know in all the world. Not because of the grandiose things but because of the small things, the intimate natural moments. The Old Man is his guide into this transitory world that he will carry inside his head and heart for all the days of his adventurous life.

I've long admired his Southport tales, and so I made a pilgrimage with my wife, Jill, to the home of Ruark's maternal grandfather, Captain Edward Atkins, one of the inspirations for the Old Man of the books. It's now the Robert Ruark Inn, a beautifully maintained yellow Victorian fenced in by white pickets at the corner of West Nash and North Lord Streets. In the parlor, beside the hearth, stands a glass showcase containing all of Ruark's books and two binders full of family letters that were discovered by the previous owner of the house.

The house is kept in pristine condition, with the original heart-pine floors and wavery leaded-glass windows. Every room seems luminous with the light from high windows, and it's easy to imagine a boy spending time in that house, devouring books from a perch in the reading alcove in the parlor, imagining the books he himself will one day write, the stories of his pilot grandfather already whispering in his head, the lessons of his boyhood in the salt marsh and coastal forest only beginning to form into words.

~~~~~~~

At Southport I also look up Mike Rice, the prime mover behind Save the Cape. I called him because all of a sudden the so-called superport plan has surfaced again. Three public hearings were held by the North Carolina Department of Transportation, one of them in Southport, and Mike Rice had his say. He invited the crowd of just under 400 people to stand up if they opposed the superport, and every single one of them did. "Of course, we were all talking to ourselves," he tells me matter-of-factly. "They were just checking off a procedural box."

He lives off Robert Ruark Drive, appropriately enough, in a gray house that backs onto the river marsh, with a gorgeous, panoramic view. "When the tide goes out, the wading birds come in," he says. "Beats looking at container ships."

Mike is both a lawyer and an engineer, with receding silver hair, a relaxed posture in jeans and dark blue sweatshirt and boat mocs, and a demeanor that exudes honesty. He speaks quietly, smiles often, and has an air of humility and earnestness about him. He's the sort of guy you'd trust with your car keys. His gaze is steady and direct in a manner that reassures you he knows what he's talking about. He is the definition of unintimidating, this foe of powerful interests. His reading glasses lend him a contemplative, professorial air.

We talk upstairs in his study, a spacious room full of light, stacked with binders, reports, books, and the other artifacts of activism. "I'm trying to save the world up here," he says softly, with a little self-deprecating smile.

He is not by nature an activist and is far more comfortable in small meetings negotiating deals, as he did for years as a transportation consultant, Wall Street deal broker, and lead negotiator for the Department of Transportation in Washington. There he arranged the licensing of deepwater oil ports: platforms located thirty miles out in the Gulf of Mexico, where the water was plenty deep for sixty-foot-draft Panamax supertankers. The oil was piped ashore—an economically and environmentally viable arrangement.

So he is no firebrand tree-hugger out to stop progress, especially not progress that involves his professional passion: transportation. His glassed-in

The Robert Ruark Inn at Southport, where the adventuring novelist learned the natural wisdom of his river pilot grandfather (author photo)

barrister's bookcase holds several shelves of HO model locomotives and rolling stock on inscribed presentation bases, gifts commemorating various deals to finance railroads. When he worked for the Department of Transportation, he had great respect for the motives and competence of his colleagues in government service. He recalls them as both altruistic and capable.

He declares, right at the outset of our conversation, "I'm not at heart an environmentalist—that's not how it started. It was just a recognition of what should *not* happen, and then of what *should* happen."

He has studied the plans for the superport, obtained crucial documents through the Freedom of Information Act. "You look at this and there are two things going on in your head. One, it would be devastating for the community, and two, it can't possibly succeed."

I tell him that my understanding after talking to people at the Army Corps of Engineers was that the superport project is dead—there's just no money, not on that scale. "Yes—it was put on hold in July 2010 when six municipalities passed resolutions opposing it," he explains.

Then: "It came back with a strength that is frightening and invisible."

Suddenly the so-called international port started showing up as a viable alternative for a deepwater port, as the North Carolina Department of Trans-

A dredge working the estuary, clearing the channel for shipping. Massive dredging would be required to build and maintain a superport at a minimum cost of $12 million per year. (author photo)

portation and State Port Authority searched the coast for options between Virginia and South Carolina borders, "as if that hadn't been done 300 years ago." And indeed, the local *Star News* announced that the results of a $2 million maritime study commissioned by the North Carolina Department of Transportation would be released in March 2012: "The maritime study is expected to identify a menu of options for improving the state's position in the global shipping industry. That could include improving existing port facilities in Wilmington and Morehead City or building a new deepwater port near Southport, among other possibilities."

His prediction came true. So the Southport superport is back on the drawing board.

Mike ticks off all that is wrong with the idea: The water fronting the site is way too shallow, and the dredging required would be monumental in scale, costing $12 million per year just to maintain; the nearest interstate is thirty miles away; the nearest railroad, about seventeen; and it is operated by the Department of Defense.

In his view—and bear in mind that he loves transportation and is a fan of commerce, and that it has been his profession for a long time—even the current port is no longer economically viable. He has graphs and pie charts that demonstrate just how little traffic goes through Wilmington—negligible compared with what passes through the ports of Charleston and Norfolk.

"It's just reckless," he concludes, "because the port of Wilmington has not been commercially significant since January of 1865."

"But doesn't the port create some traffic, some jobs, some level of valuable economic activity? Isn't that worth something?" I argue.

"No doubt it is. But is it worth the price?"

His argument is simple, and he illustrates it using the example of the Connecticut River, which used to be a thoroughfare to Hartford. Then steamships got bigger and railroads could move goods cheaper, and deepening the river was economically a nonstarter. So while other northeastern rivers are cluttered with obsolete factories, tank farms, and dirty smokestacks, there you see something very different. "You get to the mouth of the Connecticut River, it's pristine." He says, "The market leads to the least expensive alternative," and he counts all the costs, not just the dollars.

And at last we come to his ultimate goal, to create Cape Fear National Seashore. It's not a crazy idea at all—the National Park Service recommended the formation of Cape Fear National Monument way back in 1967, on the model of Cape Hatteras National Seashore. The Park Service plan would have covered most of the east side of the river—Federal Point and Fort Fisher—and they have already been preserved. Mike aims at the mainland side, where some parcels, like Orton Plantation, have been spared development because of enlightened ownership and others, such as Brunswick Town, have attained the status of historical sites.

"There is a patchwork that we feel should be brought together." For Mike Rice and his cohort at Save the Cape, we've reached a historical moment of decision. "It's a turning point, really. This area had been spared development simply because it hadn't gotten here yet."

He knows it's a hard case to make, and it may be too late; but he is persistent and levelheaded, so who knows? He says, "The history of national parks is that they were very often created over local opposition." He cites Grand Canyon, Grand Teton. "They didn't want the federal government in their backyards. It was only after it happened that they realized the enormous economic benefit."

To succeed may require someone with star power, a "front" person who can galvanize the media and public support. "I can do the grunt work," he says and smiles, "but I'm not charismatic." Maybe not, but he is awfully persuasive.

As with the Stop Titan cadre, I'm not sure he has a chance. There's heavy money on the line—$50 million and counting, the costs of buying the port site and conducting all those studies, then refinancing the whole nut. But he's got that quiet, smoldering passion, the kind that's on for the long haul. I recognize it in David Webster, Mike Mallin, Kemp Burdette, Doug Springer, Bob Maffitt, all these smart people who have been smitten by the river, to whom it truly belongs.

~~~~~~~~

Across from Southport lies Federal Point, on the northern flank of New Inlet, which runs between it and the shoals of Zeke's Island. Once upon a time, long before it was dammed, New Inlet was the favored entry point into the Cape Fear.

Federal Point was renamed Confederate Point during the Civil War. It was the natural place to build a massive fort — Fort Fisher — to anchor a system of nine forts on the lower Cape Fear with the aim of keeping the Federal fleet out of the river. Fort Fisher was the strongest, occupying a key position between river and sea. Colonel William Lamb was its twenty-nine-year-old architect and commandant. He was a gentleman of means from Norfolk, son of the mayor there, who had run unsuccessfully for mayor himself. He had some training as a military school cadet and later became a newspaperman ardently in favor of secession, but it's a mystery how he came by his remarkable engineering skills.

Rather than try to construct masonry forts on the model of Fort Caswell across the river — which had been built before the war by the U.S. Army Corps of Engineers — he understood that ramparts of sand would withstand a heavy bombardment much better than brick and mortar by simply absorbing its force. He kept a thousand men busy for two years perfecting the inverted L that became the most formidable sea-facing defense of the Confederacy.

Lamb had a great advantage over his adversaries in similar situations, an advantage that would play a part in the fort's undoing: slave labor.

Six hundred black slaves and Lumbee Indians were forced into the back-breaking travail of building the fort, shoveling hundreds of tons of sand into massive mile-and-a-half-long earthworks, raising wooden palisades nine feet high in front of the land face to block the Wilmington road, planting sharpened abatis in front of the palisades, digging deep trenches in front of all the ramparts, then hauling on man-ropes attached to derricks to swing the heavy barrels of the seven-ton Columbiads onto their mounts in the deep traverses formed by heavy timbers and sandbags on top of the ramparts.

Wilmington could not be bombarded from the sea — it was too far upriver. Once a ship got past the fort into the river, however, all bets were off.

The whole point of the fort was to keep U.S. Navy vessels from getting upriver to Wilmington, while allowing fast, shallow-draft blockade-runners to sneak into the river via either the main channel or New Inlet.

The latter was blown open by a hurricane in 1761, transforming a low-lying sandy spit called the Haul Over into a channel half a mile wide and eighteen feet deep. The Haul Over was so named because, before the hurricane opened it to the sea, captains used to beach their small craft there and haul them across the spit of land into the river, thus saving a long and treacherous voyage around Frying Pan Shoals and into the main fairway.

Because there were two entrances to the river, separated by the Frying Pan Shoals, which extend from Cape Fear on Bald Head Island some twenty-eight miles out to sea, the blockading Yankee fleet had to patrol an arc more than fifty miles long.

The blockade-runners were built with deliberately shallow drafts and powered by sidewheels, often tandem wheels, that provided amazing speed and thus maneuverability. The blockade-runner captains muffled the wheels with canvas and burned hard coal, so they couldn't be tracked by the telltale black smudge on the horizon. They either carried local pilots or—like Captain Maffitt—were themselves familiar with the unmarked passage.

The U.S. Navy was stubborn and kept adding ships, till by the end of the war more than thirty were stationed off the Cape Fear—almost as many as formed the entire Union fleet at the outbreak of the war. Of the 100 or so blockade-runners that served Wilmington during the war, after four years of interception, two-thirds of them had been captured or sunk or had foundered on the shoals.

But blockade-running was such a lucrative business that owners still risked it. In just a couple of voyages they could pay off their ship and make a hefty profit. Captains and crews shared in the profits. Even the commanders and crews of the blockading Yankee fleet got their cuts: Captured vessels and cargo were auctioned, with one-half of the proceeds going to the U.S. government and the other half divided into prize shares by rank.

By the way, this makes our hero James Sprunt something of a war profiteer. He invested in cotton bales the money he made bringing in a few barrels of molasses. This was common practice for seaman aboard blockade-runners: Buy a barrel of molasses or rum and sell it for an exorbitant price in Wilmington, where cotton could be had for just three cents a pound. Indeed, he was in good company. Colonel Lamb himself speculated in cargoes and made some tidy profits along the way, though his duties kept him from getting too deeply into the business.

By 1864, General Robert E. Lee's army was totally dependent on food and armaments arriving through Wilmington and then shipped north via the Wilmington and Weldon Railroad. North Carolina's other railroads—encompassing most of the thousand miles of track in the state—had all been built east to west to carry raw materials out of the hinterlands and finished goods back in.

Even the Wilmington and Weldon was not ideal, since it was constantly subject to attack by Union troops who occupied the coast. It was a thin lifeline, and its usefulness was limited further by the fact that the gauge of the tracks in North Carolina did not match that of Virginia railroads—it was off by an inch and a half—so that troops and goods had to detrain at the border and load onto other cars.

Nevertheless, the Wilmington and Weldon was the only remaining line of supply, and it had to be protected at all costs. And Fort Fisher was the key to protecting it. So in addition to cannons, the fort had a state-of-the-art hidden defense: an underground minefield laid across the peninsula from the river to the beach to stop troops invading down the river road from Wilmington. The mines were either standard heavy artillery shells or specially designed "torpedoes" packed with 100 pounds of black powder. The twenty-four mines could be detonated electrically using power from a battery inside the fort.

The proximity of the beach led to a vexing security problem for the Confederates. The Yankee ships patrolled just offshore, which meant that if a slave could swim out far enough, he could be picked up by one of the smaller picket boats. Indeed, on several occasions Yankee longboats landed on the beach and simply took off runaway slaves, who then enlisted in the fight.

Colonel Lamb lost one of his own slaves in this manner, with momentous consequences.

In May 1864, Charles Wesley slipped out to the beach and was picked up by sailors from the USS *Niphong*. Having helped to build the fort, he proceeded to brief the Yankees on the layout of the structure; its garrison of 800 artillerymen, regular soldiers, and junior reserves; and its armaments—44 cannons (more were still to be added, and additional reinforcements would swell the garrison to almost 2,000), including the massive ten-inch Columbiads and eleven-inch Brooke guns.

Thus an escaped slave is credited with helping engineer the downfall of the mighty fortress. In its simplicity and its turnabout toward justice, the Wesley saga is almost biblical.

In all, 82 African American men from the Wilmington area joined the United States army or navy, and a dozen of them returned to fight in the final battle of Fort Fisher. Of the 9,000 troops in the invading force who eventually stormed the redoubts, nearly a third belonged to what were called U.S. Colored Infantry regiments—and most of them were former slaves. One of the volunteer regiments, the 37th, had been raised in Kinston.

All this is not to refight the Civil War, only to make the point that here at the mouth of the Cape Fear River all the complicated elements of the war came together in one dramatic event: slavery, an economy built on a bankrupt premise, political extremism, international trade, blockade-runners and aristocrats, freedmen and conscripts, modern engineering, obsolete tactics, and a hell of a lot of firepower.

The Fort Fisher garrison was not the Confederacy's finest. The Junior Reserves—in theory consisting of boys of at least seventeen years of age, but in fact including boys as young as thirteen—were particularly vulnerable to veteran troops. John Homer High, stationed at the fort with the 18th regiment, noted in a letter to his father six months before the fort was stormed, "I am truly sorry to see such boys in service though many of them are able boddied soldiers but among them are some that can't hold their guns offhand to save their life neither can they pull the hammer back to fire without putting the breech of the gun on the ground and put their foot on the hammer to cock it."

"Offhand" was the typical way of holding and aiming the ten-pound musket while standing. In this day and age, we are used to high school boys who stand six feet tall and weigh 180 pounds, but the uniforms on display at the Museum of the Confederacy in Richmond look more like outfits for kids playing soldier: tight waists, narrow shoulders, short legs and arms. And they were the clothes worn by regular adult troops.

The battle for Fort Fisher was in fact quite a battle, or rather battles. The first invasion fleet of sixty-four warships mounting more than 600 cannons, accompanied by troop transports, maneuvered into firing position through a dense sea fog on the morning of Christmas Eve 1864. The first "shot" was actually a "powder ship"—basically a floating bomb: The USS *Louisiana* was packed with high explosives, set adrift in the river, and detonated. The force of the blast rattled windows as far away as Wilmington, seventeen miles upriver, but it did not damage the fort.

The 10,000 shells that followed, however, created a hell on earth for any defender not holed up in a bombproof bunker.

The bombardment began shortly after noon and lasted till dark, then continued on Christmas Day, intermittently, as troops swarmed ashore from small boats but were driven back by a withering fire from the fort.

The attackers thought they had killed off the garrison, but the garrison had been hunkered down in "bombproofs": thick-walled, reinforced chambers beneath the gun traverses covered with several feet of sand. The troops emerged from their underground sanctuaries full of fight, and for the Yankees it must have been like seeing a legion of men rising from the dead. They beat a hasty retreat up the beach and camped there for two more days before they could be safely pulled off in the heavy seas.

The armada abruptly sailed away the next morning, chased by a victory volley from the fort, but its departure was not a retreat, only a reprieve. Remarkably, despite the greatest bombardment in history up to that time, only five of the defenders were killed.

A new armada returned on January 13, 1865, and pounded the fort with almost 20,000 shells. This was shock and awe on a magisterial scale: blasting apart gun carriages, pulverizing the massive timbers that shored up the traverses, dismembering those unlucky enough to be caught out in the hellish rain of fire.

This time 500 of the defenders fell killed or wounded in the bombardment and subsequent onslaught of more than 9,000 Union troops. The fort was surrendered by Major General Charles Whiting, the ranking officer on the field, on January 15.

It's not much of an exaggeration to say that the Civil War was decided there and then at the mouth of the Cape Fear River. Lee's troops would thrash about for a few more months, as would the Army of Tennessee under General Joe Johnston—a ragtag ghost of its former self, pulled together from various decimated regiments and untried coastal artillery units, that would finally be put out of business at Bennett Place in April. But the Confederacy now was cut off from the outside world.

No more munitions or foodstuffs would be coming in, and equally important, no more diplomatic pouches would be going out to secure the intervention of the British or other European nations. It was only a matter of running out the clock.

For the full drama of the epic clash of ships, cannons, and onrushing hordes of Yankees, including the desperate hand-to-hand fighting in the gun pits, read Rod Gragg's thrilling book, *Confederate Goliath*, and follow it up with Chris Fonvielle's gripping coda, *The Wilmington Campaign*. Both write as if they were there dodging shells and taking notes.

Once the Yankees had secured Fort Fisher—the anchor—the Confederates simply abandoned the other eight smaller forts ranged along the river between the sea and Wilmington.

The Yankees marched upriver and fought through the artillery at Sugar Loaf Hill, where General Braxton Bragg had timidly kept his reserve troops rather than commit them to the defense of Fort Fisher when they might have done some good. U.S. Colored Infantry fought to a standstill farther on at Forks Road, close to the present site of the Cameron Art Museum, before reinforcements carried the day and they marched triumphantly into Wilmington.

I find myself walking the paths inside Fort Fisher on a chilly March day, following a tour guided by Amy Thornton, a young, knowledgeable site interpreter. She reminds us of the isolation of the fort in those days: There were no lines of vacation homes along the beach, no high-end housing developments on the river. Wilmington was a long day's slog away through sand and mud on a narrow rutted road. Or it could be reached by steamer in a couple of hours from landings on the river side.

In summer, when troops and slaves labored to build the massive sand ramparts, temperatures hovered in the high 90s and often broke 100. Swarms of malaria-bearing mosquitoes afflicted the garrison. In winter, when the fighting actually occurred, the peninsula was blasted by icy winds. Just before the first battle, a tremendous gale blew in, and after the first bombardment, which destroyed all the barracks, the storm returned, frothing the sea into whitecaps that stranded the Yankees on the beach and making life miserable for the Confederate defenders as well.

We are allowed to climb up into the traverse on the land face, guarding the sally port where the road from Wilmington ends. One of the giant cannons has been mounted on a swiveling base. To see over the parapet, you have to climb up onto a wooden platform. There you catch a breathtaking vista of the river, a long reach of the eye upriver and across, encompassing marshes and gray shallows, and beyond them the ship channel heaving with wind-driven waves. Thirty feet below, the Yankees would have been swarming up the face of the rampart, making the hard sluggish climb through sand.

The fighting was remarkably savage, overwashing the fort like a tide.

Once the first assault troops were over the ramparts, the fight went lateral, from gun traverse to gun traverse. Men fired down into the faces of other men. Inside the gunpits, the troops were so jammed together that many could not raise their muskets to fire. Others could not reload, so they were handed down muskets by their comrades and fired them off point-blank into men wearing the enemy uniform.

Meanwhile, the navy was still bombarding the fort, catching the Confederate defenders in a hellstorm of exploding metal and occasionally wiping out Federal troops with "friendly" fire.

Littered about inside the fort were hundreds of pieces of men, the toll of

Soldiers of Company E, 4th U.S. Colored Troops, who landed at Fort Fisher and led the campaign to capture Wilmington (courtesy of the Library of Congress)

the bombardment: headless corpses, stray arms and legs, pulpy unidentifiable remains. I can hardly envision such a butcher's yard, here in this beautiful place, listening to a charming and knowledgeable guide reel off statistics: how many shells, how many dead, how many hours of fighting until the nighttime surrender.

And even after surrender, the dying went on wholesale. Someone, it was never determined who, accidentally ignited the powder magazine and killed another 130 or so exhausted men. An exact count was impossible, since the huge explosion had simply vaporized the men closest to the blast. Most were probably killed in their sleep.

The thing is, because Fort Fisher was the last great bastion of the slave empire, the bloody fight meant a great deal, changed the war, probably hastened its end by many months and therefore was a kind of awful bargain that saved countless lives. Three thousand of the Union troops who assaulted the fort were African American, the so-called U.S. Colored Infantry Regiments, though they were mostly held in reserve against an attack from the rear that never came and only joined the final assault.

By overwhelming force of numbers, they helped carry the fort, then fought their way up the peninsula and marched into Wilmington in the vanguard. Observers dryly noted that the upper class of Wilmington were conspicuous by their absence at the victory parade, while hordes of blacks and working-class whites cheered lustily, many tearfully.

Fonvielle recounts how one of the veterans of the 37th Colored Infantry Regiment marched into Wilmington in triumph and spied his mother standing on the sidewalk. He had not seen her since marching off to war. He had left a slave and now was a free man who had fought to make himself so.

I linger after the tour has moved on, listening to the shrilling wind, watching the glowering sky above the river, feeling a reverence I always feel on great battlefields for what was fought over and for those who suffered so greatly in a place that has become beautiful with their passing.

The sea has taken much of the old fort, and a runway was bulldozed through what was left of the ramparts during World War II. But even reduced, it has a massiveness to it that cannot be denied. It is the ghost of a mammoth human enterprise, a stubborn monument to a bad cause, and the sea is like history itself, leveling the battleground and always winning.

Long after the Confederates had faded away into graveyards and history books, Fort Fisher gained notoriety from another inhabitant, Robert E. Harrill, known as the Fort Fisher Hermit.

Harrill was a troubled man with a history of mental illness, originally from South Carolina, who ran away from home at age sixty-two and spent the next seventeen years living in a concrete bunker on the narrow peninsula at the mouth of the Cape Fear. The bunker was a relic of Fort Fisher's role in World War II as an antiaircraft training facility. By all accounts, as a hermit, Harrill got a new lease on life. Visitors came from far and wide to hear his wisdom, and from 1955 to 1972 he held court like a kind of guru of his self-described "School of Common Sense," accepting gifts of food and drink (not liquor—he was a teetotaler) and rarely without company.

He claimed—though it's hardly verifiable—that during the latter years he was the second most popular tourist attraction in the state after the battleship USS *North Carolina*, hosting 17,000 visitors a year.

But he also claimed to have demons in his head.

He lived on clams, fish, sassafras tea, and whatever edible plants he could grub up. Apparently he got some help from the other hermit—yes, on the Cape Fear everything seems to have two names, or to have happened more than once, or to have its own secret sharer.

The second hermit was a ragged fellow named Empy Hewitt. Some referred to him as "the Wild Man" or "the Bird Man." Hewitt was a true hermit who avoided contact with other people—except, of course, his fellow hermit. Legend has it that his face had been disfigured by cancer. He could be identified by the old air force jacket he often wore. It was he who is said to have shown Harrill the abandoned concrete bunker that would become his home and serve as a kind of primitive visitors' center.

In photographs, the Fort Fisher Hermit looks like a man who has endured a hard life: His rugged, bearded face and haunted eyes seem to map the years of physical abuse at the hands of a step-grandmother; the hard-luck, low-paying jobs at cotton mills and carnivals; the son who jumped off a trestle to his death; the wife who left him; the demons he complained of inside his head. His daily uniform was simple: swim trunks and straw hat, sometimes a pair of high boots. Stray dogs seemed to gravitate to his little compound, full of trash and assorted flotsam gathered from the beach.

But as he got better known, he began to attract the wrong kind of attention. Local thugs would wait till he left his bunker and then set fire to his belongings. Kids made fun of him on the street in Carolina Beach. At one point, he claimed to have been kidnapped by two men—and to have escaped. Rumors began to make the rounds that the old man was hoarding a fortune, which he had buried near his hideout.

And then on June 4, 1972, he became the center of a gruesome mystery.

Five local boys discovered him bruised and bloody at the threshold of his bunker—dead. The camp area was scored with footprints and drag marks. A shoe was sticking out of the sand. What exactly had happened?

Some believed that local teenagers had abused the poor man until his heart gave out—maybe trying to make him give up his treasure. Fred Pickler, who knew the hermit well enough to memorialize him in a photographic memoir, worked at the time as a crime scene technician with the New Hanover County Sheriff's Department. He wanted a thorough investigation and an autopsy. But it wasn't until Harrill's son consented to an exhumation in 1984 that the body of the hermit was autopsied, and by then the results were inconclusive. Ben Steelman chronicled all this thoroughly in gripping style in various articles in the *Wilmington Star News*.

Locals have long speculated as to why no autopsy was performed at the time of his death. The most popular theory I've heard—again and again—is that it was well known who the perpetrators were, but they came from socially well-connected families, so the whole unfortunate case was hushed up.

But I have a simpler theory.

The river seems to draw mystery to it. Dark deeds and fatal attractions seem to follow the river every mile—from the deadly lure of Buckhorn Dam, to the exploding steamboat boiler at Whitehall Landing, to the collapsing highway bridge at Lillington, to the blasted ferry at Elwell's crossing, to the wagonloads of black bodies dumped into the river at Wilmington during the white supremacist coup of 1898, to the sabotaged Florida-bound airline flight, to this killing. The river has drained its share of blood. I doubt there was any conspiracy or cover-up, just the plain old problem of getting to the bottom of anything on the river, where every fact seems to have multiple causes, every action a competing crew of actors, every story several versions.

An equally mysterious killing occurred on Bald Head Island, a place so idyllic it doesn't even allow cars. Residents pedal bicycles or ride around in electric golf carts.

Just before midnight on October 22, 1999, the dispatcher at Central Communications (C-Com) for Brunswick County, of which bald Head is a part, logged this ominous sequence of transmissions:

"C-Com, 4206."

"4206?"

"10-4. Show me out with three. Stand by. Stand by, please."

The caller, designated 4206, was Officer Davina Buff Jones, a thirty-three-year-old rookie with nine months on the force.

Then she said, off-mic and without identifying herself to the dispatcher, "There ain't no reason to have a gun here on Bald Head Island, okay? You want to put down the gun? Come on, do me the favor and put down the gun."

After a squelching noise, Jones is heard to say, "Come on, you guys."

Next comes a single gunshot.

Her partner, Officer Keith Cain, found Jones lying facedown in the shadow of Old Baldy Lighthouse with a single gunshot wound to the back of her head. The shot, it was determined later, came from her own .40 caliber Glock pistol, also found at the scene—lying under her right hand.

It had been a quiet night up until then. The most excitement came from the report of a missing golf cart. Shortly before Jones was shot, three lost tourists had gotten directions from her a quarter-mile from the lighthouse. Her partner had offered to ride along on her patrol, but she had gone alone.

The local district attorney initially determined that Jones had staged her own death to look as if she had died in the line of duty, to preserve death benefits for her family. She apparently had a history of depression and other psychological issues.

But her family was adamant: She had died at the hands of three "unsubs"—unidentified subjects—probably involved in drug dealing, who eluded authorities and escaped the island at their first chance—by boat, since that's the only way off the island. The North Carolina Industrial Commission, which determines pension benefits for public employees, ultimately ruled that the cause of her death was "undetermined" and awarded double benefits, but that has not stopped those who have long campaigned to have the case reopened—and in fact, just recently a new district attorney has reopened the investigation.

"I don't believe she did it, and I'm not convinced someone murdered her," Karen Grasty, the town's former police chief, said, according to Ann Griffin of Tribune News Service. "All I know for sure is that Davina deserved better."

The oddest fact of the case was that Officer Jones was shot in the back of the head at an angle—some claimed—that would be impossible were she holding the gun herself.

So once again there is no good answer to the mystery. The district attorney cited what he considered conclusive evidence: no footprints, powder marks on the skull indicating that the barrel had been pressed against it when fired, the lack of any physical evidence that didn't belong to Jones, and of course the fact that the weapon used was her own gun. All 200 people on the island at the time were interviewed by police, and none aroused suspicion. Certainly she had emotional issues; shortly before her death, she called an ex-boyfriend to mend fences after a bad breakup.

On the other hand, clearly her partner had no qualms about letting her ride off on patrol alone, so she must have seemed to be in a normal state of mind. And she had spent time on that last evening updating her résumé—hardly the typical action of a suicide.

Or was it? Was she planning the whole evening carefully to lay the groundwork for the fatal charade she intended to act out in the lonely dark? It's well known that suicides often experience a kind of peaceful calm just before the act, as if making the decision has relieved all the stress that was wearing them down.

But the mystery of Jones's death continues to haunt the island. Part of what is so unsettling is the juxtaposition of such dark violence on an island that is upscale, laid back, and serene, more known for its golf courses, sea turtle nests, and backmarsh kayak tours than gun violence.

Whatever secrets Bald head Island holds, it is my next stop—since there I will find the Cape of Fear.

The route to the actual Cape of Fear on Bald Head Island is circuitous and expensive.

The cape, of course, is a shifty piece of real estate. In this part of the world, sand migrates south and west, as a rule, according to currents and tides, but storms tend to plough through these low islands, moving thousands of tons of sand in hours. The relentless undertow of large wave trains sucks sand off beaches and furrows it into shoals offshore. And dredging the long fairway into the ship channel undoubtedly contributes something — nobody can agree on exactly what — to the whole restless equation.

So think of the cape as an indeterminate place, partly submerged, where land turns into treacherous water. The Frying Pan Shoals extend more than twenty miles offshore. There used to be a light tower marking the outer fringe of the ship-killing sands, but it's been decommissioned and sold off to a private individual.

I once helmed a forty-six-foot sailboat under power through a shortcut across the shoals, heading north to Sag Harbor. The captain navigated. All I had to do was drive. But steering through that narrow, twisty patch of water was unnerving.

On either hand, only a couple of boat-lengths away, the steep, four-foot-high breaking waves frothed and slapped down. We crawled slowly across Cape Fear through a little furrow in the shoals, and I was glad when we finally found open water again and the depth-sounder read first twenty-five feet, then forty, then sixty, and at last off the continental shelf, no bottom.

To get to that remote spot, the Cape of Fear at the far southeastern tip of Bald head Island, we begin in Southport, my wife, Jill, and I. That's where the Bald Head Island ferry terminal is located, at Deep Point Marina. There is no bridge to Bald Head, no public ferry, and even docking your own boat in the Bald Head Island harbor will run you $20 an hour.

We purchase round-trip tickets, $23 each, and settle in to wait on the observation deck, shaded by a peaked pavilion roof. The benches are curved and comfortable, and there are white rocking chairs, the staple of beach-town porches every-

Old Baldy Lighthouse on Bald Head Island, the sentinel
marking the Cape of Fear (author photo)

where. The benches and rockers fill up with families and kids, a frisky yellow
lab and comical French bulldog, and businessmen clearly looking forward to
a week on the golf course. They converse in the accents of South Jersey, New
York, Virginia, and the Midwest. When the ferry arrives, a hundred or more
passengers, including us, swarm aboard as staff members rush cargo wagons
full of baggage down ramps and into the cargo bay. Many of the passengers
will be trammed off to vacation rentals once they arrive on the island.

I spent a long weekend on Bald Head Island a couple years back while researching and writing a story about the "Bald Head Mounties"—inspired by
a photo.

It's an arresting image, one of a suite of photographs posted above a glass-
covered display case in the Smith Island Museum of History near Old Baldy
Lighthouse: A tall young rider wearing long-sleeved Coast Guard blues, high
leather riding boots, and an infantryman's helmet sits astride a horse rearing
up on its hind legs in the surf, a dramatic Lone Ranger pose. But it's not the

Wild West. The mounted guardsman is Jack Murphy, all six feet, five inches of him. The horse is King. The time is World War II. The place is a beach on Bald Head Island.

Murphy was one of an adventurous band of farm boys, cowboys, polo players, retired cavalrymen, stunt riders, and jockeys that made up the "Coast Guard Cavalry," who scouted the beaches for trouble, armed with rifles and radios, first responders against invasion. The display case holds his scarred, lace-up cavalry boots and a rusty helmet found on the beach that matches the one in the photo, physical reminders of an era of vigilance against an enemy coming from the sea.

It's hard to imagine now an idyllic island vacation community, a place of quiet natural beauty and peaceful contemplation, as the outpost of a war effort. Hard to realize after all these years of security, even after 9/11, that in the months following the devastating surprise attack on Pearl Harbor our long, mostly undefended coastlines were considered dangerously vulnerable to attack. Following the Japanese strike on Pearl Harbor, Hitler declared war on the United States, and President Franklin Roosevelt went on the radio warning Americans on the Eastern Seaboard to be prepared for aerial bombing raids launched from forward German bases in captured Scandinavian countries.

The threat was real enough, if sometimes much exaggerated. Fleets of German *Unterseeboots*, operating in radio-controlled wolfpacks, were plundering the shipping lanes from the Gulf of Mexico to Nova Scotia seemingly at will. If the Japanese could strike unexpectedly across thousands of miles of trackless ocean, why not the Nazis?

On some moonless night over New York or Baltimore or Charleston, would the skies blossom with hordes of enemy paratroopers? The harbor fill with enemy warships?

Indeed, according to legend, a U-boat fired on the Ethyl-Dow plant at Kure Beach, just north of Bald Head, in 1943.

The other invasion danger was more insidious: spies and saboteurs.

In June 1942, two teams of English-speaking Nazi saboteurs were landed from U-boats in rubber rafts, equipped with thousands of dollars in U.S. currency and the ingredients for making bombs to blow up shipbuilding works, factories, and other targets crucial to the American war effort. A young coast guardsman named John Cullen, patrolling on foot out of the Amagansett, Long Island, station, surprised one of the teams, which had landed from the U-202.

The saboteurs tried to bribe him into silence, but instead he alarmed his station, and a reinforced patrol found a buried cache of explosives in the dunes. Not long afterward, the FBI captured the saboteurs as they attempted to make their way inland. Another team of saboteurs that infiltrated via U-boat was nabbed only a few days later in Florida.

Though beaches in populated areas were already patrolled, it was clear that the threat of enemy agents required that even remote beaches, like those on Bald Head Island, be patrolled regularly. The port of Wilmington, seventeen miles upriver, had become an important shipbuilding center. The Gulf Stream close offshore was a hunting ground for U-boat wolfpacks, the northbound highway for ships en route to New York and Halifax that would form into convoys for Britain. Bald Head Island sat squarely on the hip of a crucial shipping channel to a port vital to the war effort, where Liberty Ships still under construction on the ways could be sabotaged and valuable cargoes destroyed.

As the Atlantic war escalated, North Carolina governor Joseph M. Broughton complained of the vulnerability of the coast to President Roosevelt. Each morning, debris would wash up: abandoned life rafts, oil, even occasional bodies. Governor Broughton had long advocated for a more comprehensive beach patrol.

Fearing a new kind of invasion, military authorities beefed up their "tripwire" forces. By the end of the summer of 1942, Bald Head Island, like the entire Atlantic Seaboard, was patrolled around the clock.

The coast guardsmen who patrolled the strands were called "beachpounders." To assist the two coast guardsmen who alternated duty on Bald Head at the start of the war, a dozen or so new men were assigned to the three old buildings at Captain Charlie's Station near Cape Fear, which had been shut down but was recommissioned for the war. A new steel "skeleton lighthouse" tower was erected nearby on South Beach, with an enclosed watch room at the top, near the current intersection of South Bald Head Wynd and Silversides. The men took four-hour shifts scanning the horizons for signs of threat or vessels in distress.

In addition, on Bald Head, as in other locations with miles of wild, open beach far from population centers, the Coast Guard stationed another twenty to thirty riders and a stable of army cavalry remounts from the more than 3,000 assigned to the Coast Guard.

Think of that: the Coast Guard with three regiments' worth of horses. Jack Murphy and his comrades patrolled on horseback in pairs, in four-hour shifts.

"Well, when they decided that they needed a horse patrol to cover the beaches, they sent a memo out asking for volunteers, anybody that knew anything about horses," recalled boatswain's mate Chester Hennis, who served on Bald Head in those days before volunteering for duty in the Pacific war, in a 1995 interview for UNCW's oral history project. He came to Oak Island straight out of boot camp in New Orleans but quickly decided that Bald Head Island would be the ideal post and asked to be reassigned there. "So all these kids from Texas and Oklahoma thought they were cowboys, so they volunteered immediately. They were tickled to death. They were scared of the ocean, scared of boats, and here they're in the service and it was like a godsend to them. Man, they wanted to get on those horses and get away from the boats!"

Men and horses trained together at the Mounted Beach Patrol and Dog Training Center, in Hilton Head, South Carolina. At least two dogs, Wolfe and Gypsy, patrolled Bald Head with the mounties. Each dog was paw-printed and inducted formally into the military, complete with a service record that noted whether the dog had passed obedience training and came when it was called—no kidding.

The mounties lived in a long-gone board-and-batten beach shack with a screened-in porch "at the last palmetto tree on Bluff Island" up the East Beach. Nearby was one of two horse barns—the other was a converted boathouse on South Beach, now a private residence moved to the head of Sea Lavender Lane. Except in the coldest winter weeks, they bathed their horses daily in the saltwater to keep them from getting saddle sores in such a hot, humid climate.

According to Coast Guard directives, the job of the mounted patrols was not to repel "hostile, armed units" but, rather, to report any suspicious activities in their sectors—unauthorized boats, strangers, wreckage, anything out of the ordinary. Sometimes local fishermen came ashore, were questioned, and were allowed to go on their way. As part of the wartime navy, the beach-pounders were to work closely with their local counterparts in the army and the FBI. Their second assignment was to do what beach patrols had always done on the North Carolina coast: Be on the alert for vessels or mariners in distress and aid them in any way possible.

So they patrolled the wide-open, windy beaches on the south, east, and west of the island, crossing the sharp point of Cape Fear.

The waves break onshore at the point of Cape Fear with astonishing violence during the rising tide, more so in storm. The Frying Pan Shoals are barely submerged sand ridges on which the waves break with fury hundreds of yards offshore. Indeed, the shoals are a ship-killing ground. During rough weather, when the Atlantic gets its back up, the breakers froth in ragged lines all the way to the horizon. It's easy to imagine threat or calamity coming from the restive ocean that pounds the beach.

Since the Gulf Stream, the favorable current for northbound ships, runs so close to the North Carolina shore, and southbound vessels often steamed inshore from the stream to avoid the adverse current, the beach patrols had a ringside seat to watch the U-boat war. Almost nightly, they could see the glow of burning ships on the horizon. During the first six months of 1942 alone, seventy-two vessels were sunk off the North Carolina coast, including two German U-boats. The toll also counted thirty Allied tankers, three of them lost on the same night.

While researching the mounties, I stayed at a cottage called Mer de Rêve—Sea of Dreams—also known as Surfman's Walk #10. Like many such vacation cottages, this one had a guestbook in which occupants could record their adventures. The entry for March 17, 2005, caught my eye: "Lost at sea for 30 days, today we were forced to eat Jim. It only took 3 hours to wrestle him to the ground and knock him out, but it took several more hours to cook using the microwave. Sorry about the mess."

A companion note the next day: "We found out today how to charge up the golf cart, and it turned out the shopping center is walking distance. We had lobster for dinner. It was Jim's favorite." Signed: Hannibal Lector and Family.

~~~~~~~

No motor vehicles are allowed on the island except fire and police and maintenance vehicles. Everybody else walks, rides a bicycle, or scoots around in an electric golf cart. On our excursion, Jill and I rent #109, the last cart available, forewarned that it is not completely charged. But it will get us there and back. It's a breezy three miles from the ferry terminal down shady Federal Road through thick, lush maritime forest.

Along the way we pass the historical marker for Fort Holmes, once a formidable Confederate bastion. During the Civil War, Confederates using conscripted African American laborers built an elaborate sand fort on the western corner of the island, Fort Holmes, in honor of General Theophilus H. Holmes, to guard Old Inlet, the main channel into the Cape Fear up to Wilmington. Long guns were mounted in elaborate breastworks similar to those at Fort Fisher not far away to the north, garrisoned by the 40th Regiment of North Carolina troops under Captain John Hedrick beginning on September 9, 1863.

Bald Head Island straddled both the main channel to the Cape Fear River and New Inlet.

Thus it was strategically located to either block or cover vessels trying to enter the river. Anticipating that sooner or later the Yankees would get a foothold on Bald Head—for they had already taken the barrier islands to the north, Hatteras, Ocracoke, and Roanoke—General Charles C. Whiting, in command of the Wilmington District, fortified the island. Fort Holmes ran 1.7 miles along the eastern and southern faces of the island. At its peak it was garrisoned by about 1,700 soldiers—more than twice the garrison of Fort Fisher before it was reinforced in 1865.

But the Yankees never attacked Fort Holmes, and it was burned and evacuated by the retreating Confederates, leaving behind some vestigial earthworks and three recently disinterred remains of workers or soldiers.

Bald Head's martial history actually extends all the way back to the Revolutionary War, when the British, having been driven out of Boston, returned in May 1776 to invade the Carolinas. The British fleet, carrying Lord Cornwallis's famed 33rd Regiment of Foot, rendezvoused in the Cape Fear estuary. They established Fort George on the island. Patriot troops landed and tried to capture it, but they were driven off. Many historians consider this the first amphibious assault by American troops in U.S. history—another unlikely first for the Cape Fear River.

In our rented golf cart, Jill and I trundle on silently to East Beach, where the cape spreads out in a gorgeous soft sand beach, disappearing into a roiling sea. We clamber over the boardwalk that crosses the double dune line and step out onto the Cape of Fear.

For miles out to sea, all we can see are thrashing breakers, rearing across the sandbars and shoals in ragged lines. There is not just one definitive line of breakers but foaming ranks slamming in at several angles, cresting on the scalloped floor of the shallowing ocean. Far off to our right passes the ship channel, the channel markers barely visible at this distance. The water quiets only a little as it enters the river fairway, looking slatey and humped with wind-driven combers on this overcast day.

James Sprunt's portentous words come ringing to mind, proclaiming the name as "Fear" rather than "Fair": "There it stands today, bleak, and threatening, and pitiless, as it stood three hundred years ago, when Grenville and White came nigh unto death upon its sands. And there it will stand, bleak, and threatening, and pitiless, until the earth and sea shall give up their dead. And, as its nature, so its name, is now, always has been, and always will be, the Cape of Fear."

The tide is advancing across the beach, creating long tidepools parallel to shore in the swales of sand, then oversloshing them with new waves. The lifeboat *Cape Fear* lies overturned in the sand above the high-tide mark, next to

The author at the Cape of Fear, the "playground of billows and tempests" (Jill Gerard photo)

its identical unmarked white twin. I can only imagine this exposed arrowhead of sand as a storm, or a hurricane, piles giant waves onto the beach, flooding it all the way to the dune line and perhaps beyond. I can't quite fathom heading out to sea in weather like that to perform a rescue—not of anybody, for any reason.

The sky to seaward is suffused in mist, created by blowing spindrift.

This is the front door to the river, the first landfall west of Bermuda, 600 miles to the east.

Overlooking the cape is the Shoals, a luxurious club with bar, restaurant, pool, all the amenities—not a sight Sprunt would have recognized. The dunes fronting the club are posted and roped off to keep tourists from trampling the nests of seabirds—David Webster spent part of last week out here mapping out the nesting zone. Bald Head is also a haven for loggerhead sea turtles. Last year seventy-five nests were discovered and carefully tended by volunteers from the Bald Head Island Conservancy. All seventy-five hatched.

Down the long stretch of South Beach, kids cavort in the surf, fling footballs and flying rings at one another, screeching with delight. Surfers bob offshore on their boards, waiting for a ride. The wind is picking up. Darker clouds are moving in. Before long a quick downpour will pass over the island, slapping it with a wet hand, then disappearing.

I stare off at the breakers, the gray mist, the darkening sky, the relentless thrashing surf, thinking, what a beautiful, treacherous place.

We have just enough battery power left in our golf cart to make it back to the ferry landing and catch the commercial ferry heading back to the mainland. This is not the slick, new catamaran that carried us here a few hours ago but an older monohull boat that pitches and rolls in the restless cross-seas stirred up by wind and tide fighting against each other. Rain and wind drive us into the main saloon, where the passengers are lounging among tool-bags, backpacks, and personal coolers: housekeepers, drywallers, carpenters, masons, tilers, mechanics, hospitality staff, all the workers who make it possible for Bald Head Island to thrive, headed home after a long day of work.

Out the window I watch the river, gray and heaving, listen to the engines labor against all that current, all that water, upriver to our landing.

On our drive home, we cross the Cape Fear River yet again. High on the bridge, our SUV buffeted by the wind, we can spy the McAllister tugboat fleet below us, see the blue and orange cranes of the port downriver.

But my mind is on the thundering lines of breakers at the far reach of Bald Head Island, the Cape of Fear.

# PART 5

# Finishing at the Starting Point

I don't know exactly why it has seemed so important to travel the whole river, start to finish. Maybe it has to do with wholeness, with completion. And so I have made it *almost* all the way—from Buckhorn Dam to the Cape of Fear—and all the water that carried me has spilled into the sea. In that sense, we made the journey together, and the river I traveled with is gone, replenished each day by a new river, a continuum of rivers, existing both in one single intense moment and across the millennia.

16

We live in a world of such fragmentation and compartmentalization that at times I find it exhausting and yearn for the completeness and sense that something is all one thing—and only one thing.

One of the big reasons our natural environment has taken such a hit over the generations is it has been thought of and dealt with in pieces, chopped up into segments that can easily be labeled and disposed of—like the Titan Cement permits. Even on the university campus where I have worked for more than twenty years, we typically consider natural spaces either as mere scenery or future building sites—not as parts of a single connected ecosystem of intrinsic value beyond our pleasure or use.

David Quammen begins his brilliant book *Song of the Dodo* by asking his reader to imagine a beautiful Persian carpet, say, twelve by eighteen feet square. Now take a sharp knife, he says: "We set about cutting the carpet into thirty-six equal pieces, each one a rectangle two feet by three." We wind up with the same 216 square feet of carpetlike stuff. "But what does it amount to?" he asks. "Have we got thirty-six nice Persian throw rugs? No. All we're left with is three dozen ragged fragments, each one worthless and commencing to come apart."

He is making a point about habitat, of course—about the need for contiguous terrestrial habitat, unbroken by roads and clear-cuts and development, where species can thrive. But it's a truth that applies equally to a river, or a life—chop it up into segments, and you literally destroy its integrity, the very wholeness of the thing that gives it value.

It seemed to me from the beginning important to consider

the river as a whole thing, indeed, to think of the entire watershed as all one thing, like the cardiovascular system in your body.

It may seem trivial, a matter of no big deal, to spoil one little trickling creek, to dam one segment of a channel. But think how a blockage in a single artery can cripple or kill you.

Likewise, clear-cutting a few miles of stream banks along a river that has 200 miles of it may not seem like a problem, but that green stuff, trees and foliage, grasses and wildflowers, is the lungs of the watershed and the habitat for all the critters who live there.

So when Titan Cement wants to scour out a giant open-pit mine on a sensitive part of the Northeast Cape Fear, and the effluents that are released into the air are certain to wind up in that river and farther downstream in the Cape Fear, people are right to be concerned. For though the project would take up only a fraction of the real estate of the extensive watershed, its consequences would be felt along the course of every mile of water downstream, as well as in the aquifer underlying the greater Wilmington area that provides drinking water for many of the city's inhabitants.

And so completing the journey—traveling the miles from the Deep River on down past Mermaid Point to Buckhorn Dam, where we started—remains crucial as a metaphorical affirmation of this philosophy of wholeness, of integrity.

And in a practical sense, were I not to run the last—really the first—few miles on the Deep River, I would miss the contrast between the legendary Mermaid Point—sand and soothing, ethereal music—and the real one—a clamor of hard-edged industry backing up the live water into a muddy cooling pond for a power plant.

So the journey is almost complete now and the book is forming, for a book is a kind of watershed with a main channel that is fed by all the tributary ideas and themes and facts, each falling toward the main channel by its own kind of gravity. And this book, like the river inside it, is a messy, overwashing thing that spills over its banks and floods into soggy ground on either side.

And the story is more than the main channel.

It's a kind of interconnected web of stories: the history of the early explorers, the economy of the river that later settlers founded, the geology of the river bottom and its falls, the quality of its water, the human culture that took root along its banks and interacted, sometimes disastrously, with the native plants and animals that lived along and in the river—driving to extinction the Carolina parakeet, for instance, and introducing cultivation of rice that could only be sustained with slave labor and has produced beautiful, abandoned fields of wild grass haunted by alligators.

It's a personal story of feeling the current on your body, manhandling you down rapids and through chutes. It's the chronicle of engineering the river for navigation, in the process making insurmountable obstacles for spawning sturgeon and striped bass.

The river muscles canoes through the rocky teeth of white-water rapids and carries leviathan cargo ships on its broad back. It is bracketed at both ends by man-made power plants that change the nature and course of the river. It has been deepened, straightened, dammed, channeled into millraces and locks, but never quite tamed.

And how could it ever be? The river is such an elemental force, deceptively powerful even in its meandering lower reaches, where it seems lazy and sluggish. Every second of every day, on average, between 5,600 and 6,000 cubic feet of river water empty into the sea. That's more than 42,000 gallons per second. So in twenty-four hours, between 3.6 billion and 3.9 billion gallons of water drain out of the Cape Fear.

Every day, year after year, century after century.

And one thread is the story of where we go from here. How wild will the Cape Fear remain?

Even a mile out of the city where I live, the riverbank seems wild and daunting, though that's somewhat of a facade. The buffer of vegetation might stretch only a few hundred yards before giving way to cleared fields, development, factories. Still, the illusion is valuable to the traveler's experience, and in fact even a narrow buffer helps to filter out the sediment and pollutants that otherwise would enter the stream.

All down the river, we have been reminded that civilization is never very far off. Round a corner and all at once a bridge appears. Bridges are one of the very few landmarks on the river, and again, one wonders why. The Erie Canal offers mile markers and helpfully identifies the roads crossing on the bridges and the names of the towns as you pass into and out of them.

When the river was the real highway to the interior, for some 300 years from the seventeenth century through the mid-twentieth, signs and landmarks abounded, announcing steamboat landings, factory docks, and the names of counties and towns. The towns faced the river then. Now too many of them seem to have turned their backs on it—it is no longer useful for commerce, not until Wilmington and below.

And now that I have been to the sea, walked upon the actual Cape of Fear, it's time to return to the source, the place where the river begins. And paddle alone until I reach the place where we started our adventure.

~~~~~~~

Jill and I leave home around 8:00 A.M. on a beautiful June morning, slip over the Cape Fear Memorial Bridge at 8:27 (I can't break the habit instilled in me by David of logging every bridge crossing) on the stem of the Y the river makes as it diverges into the northwest main channel and the Northeast Cape Fear, and by 8:29 we're over the U.S. 421 bridge heading north, the Wilmington waterfront reeling by across the river to our right, backlit by the low sun. We follow U.S. 421 to U.S. 401 at Lillington, turn onto N.C. 42, thence to Lower River Road. Turning right again, we arrive suddenly at the Old Route 1 put-in on the Deep River.

Jill helps me carry the kayak about 500 feet down a muddy, rutted, four-wheel-drive track to the landing site just above the bridge. I get off without incident at 1:28 P.M. and begin my solo journey of the last leg.

As I begin paddling, I experience an odd moment of vertigo, for there's so little current that I have to remind myself that indeed I am paddling in the right direction, downstream.

If all goes as planned, in two or three hours I will have covered almost nine miles to Buckhorn Dam.

On my solo journey, short as it will be, I need to remind myself of first principles:

First: *The journey is the thing*.

I am quite excited to *arrive*, to be there and fulfill the trip, so I need to consciously slow myself down. I know Jill is waiting for me at Buckhorn, and I don't want to make her day an ordeal of waiting and worrying, so I don't want my paddle to be too leisurely either. I also don't know precisely how far the distance is that I must cover. The guidebooks differ somewhat on that score and in my growing experience do not exactly conform to the reality that you find on the river. Things take longer or shorter than advertised.

Second: *The journey requires its own rhythm*. The first part of my journey is devoted to finding my rhythm—a kind of analog to coming of age, if you will, trying things out until the right individual stroke is found.

My boat is a twelve-footer, short for an open-water kayak, too long and v-bottomed for white water. I know I won't find any white water above Buckhorn, since the river is so backed up and deep it is actually labeled Buckhorn Lake on the map. Much depends on how you take your seat, offering your back the best support to prevent fatigue and maintain good balance in moving water.

Much also depends on how you hold your paddle. I find that a wide, fairly relaxed grip works best. I can pull short, steady strokes, resting every so often to listen to the bow slice the water ahead. Once I get the boat up to hull speed—the fastest velocity a hull can move through the water as determined by its bow wave—paddling harder won't make it go any faster.

Oddly, though there is no discernible current or wind, whenever I rest for even a couple of moments, the bow wants to pull right, as if drawn by an invisible magnet set into the bank. Later it will nudge left, which I don't mind, since ultimately I have to pull in on the left side of the river to avoid the dam, and one paddle stroke on the left side will correct my course. But when the bow pulls right, I sometimes have to use a stop stroke on the left side to turn the boat back onto the right heading, losing momentum.

Once I get the rhythm down, it feels like achieving a kind of identity: *This is how fast I go, this is the stroke I make, this is the character of my movement through the water and the wake I leave as a telltale of my passing.*

I stop thinking about paddling. I just become myself, someone whose mission and identity for the next little while is propelling a red-and-white kayak down the Cape Fear River toward a dam and a book. I become myself, in a sense, much as a man finally stops being a boy trying on roles and identities, trying to get his feet under him and his face on for the world, and all at once realizes that he has become who he was always going to be, and has now been for some time before actually knowing it.

In that sense, paddling is like so many other endeavors that require a melding of physical activity with mental acuity—sailing a small boat, playing a guitar, hitting a baseball. At the moment when you no longer have to think about doing it and you just instinctively do it, it becomes much more satisfying and real.

This period of establishing of the rhythm takes fully half an hour.

I have not been thinking about paddling for some time before I realize that I have not been thinking about paddling for some time.

Almost immediately when I put in, a great blue heron erupts from a snag nearby and flies away downriver. He leads me all the way down the Deep River—flying ahead a couple of hundred yards, lighting just long enough that I can almost catch up, then off he flies ahead, scout and escort.

I'm glad to have his company—or hers, as the case may be—for the Deep is a brooding and sullen river, its banks impenetrably overgrown for the length that I paddle it. In that spot it seems a dead river, or that the real river lies buried under the thousands of gallons of standing water backed up by the dam, not a live river on the surface but a flat, calm, pollen-dusted lake of brown water.

As I'm paddling down the Deep, I pass one lone fisherman, a young guy, his skiff nosed into shore, fishing for lunkers under the cutbank (as we saw so many fishermen farther on fishing the ledges just off the banks, some from lawn chairs, others from small boats, going for catfish). All along the river, favorite fishing spots are marked by red, blue, or orange streamers tied to overhanging branches.

I ask the lone fisherman, "Catching much fish?"

He replies, "Just some small ones." Then he says, deadpan, "Doing much paddling?"

I smile. "Yeah, a little bit," I say, and think, "and I ought to do more."

Everybody ought to paddle more. If everybody in the basin spent even a single day on the Cape Fear River, they would be astonished at its wildness, captured by its beauty, and jealously protective of it as their own, not some abstraction on a map. If only our county commissioners and legislators could be induced to paddle the quiet, shady tributaries, they would not be quite so ready to sell off that legacy for a few jobs or a boost in the tax base. If the mayors of our river towns could turn their towns back toward the river that runs through their communities, they would glimpse the treasure spun out of water and gravity, lush thicket and birds, shad and turtles, otters and mink. The treasure on their doorstep.

They would *get* it.

The heron stays with me for the better part of an hour as I make it to storied Mermaid Point, the confluence, once a subject of fanciful folklore. Now it is an overgrown peninsula in midstream marked by a stove-in dock and the bleached trunk of a downed tree just off the bank. The bank is hidden under a tangle of underbrush and poison ivy, a difficult landfall at best.

There are no comely mermaids combing out one another's long hair, no otherworldly siren song.

Indeed, just the opposite. For half an hour or so I have been hearing a steady rumbling surge. But I know that no white water lies ahead above the dam, and anyway I'm too far from the dam for the din of the rock garden below it to carry.

Just before arriving at Mermaid Point, I spy them, the two tan smokestacks ringed with black at the tops of the Progress Energy power plant rising above the treeline to my left. As I round Mermaid Point, I can see it plainly, the ugly concrete edifice of the power plant, issuing a steady roaring hum on the Haw River side. My heron escorts me past the two great cooling-water intake gates, each 10 feet wide by 8 feet high. The river here has an average depth of 11 feet and a width of about 300 feet. The cooling system of the plant is designed to suck in about 299,000 gallons of water per minute, 430 million gallons per day—at this point, about a fifth of the river's total flow.

From down on the river, the plant seems like a live, malevolent thing, though my brain tells me it serves a useful human purpose, that without power plants we'd all be living in the dark. Still, I hurry past those giant sluice gates, unreasonably anxious about being sucked through the grating into the labyrinth of the throbbing leviathan. Once I pass the monstrous gates, my heron turns and flies back practically right over my head, so I can see the alertness in his eye and the beautiful blue-gray shadings of his great wings.

The great blue heron has a call that sounds like that of a pterodactyl, or to be accurate, what I imagine one of those flying dinosaurs would sound like—a startling *yawwk!* On this occasion, the heron glides past eloquently silent.

I spot only one water snake—an eighteen-inch-long pale green creature sidewinding through the water with his head raised ever so slightly off the surface. I've been seeing plenty of water-skippers and a few birds, but it's the still of the day and hot, 92 degrees or so, with barely a breath of wind to match the stalled current.

I'm working harder than I realize, paddling a steady rhythm, moving fast through the gelid water. My arms will still feel rubbery, hours later, as I jot these notes into my moleskin notebook, as I ponder my little journey and the legend of the mermaids and the enchanted beach drowned by a dam that would have kept the mermaids from ever swimming so far up the river—or getting back down again.

The Mermaid Point area is, like the Deep, a backwater—a sparsely inhabited country of farms and deep woods broken by pastures and edged by dirt roads. But like so many places along the Cape Fear, it bears the clues of a more complicated history, the telltales of a region that once had grandiose ambitions, of a town that once was, and of a future that might have been but never quite came true.

Twice, boosters of the region tried to claim for it signature distinctions—and twice they failed. The curious abortive history is related by Dennis Daniels in his article "Loss of a Town."

The first time, in 1788, Thomas Person, representing Granville County at the state constitutional convention at Hillsborough in Orange County, made a bid for the "fork of the Haw and Deep Rivers" to become the site of the new state capital. But after due deliberation, the delegates chose to establish Raleigh as the capital instead, in nearby Wake County.

The more important business of the convention was to ratify the new federal constitution, but after robust debate, ratification failed by a vote of 184 to 84. The antifederalists were concerned that the national constitution, as then proposed, contained no bill of rights to protect individuals and states from excessive taxation and other abuses feared from a strong federal government. In some strange fit of prescience, they were laying the groundwork for secession three generations later.

It would take another convention, downriver at Fayetteville, to finally ratify the U.S. Constitution in North Carolina.

The second bid for distinction came four years later, in 1792, when a new committee was charged with the task of establishing what would become the first public university in the nation when it opened the following year. Money was offered to the committee who were deciding where to build the university if they would site it at the confluence of the Deep and the Haw. It's unclear who exactly was behind this bald-faced attempt to buy prestige, but once again, progress went elsewhere, this time to New Hope Chapel Hill.

But the confluence of rivers inspired yet another scheme, this one commercial. The idea was to make the Cape Fear navigable from the sea all the way upriver to Mermaid Point, to establish a port city at the fork, and for that city to become a kind of inland entrepôt, transhipping goods overland from the river and in turn shipping raw materials, especially coal and lumber, downriver to the sea.

Thus was chartered the Deep and Haw River Navigation Company, which renamed itself the Cape Fear Navigation Company, in 1797.

And thus was born a town originally named Lyons and later changed to Haywoodsborough and finally simply Haywood, after a long-serving state treasurer named John Haywood. (Even then, state officials had begun the tradition of getting things named for themselves—roads, bridges, towns. Further, they followed the tradition of so many river towns, including Wilmington and Fayetteville, of trying on names until they got it right.) Haywood himself was among the first to purchase some of the town's 294 lots.

His investment was not altruistic. Like the speculators out west who were privy to the planned path of the railroad, he and his cohort hoped to flip the lots for a handy profit once the river traffic sailed into town.

And there was some early success, enough to tease the investors with the promise of hefty profits in the offing. The *Haywood Packet* reached the town on May 21, 1800, after a voyage of eleven days from Wilmington. Daniels reports that it rained for ten of those days. I imagine those miserable rivermen poling their heavy boat up against the rushing current, driving uphill all the way (Pull and Be Damned); laboring against the swell of runoff water; being lifted over the rocky teeth of the river in some places, getting hung up on snags in others; squinting into the spring deluge to recognize landmarks and avoid dangerous ledges.

Other boats made the trip in about a week. But the Cape Fear is a stubborn river, floored by rock ledges in its upper reaches, hard to navigate even in moderate water. In drought and flood, it becomes impassable above Fayetteville. So by 1834, the Cape Fear Navigation Company gave up. It could not find a way to get all that Chatham County coal downriver at a profit.

It's a funny thing about failure: It often inspires others to prove that the thing in question can be done, if only the right people with the right know-how take it on.

It took fifteen years, but in 1849 a new company negotiated for navigation rights along the upper Cape Fear. Calling itself the Cape Fear and Deep River Navigation Company, it was confident that it could accomplish what its predecessor had tried and failed to do in more than thirty years. Using a corps of forty slaves hired from their owners, the directors of the new company built locks and dams—many of the large, rectangular rocks we banged into during our descent of the river were undoubtedly the ruins of those early engineering efforts—and through what would seem to be sheer stubborn will, in April 1856 they shipped the first load of coal downriver aboard the *John H. Haughton*, just as they had promised. Meanwhile, the real John Haughton made $1,438 renting out his slaves to the company.

The *Wilmington Herald* applauded the feat: "Bring out the big guns and let us be ready to give the *Haughton* a 'feu de joie' on the arrival at our port with the first cargo of native black diamonds."

The following month the *Fayetteville Observer* reported that the captain of the *Haughton*, Angus McDiarmid, got into an altercation with a slave who had jumped ship on the voyage upriver, then returned to the boat for the downriver passage: "Captain McDiarmid was in the act of tying him, when he resisted, got the rope entangled around McDiarmid's body, and pitched him into the river." The body was not recovered.

In commerce as in life, timing is everything. By the time the Cape Fear and Deep River Navigation Company hit its stride, the Union was in trouble. The Civil War broke over the Cape Fear region in a catastrophic storm of battles—Fort Fisher, Wilmington, Fayetteville, Averasboro, Bentonville—disrupting river traffic and, more important, making it impossible to undertake large-scale navigation projects such as dredging and lock-building.

During the war, railroads became crucial for moving troops and supplies, and the North was churning out locomotives and rolling stock and laying track in places where only dirt paths had once been the only mode of travel. By the end of the war railroads were putting riverboats out of business, not just on the Cape Fear, but as far north as the Erie Canal and as far west as the Mississippi. The war and railroads took Mark Twain off the river and set him on the path to becoming arguably the first great truly American writer, writing with the eye and temperament of a riverboat pilot in the idiom of a region that lived by storytelling.

No battles were fought over Haywood.

The town wasn't important strategically; no arms were stockpiled there, and the river in that region was inconvenient for navigation. The little town simply languished. At the end of the war, it endured exactly one day of Union occupation. To add insult to injury, the railroad bypassed Haywood, locating a station and switching yard about two miles north, at the present site of Moncure, not far from where I launched my red kayak to bring my own river trip to closure. The town withered and the government evaporated sometime in the 1900s, leaving behind the ghost of a dream of grandeur.

Haywood did enjoy one final, fleeting distinction.

In the chaotic years following the Civil War, during the period called, with varying degrees of irony, Reconstruction, Haywood became a small outpost of racial tolerance. Whites and blacks met together as part of the Union League, supporting President Ulysses S. Grant and the Republican Party. They even voted together at the same venue.

But in that country at that hour of history, the idyll could not last. The Ku Klux Klan, brainchild of General Nathan Bedford Forrest and a cohort of diehard Confederates, came alive in North Carolina. Led mainly by former Confederate officers, it claimed to be the legal government, conducting "trials" and meting out sentences that ranged from tarring and feathering to hanging. In one case, a dozen Klansmen seized state senator John W. Stephens in the Caswell County Courthouse, then stabbed and choked him to death. Wyatt Outlaw, a prominent black Unionist, was dragged from his home and lynched, as were other black leaders. The Klan drove the races apart, conducting open war, until finally 100 Klan leaders were rounded up by order of Governor William W. Holden—whose reward was to be impeached and removed from office. The bloody melodrama would be replayed downriver at Wilmington a generation later.

As for Haywood, the little town at the head of the river simply faded away.

~~~~~~~~~~

Beyond Mermaid Point I'm on a new river: the Cape Fear.

Despite the fact that there's no great cascading confluence, as there is, say, where the Potomac and Shenandoah Rivers come together in the boiling rapids of Harpers Ferry, I feel a thrill of exuberance to be at the place where the big river is born.

The Deep seemed sullen and still and spooky, its banks looming like dark walls, impenetrable jungle like you might expect in some Heart of Darkness story, the water still and stagnant, dusted with pollen and leaf litter and mulch, mud-murky.

It felt, well, *deep*, and oddly unsettling.

The Cape Fear smells different somehow, fresher. A breeze is stirring, fitfully, the sky clouding up and the air cooling off for awhile.

I then turn out of a bend and there, all at once, completely formed, is what looks like the oldest, rustiest, most disused railroad bridge in the world—yet it carries freight on a line that goes west, then splits, one spur going south to Sanford, the other to Greensboro.

There is something about the way a bridge comes at you on the river like that—an all-at-once phenomenon, not something you gradually steal up on. It reveals itself full-blown, an artificial concrete fact planted squarely across the water, an intersection of the world with your river.

I've been told that the way to find the old river fords is to go to the nearest highway bridge and then walk upriver or down until the bank drops away. A bridge is never on the site of a ford. A bridge wants to have high sides and a well-defined cut on which to brace itself. A ford wants to amble down to the river on a not-too-steep path and then walk across in shallow, wide water without too much current to carry you off your feet.

I squint upward at the bridge, but there's no sign of a locomotive.

I paddle on beyond the railroad bridge, watching the muddy water roil off my paddle blade. When I strike the next bridge, I'm already back at Route 42. Square in the middle of its approach hangs a sign:

DANGER DAM
2 MILES AHEAD

I suddenly am assaulted by second thoughts.

The sign seems so definite, so official. In my mind, I'm reeling back all of Ethan's lessons about hydraulics, how deceptively dangerous a dam can be, how it can hold you in a current that recirculates and never lets you go. I've felt the force of the river more than once, pulling my kayak to one side or the other, spinning our old Grumman canoe, flipping us out into the cold water and bearing us downstream with irresistible power.

I've read Chaos Theory and understand one basic tenet: Order—a steady

A railroad bridge "reveals itself full-blown, an artificial concrete fact planted squarely across the water, an intersection of the world with your river." (Amy Williamson photo)

and predictable current, say—turns into turbulence—a boiling maelstrom of whirlpools and swift eddies—instantly and without warning. It does not happen gradually. One moment you are floating along, completely under control; the next you are being spun and thrown and sucked under and spat out again.

Just above the dam, the river is broken by islands and strainers, and there's no predicting how the currents are going to behave as they approach the fall line of the dam, quickening with gravity.

I pull into the deserted Wildlife ramp, and as I step out of the kayak, my legs are so jellied that they collapse under me and I sit down hard in a foot of cool water.

I try to raise Jill on the cell phone to let her know I have decided not to chance the dam—feeling a bit afraid, frankly, and also sheepish for feeling afraid. But I fear that will leave me with a frustrating sense of lack of completeness, and so it's lucky that the phone doesn't work (though we're only half an hour from the second-largest metro area in North Carolina).

No service. So I soldier on, feeling this must surely be an omen. I am meant to finish the journey, every last yard of it. I'm careful to stay far left so as to not get caught in the midstream rush of water toward the broad back of the dam.

As I approach the last mile above Buckhorn, a new great blue heron appears. He does the same routine as his earlier cousin, hopping ahead of me in short bursts of flight. He finally lights on a snag pile just upstream of the dam on the far left side. When I reach the snag and am in good position for the take-out, he erupts into flight and makes a beeline across to the other bank.

While my rational mind understands it's a nice, picturesque coincidence, part of me can't help but see the big, beautiful fishing bird as a lucky omen, like dolphins in the estuary, which always seem to show up just before the weather improves, harbingers of wind from the right direction, a settling sea, the glass rising.

The escorting herons give me a sense of being watched over, looked out for, on my short, solitary journey.

From the last bridge and the danger sign, I've paddled forty-five minutes to reach the dam. I try to pull left too soon, mistaking the channel for the one to the take-out, but get hung up in a swamp of plants. So I back out and take directions from Jill, who is standing high on the observation platform on the left side of the dam and can see what I cannot from her aerial vantage point.

Come in closer, she motions, so I paddle toward her. I hug the left bank, wary of the long, fast fall over the dam and the surprising power of running water—and it's fitting that the last hundred yards of a journey that has taken me more than 200 miles should be the most hazardous.

Then I ease the bow in through a cut in the foliage next to a water gauge below the twelve-foot-long walls of the dam embankment. I give a final thrust of the paddle, and the bow grounds home. I've made it! The journey is at last complete.

Upon the bluff of the dam, I spy Jill, short red hair riffling in the breeze, blue eyes sparkling, and a big Irish smile on her freckly face. Jill scrambles down off the dam to find me.

I stick out my paddle and test the bottom on the right side—shallow and sandy. Good—I worried that it would be the boot-sucking mud we encountered so often along the river. I step carefully out on the left—but suddenly my foot cannot find bottom. I keep stepping and fall off-balance, topple headlong out of the boat into four feet of water, and gash my shin on the tide gauge. I thrash about, more surprised than anything, while Jill stands on the bank and laughs like a crazy woman. She insists that I pose for a heroic photo, which I do, drenched and dripping and bleeding and laughing with her.

The river grabbed me one last time and reminded me of its power.

In two hours and forty-five minutes, I've averaged a little over three miles per hour, even with my nervous stopover. A walking pace.

As we haul the boat up and across the rocky berm of the dam, my river sandals slipping on mud and the broken glass a generation of drunks has left

"I am meant to finish the journey, every last yard of it." (Jill Gerard photo)

there from shattered beer bottles, it begins to rain. A drizzle at first, then a cloud-bursting downpour, a hard, drumming rain of the kind we camped in just above Fayetteville on our cobble bar.

We lay the boat behind the truck and tumble in, crank up the air conditioning as it rains even harder, if that's possible. I suck down a cold soft drink and we laugh some more. Jill was not worried about me much, but I was alone out there, and however placid the waters seemed, if something happened, I was on my own. There was no savvy river guide to haul my ass out of the drink. And a little thing, when it happens to you alone, can quickly become a much bigger problem.

As a case in point, a long spit from the take-out, my kayak suddenly grounded on a submerged log and began to tip. I reached into the water, steadied my weight on the log, and slipped us over. But I could easily have moved the wrong way in a moment of panic and capsized the boat within a dozen feet of shore.

And here is the place to ask why there is no safe take-out above the dam: a truckload of sand, a sign, and maybe some steps up and across the dam like the ones the Army Corps provides at the locks.

And why all the trash? Buckhorn is a beautiful spot. It has fishing rocks, the dam, and a long, sandy beach where boaters put in kayaks, canoes, and small runabouts, and where fishermen camp away their summer days. But it's a dumping ground for trash and garbage. How about some trash cans and a toilet?

How about some recognition that this is a special place, the intersection between wilderness and people, the only wild place many of its visitors will ever know, the place where they will learn to respect — or not — this river and all others? This is the place where their kids will form their ethic of stewardship or exploitation, take responsibility or leave it up to someone else, and the message of such neglect is all wrong.

Like so many places on the Cape Fear, it seems oblivious to the treasure that is the river. But even the trashy landing can't take away from the pull of the river.

The lined pages of my moleskin notebooks have been steeped in the river, browned by the tannin, stiffened by the wetting and drying, redolent with river mud and sunlight, as I hope these pages will be.

This journey has been a line, a vector driven by gravity and the pull of the tides. But it has also been a circle, and I find at the end of my journey I am back at the beginning of it, the place where the boats first splashed into the live water of the Cape Fear River—tired, pleased, renewed, invigorated, and feeling the current of the big river in my blood.

I'm safe, elated, my head full of sights and sounds and ideas. I'm also wet, muddy, my river shoes full of sand, sodden, only a few minutes removed from being fully immersed in the river.

When the rain quits, I can barely lift my end of the boat onto the roof of the Pathfinder. Jill just laughs and points out that my arm muscles are wiggling, is if jolted by little electric surges inside my skin. I laugh along with her, for a long time, the physical laughter of relief and company after solitude. All my muscles are rubbery and used up.

It feels like that night on our cobble bar, huddled against the downpour, sipping wine out of plastic cups and feeling that splendid joy of having arrived under your own power at a remote place. I feel that joy now, a deep, lingering satisfaction that can't be got secondhand. You have to give yourself to the journey, let the current take you.

The river had me, then it let me go.

# Selected Sources

## Books

Alden, Peter, and Gil Nelson. *National Audubon Field Guide to the Southeastern States.* New York: Alfred A. Knopf, 1999.

Barrett, John G. *Sherman's March through the Carolinas.* Chapel Hill: University of North Carolina Press, 1956.

Bellamy, Ellen Douglas. *Back with the Tide: Memoirs of Ellen Douglas Bellamy.* Edited by Janet K. Seapker. Wilmington, N.C.: Bellamy Mansion Museum of History and Design Arts, 2002.

Bellamy, John D. *Memoirs of an Octogenarian.* Charlotte, N.C.: Observer Printing House, 1942.

Bonney, Rachel A., and J. Anthony Paredes, eds. *Anthropologies and Indians in the New South.* Tuscaloosa: University of Alabama Press, 2001.

Burroughs, Franklin. *The River Home: A Return to the Carolina Low Country.* Athens: University of Georgia Press, 1992.

Butler, Carrol B. *Treasures of the Longleaf Pines Naval Stores.* Shalimar, Fla.: Tarkel Publishing, 1998.

Carr, Dawson. *Gray Phantoms of the Cape Fear: Running the Civil War Blockade.* Winston-Salem, N.C.: John F. Blair, 1998.

Cecelski, David S. *The Waterman's Song: Slavery and Freedom in Maritime North Carolina.* Chapel Hill: University of North Carolina Press, 2001.

Cecelski, David S., and Timothy B. Tyson, eds. *Democracy Betrayed: The Wilmington Race Riot of 1898 and Its Legacy.* Chapel Hill: University of North Carolina Press, 1998.

Conser, Walter H., Jr. *A Coat of Many Colors: Religion and Society along the Cape Fear River.* Lexington: University Press of Kentucky, 2006.

Evans, W. McKee. *Ballots and Fence Rails: Reconstruction on the Lower Cape Fear.* Chapel Hill: University of North Carolina Press, 1967.

Ferguson, Paul. *Paddling Eastern North Carolina.* Raleigh: Pocosin Press, 2007.

Fisher, R. H. *Biographical Sketches of Wilmington Citizens.* Wilmington, N.C.: Wilmington Stamp and Printing Co., 1929.

Fonvielle, Chris E., Jr. *The Wilmington Campaign.* Campbell, Calif.: Savas, 1997.

Gessner, David. *My Green Manifesto: Down the Charles River in Pursuit of a New Environmentalism.* Minneapolis: Milkweed Editions, 2011.

Gould, William B., IV. *Diary of a Contraband.* Stanford, Calif.: Stanford University Press, 2002.

Gragg, Rod. *Confederate Goliath: The Battle of Fort Fisher.* New York: HarperCollins, 1991.

Hadden, Sally E. *Slave Patrol*. Cambridge, Mass.: Harvard University Press, 2001.

Hadley, Wade H., Jr. *The Story of the Cape Fear and Deep River Navigation Company, 1849–1873*. N.p.: Chatham County Historical Society, 1980.

Hairr, John. *Bizarre Tales of the Cape Fear Country*. Fuquay-Varina, N.C.: Triangle Books, 1995.

———. *Harnett County: A History*. Charleston, S.C.: Acadia, 2002.

———. *North Carolina Rivers: Facts, Legends, and Lore*. Charleston, S.C.: History Press, 2007.

Hall, Lewis Philip. *Land of the Golden River: Historical Events and Stories of Southeastern North Carolina and the Lower Cape Fear*. Wilmington, N.C.: Wilmington Printing Co., 1975.

Hartzer, Ronald G. *To Great and Useful Purpose: A History of the Wilmington District U.S. Army Corps of Engineers*. Wilmington, N.C.: U.S. Army Corps of Engineers, 1984.

Herring, Ethel. *Cap'n Charlie and the Lights of the Lower Cape Fear*. Winston-Salem, N.C.: Hunter, 1967.

Herring, Ethel, and Carole Williams. *Fort Caswell in War and Peace*. Wendell, N.C.: Broadfoot's Bookmark, 1983.

Hudson, Charles M., ed. *Ethnology of the Southeastern Indians*. New York: Garland, 1985.

Hughes, Nathaniel Cheairs, Jr. *Bentonville: The Final Battle of Sherman and Johnston*. Chapel Hill: University of North Carolina Press, 1996.

Jackson, Claude V., III. *The Big Book of the Cape Fear River*. Wilmington, N.C.: Dram Tree Books, 2008. Originally *A Maritime History and Survey of the Cape Fear and Northeast Cape Fear Rivers, Wilmington Harbor, N.C.* Vol. 1. Kure Beach, N.C.: North Carolina Department of Cultural Resources, Division of Archives and History, Underwater Archeology Unit, and the U.S. Army Corps of Engineers, 1996.

Koch, Frederick Henry, et al. *A Pageant of the Lower Cape Fear*. Wilmington, N.C.: Wilmington Printing Company, 1921.

Lee, Lawrence. *The History of Brunswick County North Carolina*. N.p.: Brunswick County American Revolution Bicentennial Committee, 1976.

———. *The Lower Cape Fear in Colonial Days*. Chapel Hill: University of North Carolina Press, 1965.

Lennon, Donald R., and Ida Brooks Kellam, eds. *The Wilmington Town Book, 1743–1778*. Raleigh: Division of Archives and History, North Carolina Department of Cultural Resources, 1973.

Lerch, Patricia Barker. *Waccamaw Legacy: Contemporary Indians Fight for Survival*. Tuscaloosa: University of Alabama Press, 2004.

McEachern, Leora H., and Isabel M. Williams, eds. *Wilmington–New Hanover Safety Committee Minutes, 1774–1776*. Wilmington, N.C.: Wilmington–New Hanover County American Revolution Bi-centennial Association, 1974.

McNeil, Jim. *Masters of the Shoals: Tales of the Cape Fear Pilots Who Ran the Union Blockade*. Cambridge, Mass.: Da Capo Press, 2003.

Meredith, Hugh. *An Account of the Cape Fear Country, 1731*. Edited by Earl Gregg Swem. Perth Amboy, N.J.: Charles F. Heartman, 1922.

Moore, Louis T. *Stories Old and New of the Cape Fear Region*. Wilmington, N.C.: Friends of Louis T. Moore, 1968.

Myover, J. H. *A Short History of Cumberland County*. N.p., 1905.

National Audubon Society. *National Audubon Society Field Guide to Birds, Eastern Region*. New York: Alfred A. Knopf, 1994.

Oates, John A. *The Story of Fayetteville and the Upper Cape Fear*. Fayetteville, N.C.: N.p., 1950.

Outland, Robert B. *Tapping the Pines: The Naval Stores Industry in the American South*. Baton Rouge: Louisiana State University Press, 2004.

Paredes, Anthony J., ed. *Indians of the Southeastern United States in the Late Twentieth Century*. Tuscaloosa: University of Alabama Press, 1992.

Peacock, James L., and James Sabella, eds. *Sea and Land: Cultural and Biological Adaptations in the Southern Coastal Plain*. Athens: University of Georgia Press, 1988.

Quammen, David. *Song of the Dodo*. New York: Scribner, 1996.

Ramsey, Cindy Horrell. *Boys of the Battleship North Carolina*. N.p.: John F. Blair, 2007.

Ross, Malcolm. *The Cape Fear*. Rivers of America Series. New York: Holt, Rinehart and Winston, 1965.

Seapker, Janet, ed. *Time, Talent, Tradition: Five Essays on the Cultural History of the Lower Cape Fear Region, North Carolina*. Wilmington, N.C.: Cape Fear Museum, 1993.

Sprunt, James. *Chronicles of the Cape Fear River, 1660–1916*. Raleigh: Edwards & Broughton Printing Co., 1916.

———. *Tales and Traditions of the Lower Cape Fear, 1661–1896*. 1896. Reprint, Spartanburg, S.C.: The Reprint Company, 1973.

Steinbeck, John. *Travels with Charley in Search of America*. New York: Viking Press, 1962.

Trotter, William R. *Silk Flags and Cold Steel*. Winston-Salem: John F. Blair, 1988.

Tushingham, Shannon, Jane Hill, and Charles H. McNutt, eds. *Histories of Southeastern Archaeology*. Tuscaloosa: University of Alabama Press, 2002.

Waddell, Alfred Moore. *A History of New Hanover County and the Lower Cape Fear Region*. N.p., 1909.

Watson, Alan D. *Wilmington, North Carolina, to 1861*. Jefferson, N.C.: McFarland & Company, 2003.

Watters, Fanny. *Plantation Memories of the Cape Fear River Country*. Wilmington, N.C.: New Hanover Printing and Publishing/Lower Cape Fear Historical Society, 1944, 1961.

Watts, Alan. *Reading the Weather*. New York: Dodd, Mead, 1987.

Wheeler, John H. *Historical Sketches of North Carolina*. Philadelphia: T. K. & P. G. Collins, Printers, 1851.

Works Progress Administration. *The WPA Guide to the Old North State*. 1939.

## Articles

Adams, Kevin. "Paddling the Black." *Our State*, March 2010.

Cain, Robert J. "Cotton for the Kaiser: James Sprunt, Contraband, and the Wilmington Vice Consulate." *North Carolina Historical Review* 74, no. 2 (April 1997).

Clawson, T. W. "The Sprunt House: The Historical Place in Wilmington Where the President of the United States Will Breakfast November 9th." *Evening Dispatch*, October 3, 1909.

Daniels, Dennis. "The Loss of a Town." North Carolina Museum of History, Office of Archives and History, N.C. Department of Cultural Resources, 2005.

Ferguson, Paul. "Searching for Methuselah." www.pocosinpress.com/Methuselah.pdf.

Griffin, Anna. "Bald Head Island Mystery: Who Killed Davina Jones?" Knight Ridder Newspapers, Knight Ridder/Tribune News Service, June 5, 2002.

La Vere, David. "Recalling the Tuscarora War." *Wilmington Star News*, September 22, 2011.

Mallin, Michael A., Virginia L. Johnson, Scott H. Ensign, and Tara A. MacPherson. "Factors Contributing to Hypoxia in Rivers, Lakes, and Streams." *Limnology and Oceanography* 51, no. 1, pt. 2 (2006): 690–701.

Mallin, Michael A., Martin H. Posey, G. Christopher Shank, Matthew R. McIver, Scott H. Ensign, and Troy D. Alphin. "Hurricane Effects on Water Quality and Benthos in the Cape Fear Basin." *Ecological Applications* 9, no. 1. (February 1999): 350–62.

Menius, Arthur C., III. "James Bennitt: Portrait of an Antebellum Yeoman." *North Carolina Historical Review* 58, no. 4 (October 1981).

Mintz, Mary. "Whitehall Road." Bladenroadwork.pbworks.com.

National Oceanic and Atmospheric Administration Central Library. "The Rebirth of the Survey." National Oceanographic Data Center, http://www.lib.noaa.gov/noaainfo/heritage/coastsurveyvol1/HASSLER3.html#FIRST. January 3, 2012.

North Carolina Museum of History. "Babe Ruth." 2005.

Odom, Reverend Nash A. "Steamboats on the Cape Fear." Bladen County Historical Society.

Rawlins, Wade. "Rising Sea Level Redefines N.C. Coast." *Raleigh News and Observer*, June 3, 2007.

Sato, Ayako. "Public Participation and Access to Clean Water: An Analysis of the CAFO Rule." *Sustainable Development Law and Policy* 5, no. 1 (Winter 2005).

Yarborough, Jenny. "For the Birds." *Wrightsville Beach Magazine*, July 2011.

———. "More Hog Farms Built in Past Ten Years Despite Moratorium." *Daily Southerner*, March 23, 2007.

## Newspapers

*Chatham County Record*, June 21, 1906; April 25, 1907
*Fayetteville Observer*, February 18, 1858
*Harnett County News*, 1920
*Illustrated London News*, 1864
*Wilmington Chronicle*, 1844
*Wilmington Herald*, 1856
*Wilmington Star News*, June 7–10, 1921; 1977; May 27, 2009

## Dissertations

McDuffie, Jerome. "Politics in Wilmington and New Hanover County, 1865–1900:
    The Genesis of a Race Riot." Ph.D. diss., Kent State University, 1979.
Wood, Richard Everett. "Port Town at War: Wilmington, North Carolina, 1860–
    1685." Ph.D. diss., Florida State University, 1976.

## Other Documents

Clawson, Colonel Thomas W. "The Wilmington Race Riot of 1898."
Cutting, Douglas. "Pilot." Unpublished manuscript.
*Directory of Wilmington, N.C., 1897*. J. L. Hill's Printing Company.
"Giovanni da Verrazano, Letter to King Francis I of France 8 July 1524 reporting on
    his voyage to the New World." Translated by Joseph B. Cogswell, Esq., of the N.Y.
    Historical Society &c., 1841.
High Family Papers, 1861–1865. Accession Number 48 of the Manuscripts Collection,
    Special Collections Department, William Madison Randall Library, University of
    North Carolina, Wilmington.
"A Look at the Environmental Issues Raised by a New Channel in the Cape Fear
    River for the Proposed North Carolina International Terminal." Risingwater
    Associates, Southport, North Carolina, and Old Saybrook, Connecticut, 2010.
Minutes of the meeting of the Association of Members of the Wilmington Light
    Infantry, Lumina Hotel, Wrightsville Beach, December 14, 1905.
"Report of the Commissioners Sent from Barbadoes in 1663 to Explore the Coast."
    Signed by Anthony Long, William Hilton, and Peter Fabian.
Wood, Jane D., "Data about James Sprunt, LL.D." Historical Society of the Lower
    Cape Fear, n.d.

# Acknowledgments

No project of this scope can succeed without the generous help and cooperation of scores of people. Most prominent among them are my paddling and motorboating companion: Dr. W. David Webster, UNCW Department of Biology and Marine Biology; Ethan Williamson, river guide and paddling companion; Amy Williamson, paddling companion and expedition photographer; Frank Chapman, my guide to the lower Cape Fear; Virginia Holman and Curry Guinn, my guides to the Black River; Cape Fear river keeper Kemp M. Burdette; David Perry, editor in chief at UNC Press, who believed in the book from idea to manuscript and shepherded it into being; my stepchildren Ashley Marie and Patrick Joseph Leahman, for their moral support and good company on research jaunts; and especially my wife, Jill Gerard, for boundless enthusiasm, unwavering support, and the practical wisdom to make many complicated arrangements.

Thanks to David Cecelski and other colleagues whose names remain unknown to me who read the initial proposal and the manuscript on behalf of UNC Press and contributed valuable editorial suggestions to improve it.

In addition, I am deeply grateful for the time, effort, and expertise contributed by the individuals and institutions listed below.

## People

David Avrette, owner of Howard's barbecue in Lillington, N.C.
Caitlin Bell-Butterfield, Editorial Assistant, UNC Press
Lisa Bertini, Administrative Assistant, UNCW Department of Creative Writing
Jeff Bockert of the North Carolina Civil War Sesquicentennial Committee
Kim Bryant, Design Director/Assistant Production Manager, UNC Press
Diane Cobb Cashman, Archivist, Historical Society of the Lower Cape Fear
Gerald E. Compeau Jr., Captain of R/V *Seahawk*
Douglas Cutting, writer and fishing guide
Phil Edge, Lockmaster, Huske Lock and Dam #3
Will Flowers, driver
Richard Folsom, fellow paddler and storyteller
Dr. Chris Fonvielle, UNCW Department of History
Colleen Griffiths, Archivist, Historical Society of the Lower Cape Fear
John Guss, Site Manager, Bennett Place Historic Site
Linda Hickok, Lead Environmental Specialist, Progress Energy
Megan Hubbard, Office Administrator, UNCW Department of Creative Writing
Jeff Kleinman of Folio Literary Management
Dr. David La Vere, UNCW Department of History

Si Lawrence III, Information and Communication Specialist II,
    Fort Fisher State Historic Site
Dr. Patricia Lerch, UNCW Department of Anthropology
Keira Lombardo, Vice President of Investor Relations and Corporate
    Communications, Smithfield Foods, Inc.
Alan Long, fisherman
Robert D. Maffitt, Wilmington Ambassador
Candace McGreevy, Executive Director, Historical Society of the Lower Cape Fear
Kyle Robert Mustain, driver
Liza Palmer, UNCW reference librarian
Jerry Parnell, Coordinator of UNCW Special Collections
David Reid, Director, Museum of the Cape Fear Historical Complex
Mike Rice, Save the Cape Foundation
Dale Ryals, Cape Fear River Adventures
Doug Springer, Captain, *Wilmington*
Ben Steelman, *Wilmington Star News*
Amy Thornton, Historic Sites Interpreter, Fort Fisher Historic Site
Mike Wicker, U.S. Fish & Wildlife Service
Paul Woodbury, port and waterways engineer
Frank Yelverton. U.S. Army Corps of Engineers

## Institutions
The Battleship *North Carolina* Historic Site
The Bellamy Mansion and Museum of Design Arts
The Bennett Place Historic Site, Durham, N.C.
Brunswick Town Historic Site
The Cape Fear Museum
Cape Fear River Watch
The College of Arts and Sciences, UNCW
The Department of Creative Writing, UNCW
The Federal Point Historic Preservation Society
Fort Fisher State Historic Site
The Historical Society of the Lower Cape Fear
The North Carolina State Department of Archives and History
Old Bluff Church, Wade, N.C.
Orton Plantation
The Robert Ruark Inn, Southport, N.C.
The Southern Historical Collection, William Round Wilson Library,
    UNC Chapel Hill
Special Collections, William Madison Randall Library, UNCW
The U.S. Army Corps of Engineers